David Copperfield and *Great Expectati*
most famous novels. In both books, th
ing tale of his education by life, preser
scenes, and tackles profound moral, so

Part I of this essential study:

- provides lucid and penetrating analyses of key passages
- discusses the crucial topics of patriarchy, class, obsession, eccentricity, death, breakdown and recovery
- summarizes the methods of analysis and offers suggestions for further work.

Part II supplies key background material, including:

- an account of Dickens's life and works
- a survey of historical, cultural and literary contexts
- samples of significant criticism.

Also featuring a valuable Further Reading section, this volume provides readers with the critical and analytical skills which will enable them to enjoy and explore both novels for themselves.

Nicolas Tredell is a freelance writer and formerly taught Literature, Film, Drama and Cultural Studies at the University of Sussex.

Analysing Texts is dedicated to one clear belief: that we can all enjoy, understand and analyse literature for ourselves, provided we know how to do it. Readers are guided in the skills and techniques of close textual analysis used to build an insight into a richer understanding of an author's individual style, themes and concerns. An additional section on the writer's life and work and a comparison of major critical views place them in their personal and literary context.

ANALYSING TEXTS

General Editor: Nicholas Marsh

Published

Further titles are in preparation

Analysing Texts
Series Standing Order ISBN 978–0–333–73260–1
(*outside North America only*)

You can receive future titles in this series as they are published by placing a standing order. Please contact your bookseller or, in the case of difficulty, write to us at the address below with your name and address, the title of the series and the ISBN quoted above.

Customer Services Department, Macmillan Distribution Ltd,
Houndmills, Basingstoke, Hampshire. RG21 6XS, UK

Charles Dickens:
David Copperfield /
Great Expectations

NICOLAS TREDELL

palgrave
macmillan

First published 2013 by
PALGRAVE MACMILLAN

Palgrave Macmillan in the UK is an imprint of Macmillan Publishers Limited,
registered in England, company number 785998, of Houndmills, Basingstoke,
Hampshire RG21 6XS.

Palgrave Macmillan in the US is a division of St Martin's Press LLC,
175 Fifth Avenue, New York, NY 10010.

Palgrave Macmillan is the global academic imprint of the above companies
and has companies and representatives throughout the world.

Palgrave® and Macmillan® are registered trademarks in the United States,
the United Kingdom, Europe and other countries.

ISBN 978–1–137–28324–5   hardback
ISBN 978–1–137–28323–8   paperback

This book is printed on paper suitable for recycling and made from fully
managed and sustained forest sources. Logging, pulping and manufacturing
processes are expected to conform to the environmental regulations of the
country of origin.

A catalogue record for this book is available from the British Library.

A catalog record for this book is available from the Library of Congress.

Typeset by MPS Limited, Chennai, India.

FOR ANGELA

'the dear presence, without
which I were nothing'

Contents

General Editor's Preface

This series is dedicated to one clear belief: that we can all enjoy, understand and analyse literature for ourselves, provided we know how to do it. How can we build on close understanding of a short passage, and develop our insight into the whole work? What features do we expect to find in a text? Why do we study style in so much detail? In demystifying the study of literature, these are only some of the questions the *Analysing Texts* series addresses and answers.

The books in this series will not do all the work for you, but will provide you with the tools, and show you how to use them. Here, you will find samples of close, detailed analysis, with an explanation of the analytical techniques utilised. At the end of each chapter there are useful suggestions for further work you can do to practise, develop and hone the skills demonstrated and build confidence in your own analytical ability.

An author's individuality shows in the way they write: every work they produce bears the hallmark of that writer's personal 'style'. In the main part of each book we concentrate therefore on analysing the particular flavour and concerns of one author's work, and explain the features of their writing in connection with major themes. In Part II, there are chapters about the author's life and work, assessing their contribution to developments in literature; and a sample of critics' views are summarised and discussed in comparison with each other.

Some suggestions for further reading provide a bridge towards further critical research.

Analysing Texts is designed to stimulate and encourage your critical and analytic faculty, to develop your personal insight into the author's work and individual style, and to provide you with the skills and techniques to enjoy at first hand the excitement of discovering the richness of the text.

NICHOLAS MARSH

Acknowledgements

As always, my warmest thanks go to my beloved wife Angela for our many Dickensian discussions and explorations; we still have a ticket to the Doughty Street Dickens Museum in London from the time when entrance cost 45p, which gives some idea of how long we have been interested in this writer!

I am most grateful to Sonya Barker at Palgrave Macmillan for inviting me to write this book and supporting its composition; to Nicholas Marsh, the series editor, for his heartening and perceptive observations on the proposal and completed draft; to Juanita Bullough for her careful and sympathetic editing of the typescript; and to Felicity Noble at Palgrave Macmillan for her prompt, friendly and professional assistance.

I would also like to express my gratitude to the late Denis Froelich, my student, mentor and friend, for our lively and much-missed debates about Dickens and other novelists past and present.

Note on Quotations

Quotations are from *David Copperfield* (Penguin, 1985) and *Great Expectations* (Penguin, 1965 edition). In references, the titles are abbreviated to *DC* and *GE*.

All quoted definitions of words are from the *Oxford English Dictionary*, unless otherwise stated.

All quotations from Shakespeare are from the RSC/Macmillan *Complete Works* (2007).

Introduction

David Copperfield and *Great Expectations* are two of Dickens's most popular novels. Both are examples of the *Bildungsroman*, the novel of personal development and education by life, but they do not simply adopt an established form – rather, they enlarge and enrich ideas of what the *Bildungsroman* can encompass and set precedents and standards that future writers of *Bildungsromane* will seek to emulate, surpass and challenge. Both have first-person narrators who look back on their experiences as boys and young men from a later perspective, employing sophisticated adult language in their descriptive prose, withholding information to create suspense and produce dramatic climaxes, and moving between vivid re-creation of their earlier impressions and feelings and more distanced views.

Both *Copperfield* and *Expectations* have characteristic Dickensian qualities: an eloquent command of language, in terms of sentence structure, punctuation, rhythm, imagery and symbolism; complex plots packed with twists, turns, complications and surprises; a rich generic mixture that weaves into the *Bildungsroman* elements of comedy, tragicomedy, realism, romance, fairy tale, fantasy, melodrama, gothic fiction and thriller; obsessive, grotesque and eccentric characters who incarnate extreme psychological states linked to key elements of Victorian society; vividly realized settings – landscapes, cityscapes and interiors – that echo and amplify the emotional states and ethical and social issues the novels explore; an emotional and tonal range that includes joy, laughter, love, loss, terror, sublimity, pathos and pain; and a concern with the proper way to live one's life and organize society.

1

Both novels powerfully portray isolated childhoods in which the protagonists suffer physical and psychological violence from some of those who should care for them. Both trace patterns of upward mobility as the protagonists achieve greater prosperity and social status. Both move between rural settings close to river and sea and the metropolis of London. Both show their protagonists experiencing shocks, setbacks and losses that culminate in breakdowns from which they eventually make some kind of recovery.

There are also, however, marked contrasts between *Copperfield* and *Expectations.* The tone of the later novel is comparatively chastened and its narrative is more strongly focused than *Copperfield* on characters and events which contribute to the exposition of its plot and the exploration of its themes. In *Copperfield* the narrator often makes the reader aware that he is writing from a later perspective, looking back, remembering and re-creating; in *Expectations* the narrator reminds the reader of this less often. Both David and Pip suffer many vicissitudes from childhood onwards; but David eventually becomes a successful writer and, after losing his first wife and his beloved friend, ends as a happily married man with children; Pip, after the confiscation of his fortune, pursues a modest business career in the colonies, stays single, and faces an uncertain matrimonial future at the famously ambiguous end of the novel.

In *Part I,* 'Analysing *David Copperfield* and *Great Expectations*', we select short extracts from each novel for close analysis and explore the ways in which they use the resources of language to develop their novels' themes. We aim to build up an increasingly rich understanding of each novel, and of the comparisons between them, which starts from, and returns to, the details of the texts.

In *Part II,* 'The Context and the Critics', we shall explore the biographical, historical, cultural and critical contexts of the novels. There is a summary of Dickens's life and works, a survey of the historical, cultural and literary contexts of his oeuvre, a sample of key critical views and suggestions for Further Reading to guide readers through the rich and extensive field of writing about Dickens.

PART I

ANALYSING *DAVID COPPERFIELD* AND *GREAT EXPECTATIONS*

1

Sons and Patriarchs

Near the start of both *Copperfield* and *Expectations*, the protagonist of each novel, then a small, vulnerable, fatherless boy, encounters a threatening, quasi-paternal male figure that suddenly appears in his life: Murdstone in the case of David, Magwitch in the case of Pip. The fathers of both boys are dead; while David's mother is alive and feels affection for her son, she is not a strong character and cannot protect him from her second husband; David's nurse, Peggotty, is deeply loving but limited in what she can do by her social position and temperament. Pip has lost not only his father but also his mother and five little brothers; he lives with his surviving sister, over twenty years his senior, and her husband, Joe Gargery, the blacksmith; but Mrs Joe, as she is known, is callous, quick to administer corporal punishment, incurious and unimaginative, and while Joe is loving towards Pip, in a way that is both boyish and maternal, he dare not stand up to his wife when she bullies her younger brother, fearing that to do so would only make matters worse.

Both David and Pip are in situations that make them vulnerable to the intervention of domineering men who are capable of verbal and physical violence and who, in different ways, play the patriarchal role traditionally assigned to the father. Murdstone, with a veneer of religiosity and respectability, insinuates himself into David's household and becomes David's stepfather, but, as this chapter will later show, he and his stepson soon come into violent conflict; Magwitch starts by laying violent hands on Pip but later becomes Pip's secret benefactor, his 'second father', as he describes himself in the great recognition scene in chapter 39 of *Expectations*, which we will discuss in chapter 4 of this book. In both cases the encounters of the young protagonists with these patriarchal figures changes their lives. We can see harbingers of this change in the first passage we analyse, from *Copperfield*, which evokes David's initial meeting with Murdstone.

The Wrong Hand: *David Copperfield*, pp. 66–8

'But if you marry a person, and the person dies, why then you may marry another person, mayn't you, Peggotty?'

'You MAY,' says Peggotty, 'if you choose, my dear. That's a matter of opinion.'

'But what is your opinion, Peggotty?' said I.

I asked her, and looked curiously at her, because she looked so curiously at me.

'My opinion is,' said Peggotty, taking her eyes from me, after a little indecision and going on with her work, 'that I never was married myself, Master Davy, and that I don't expect to be. That's all I know about the subject.'

'You an't cross, I suppose, Peggotty, are you?' said I, after sitting quiet for a minute.

I really thought she was, she had been so short with me; but I was quite mistaken: for she laid aside her work (which was a stocking of her own), and opening her arms wide, took my curly head within them, and gave it a good squeeze. I know it was a good squeeze, because, being very plump, whenever she made any little exertion after she was dressed, some of the buttons on the back of her gown flew off. And I recollect two bursting to the opposite side of the parlour, while she was hugging me.

'Now let me hear some more about the Crorkindills,' said Peggotty, who was not quite right in the name yet, 'for I an't heard half enough.'

I couldn't quite understand why Peggotty looked so queer, or why she was so ready to go back to the crocodiles. However, we returned to those monsters, with fresh wakefulness on my part, and we left their eggs in the sand for the sun to hatch; and we ran away from them, and baffled them by constantly turning, which they were unable to do quickly, on account of their unwieldy make; and we went down into the water after them, as natives, and put sharp pieces of timber down their throats; and in short we ran the whole crocodile gauntlet. *I* did, at least; but I had my doubts of Peggotty, who was thoughtfully sticking her needle into various parts of her face and arms, all the time.

We had exhausted the crocodiles, and begun with the alligators, when the garden-bell rang. We went out to the door; and there was my mother, looking unusually pretty, I thought, and with her a gentleman with beautiful black hair and whiskers, who had walked home with us from church last Sunday.

As my mother stooped down on the threshold to take me in her arms and kiss me, the gentleman said I was a more highly privileged little fellow than a monarch – or something like that; for my later understanding comes, I am sensible, to my aid here.

'What does that mean?' I asked him, over her shoulder.

He patted me on the head; but somehow, I didn't like him or his deep voice, and I was jealous that his hand should touch my mother's in touching me – which it did. I put it away, as well as I could.

'Oh, Davy!' remonstrated my mother.

'Dear boy!' said the gentleman. 'I cannot wonder at his devotion!'

I never saw such a beautiful colour on my mother's face before. She gently chid me for being rude; and, keeping me close to her shawl, turned to thank the gentleman for taking so much trouble as to bring her home. She put her hand to him as she spoke, and, as he met it with his own, she glanced, I thought, at me.

'Let us say "good night", my fine boy,' said the gentleman, when he had bent his head – *I* saw him! – over my mother's little glove.

'Good night!' said I.

'Come! Let us be the best friends in the world!' said the gentleman, laughing. 'Shake hands!'

My right hand was in my mother's left, so I gave him the other.

'Why, that's the wrong hand, Davy!' laughed the gentleman.

My mother drew my right hand forward, but I was resolved, for my former reason, not to give it him, and I did not. I gave him the other, and he shook it heartily, and said I was a brave fellow, and went away.

At this minute I see him turn round in the garden, and give us a last look with his ill-omened black eyes, before the door was shut.

We shall start by analysing the dialogue, as it is prominent in this passage. In talking to each other, David and Peggotty use some non-standard kinds of English; both employ the contracted form 'an't' for 'are not' and David says 'mayn't you' instead of 'may you not'. But there is a distinction between the child and the nurse: Peggotty has difficulty in pronouncing the unfamiliar word 'crocodiles', in contrast to David, who has been reading aloud to her about them and has clearly mastered the pronunciation; this establishes him as a character who already enjoys a higher degree of literacy and articulateness than Peggotty. Nonetheless, David is able to talk to Peggotty with more directness than he can talk to his mother and the nameless gentleman; with them he speaks only twice, curtly, and in Standard English forms: 'What does that mean?'; 'Good night'. But both with Peggotty and, though to a lesser extent, with the gentleman, David's direct-speech dialogue is largely in the interrogative mode – that is, he is asking questions.

These questions are about adult topics. The first questions concern the nature of marriage and the constraints on who may marry whom. The second question is about why a gentleman might feel that David is highly privileged to receive a kiss from his mother. To David's questions about marriage, Peggotty answers evasively; to his question about whether she is cross with him because of his questions, she answers, not with words, but with an all-embracing gesture that is hugely reassuring to the vulnerable young boy but compounds her evasiveness on the topic of marriage – immediately after the hug, she speaks in a way that seems intended to pre-empt further interrogation on the matter. To David's question to the unknown gentleman, about the meaning of what the latter has just said, he receives, not a reply, but another gesture that is not affectionate but implicitly patronizing. Peggotty does at least try to offer some verbal response to David's questions, even while trying to close the issue; but the gentleman does not reply verbally to David's initial question, and he and David's mother offer the boy, not explanations, but only remonstrations, exclamations and imperatives ('Oh, Davy!'; 'Dear boy!'; 'Let us say "good night", my fine boy'; 'Let us be the best friends in the world!'). In the dialogue, the way in which David's questions are answered evasively or not at all and his inability to extract straight answers from adults suggest his limited knowledge of grown-up life and his comparative powerlessness.

It is also notable that the unknown gentleman's first words to David are not in dialogue but in the more distanced mode of indirect speech, which is woven into the narrative prose of the novel. Moreover, the narrator makes it clear that he is not claiming to recall the gentleman's words precisely but is offering an approximation from a later, adult viewpoint; as he says, 'my later understanding comes, I am sensible [that is, I notice or appreciate], to my aid'. This further distances the unknown gentleman by implying that he speaks in a way that is not quite comprehensible to a young boy. Indeed, his words contain an inappropriate sexual reference (the gentleman is implying that David is fortunate to be kissed by such a woman in the way that an adult male might be fortunate to be kissed by her). His parting compliment to David – that he is a brave fellow – is also rendered in indirect speech, as if David, at the end of his first meeting with the unknown gentleman, were pushing the compliment away from him. Mrs Copperfield's gentle chiding of him, and her thanking of the gentleman, are also presented in indirect speech, as if to indicate that she, too, is becoming distanced from David.

The narrative prose of the passage shows an extensive command of vocabulary and syntax that signals the voice of the adult narrator. We have just seen how at one point, David makes it explicit that he is interpreting childhood experience – in this case, the words of the unknown gentleman – with adult understanding. A second shift into the present tense occurs in the last sentence of the extract: 'At this minute' – that is, the minute at which David is writing – 'I see him turn round in the garden and give us a last look'. Here, however, the effect is not one of detachment, of the adult standing back from earlier experience and commenting upon it reflectively; rather, the use of the present tense, combined with the relatively simple, largely monosyllabic vocabulary – only four of the words in this 27–word sentence have more than one syllable – serve to close the gap between past and present, to show David plunged back into the experience in all its painful immediacy. For much of the passage the narrator stays within the child's limited understanding of the situation while letting the reader infer what is actually happening – that is, that the unknown gentleman is courting David's widowed mother with the idea of marrying her. The extract thus offers a kind of double vision in which the reader sees David's experiences from both his boyhood and his adult perspectives.

The extract contains two especially elaborate paragraphs of narrative prose: the first describes Peggotty's embrace of David, the second evokes David's reading aloud of the story about the crocodiles. The first of these paragraphs opens with a long multiple sentence, punctuated by semicolons, which takes David from anxiety at having perhaps angered Peggotty to a sense of relief and reassurance that she still loves him. In this sentence, the implications of the adjective 'short', referring to her truncation of the discussion about marriage, are compensated by 'opening', where the present participle supplies a sense of greater expansiveness than the use of a finite verb ('opened') would have done; while the closing words of the sentence, 'gave it a good squeeze', with its monosyllables and its alliteration of 'gave' and 'good', convey a sense of safe enclosure. The repetition of the phrase 'a good squeeze' in the next sentence emphasizes this. This sentence goes on to make the general point that the buttons on the back of Peggotty's gown always fly off whenever she slightly exerts herself, comically conveying Peggotty's plumpness and the constriction of her gown. An example of this general point, specific to the present instance, follows: two of her buttons fly off when she squeezes David. This symbolizes both the amplitude of her affection (two buttons, not just one) and her lack of opportunity to express it, as a respectable woman without a husband or children of her own. The present participles in the last sentence of the paragraph ('bursting', 'hugging') reiterate the ideas of exuberant expansiveness and affectionate closure.

In the paragraph about the crocodiles, the sentence that starts 'However, we returned' is, at 79 words, the longest sentence of the extract. There is a significant shift in this sentence from the first- and third-person pronouns ('I', 'she', 'he'), which are used elsewhere in the extract, to the first-person plural, 'we', as if David were talking about an experience that he and Peggotty share – or that David would like to share with her, since it later becomes apparent that Peggotty's thoughts are elsewhere. The sentence goes on to describe the imaginary adventure that David is reading aloud as if it were a real one ('we returned'; 'we left'; 'we ran away'); this suggests David's capacity to become absorbed in fictional and in this case exotic narrative (the hinterland of the British Empire is implied here, as in other parts of Dickens). But after the long sentence ends, the next one immediately abandons 'we' for an

'I' stressed by its italicization; this shift of pronoun indicates David's awareness of his distance from Peggotty and of the fact that, despite the previous use of the first-person plural, the imaginative experience has *not* been shared. A description that demonstrates Peggotty's distraction follows, as she seems to be lost in thought and keeps sticking her needle into her face and arms, as if inadvertently mortifying herself for improper thoughts – thoughts, we may infer, about Mrs Copperfield's possible remarriage.

The extract then returns to shorter paragraphs and sentences without semicolons, as David moves from his imaginary world and from Peggotty's company to the reality of his mother and the unknown gentleman – though there is an implicit link, which later events in the novel will draw out, between that gentleman and the predatory crocodiles and alligators. The description of how David's mother stoops on the threshold to take him in her arms and kiss him is much more straightforward and subdued than the account of Peggotty hugging David – no bursting buttons here; the kiss may be deeply felt but could be, from the description, merely conventional. Moreover, while Peggotty's embrace of David excludes others and encloses the two parties, even if only for a brief space, in a world of their own, David's possession of his mother's hand is threatened by the gentleman's attempt to touch hers. David signals his aversion to the gentleman by pushing his hand away, refusing to release his mother's hand and to present the correct hand for the gentleman to shake. As if inverting a colloquial phrase, Dickens shows how David and the unknown gentleman get off, not on the wrong foot, but on the wrong hand.

The diction of the passage, the words that it uses, also help to convey the sense that something strange and unprecedented in David's experience is happening. The adverb 'curiously' occurs twice, applied to the way David looks at Peggotty and to the way she looks at him. The phrase 'so queer' stresses the extremely peculiar nature of Peggotty's expression. The adverb 'unusually', applied to his mother's prettiness, further reinforces the sense that an extraordinary event is occurring, and this sense of the unusual develops into a sense of the unprecedented in the statement that David 'never saw such a beautiful colour on my mother's face before'. This signifies to the adult reader the way in which the gentleman's presence has excited Mrs Copperfield.

It is also notable that the adjective 'beautiful' is used twice in this extract; here, and in the earlier description of the gentleman's 'beautiful black hair and whiskers'. This creates a subtle link between the man and the woman – a harbinger of their future marriage – as well as suggesting the physical attractiveness of the husband-to-be and signalling his masculinity through the mention of his 'whiskers'. But the adjective 'black' assumes more negative connotations in the last sentence of the extract, where the adjective 'ill-omened' precedes it; the gentleman is taking on the characteristics of a villain of melodrama. The finite verb 'shut' at the end of that sentence contrasts with the present participle 'opening' earlier in the extract and, in the context, takes on two contradictory meanings: for the moment, the threatening male figure has been shut *out*; but he may later become the one who shuts *in* David and his mother.

The term 'gentleman', which is used seven times in the extract, is an especially significant one in both *Copperfield* and *Expectations*. Both novels explore the potential contradiction between the social and ethical implications of the term. On one level, 'gentleman' signifies a man of good social position, especially one who enjoys wealth and leisure; on another, it signifies an honourable, morally good man. Even in this first encounter, the reader may suspect that Mrs Copperfield's suitor is not a gentleman in the ethical sense – and the sexually suggestive element in his remarks, made in the presence of a child, indicates that he is not altogether a gentleman in the social sense either. In the next passage, from the first chapter of *Great Expectations*, we see an encounter between a boy protagonist and a man with no pretensions to gentility, the convict whom he will later come to know as Abel Magwitch.

A Fearful Man: *Great Expectations*, pp. 35–6

Ours was the marsh country, down by the river, within, as the river wound, twenty miles of the sea. My first most vivid and broad impression of the identity of things, seems to me to have been gained on a memorable raw afternoon towards evening. At such a time I found out for certain, that this bleak place overgrown with nettles was the churchyard; and that Philip Pirrip, late of this parish, and also Georgiana wife of the above, were dead and buried; and that Alexander, Bartholomew, Abraham, Tobias, and Roger, infant children of the aforesaid, were also dead and buried; and that the dark flat wilderness beyond the churchyard, intersected with dykes and mounds and gates, with scattered cattle feeding on it, was the marshes; and that the low leaden line beyond, was the river; and that the distant savage lair from which the wind was rushing, was the sea; and that the small bundle of shivers growing afraid of it all and beginning to cry, was Pip.

'Hold your noise!' cried a terrible voice, as a man started up from among the graves at the side of the church porch. 'Keep still, you little devil, or I'll cut your throat!'

A fearful man, all in coarse grey, with a great iron on his leg. A man with no hat, and with broken shoes, and with an old rag tied round his head. A man who had been soaked in water, and smothered in mud, and lamed by stones, and cut by flints, and stung by nettles, and torn by briars; who limped, and shivered, and glared and growled; and whose teeth chattered in his head as he seized me by the chin.

'O! Don't cut my throat, sir,' I pleaded in terror. 'Pray don't do it, sir.'

'Tell us your name!' said the man. 'Quick!'

'Pip, sir.'

'Once more,' said the man, staring at me. 'Give it mouth!'

'Pip. Pip, sir.'

'Show us where you live,' said the man. 'Pint out the place!'

I pointed to where our village lay, on the flat in-shore among the alder-trees and pollards, a mile or more from the church.

The man, after looking at me for a moment, turned me upside down, and emptied my pockets. There was nothing in them but a piece of bread. When the church came to itself – for he was so sudden and strong that he made it go head over heels before me, and I saw the steeple under my feet – when the church came to itself, I say, I was seated on a high tombstone, trembling while he ate the bread ravenously.

With this extract, in which dialogue, though vital, is less prominent than in the previous one we discussed, we can start by considering the narrative prose. The sentences in the narrative prose vary between fairly straightforward declarative sentences – 'There was nothing in them [Pip's pockets] but a piece of bread' – and three more extensive sentences that we shall look at in more detail: first, the especially elaborate sentence in the first paragraph that starts 'At such a time I found out'; secondly, the sentence in the third paragraph starting 'A man who had been soaked'; and thirdly, the long concluding sentence of the extract, with its interpolation.

The especially elaborate sentence (124 words) in the first paragraph develops the experience of Pip's 'first most vivid and broad impression of the identity of things' that he has summarized in the previous sentence. It starts with a phrase which indicates time – 'At such a time' – and a main clause 'I found out for certain'; seven relative clauses, introduced by 'that', then follow, all dependent on the first clause for their complete meaning. Each of these dependent clauses gives an example of 'the identity of things' that Pip has discovered for the first time. Four of these are elements of the landscape: the churchyard; the marshes; the river; the sea (we can easily imagine them as parts of a landscape painting). Two of the elements are not physical aspects of the landscape but objects of cognition with a strong emotional charge: the fact of death, of parents and siblings, respectively. The last element is of Pip's own identity as a small human being in the landscape, vulnerable to fear, shivering and starting to cry. So Pip becomes aware of the landscape and the names for parts of the landscape, and of the primal facts of death and life – his own. The question of identity raised at the outset of *Great Expectations* is important throughout the novel as Pip moves from the forge to the metropolis, from labour as a skilled artisan to leisure as a gentleman of private means, and from the belief that his benefactor is a lady to the certainty that he is an ex-convict. It is significant that when Pip falls gravely ill, the issue of 'identity' recurs as a plural noun, as we shall see in chapter 6 of this book.

In the third paragraph, the first two sentences are not, strictly speaking, sentences at all, since they contain no finite verb; but together with the third sentence, they help to form a progression; the second is slightly longer than the first, the third longer than the first two sentences combined. The first sentence starts with an indefinite article, an adjective and a noun – 'A fearful man'; the ambiguity of 'fearful', which can mean to show or to cause fear, suggests the double aspect of Magwitch, who is both terrifying and terrified, hunter and hunted, victimizer and victim; although the frightening aspect is uppermost here, the frightened aspect soon starts to become apparent.

The next two sentences start in a similar but simpler way, dropping the adjective and presenting 'A man', giving him a primal quality. The first sentence describes the signs that he is a convict; the 'coarse grey', presumably of his prison garb, and the 'great iron on his leg'. The second sentence concentrates on his lack of clothing: no hat, broken shoes, an old rag round his head. The third, longer sentence starts by changing the emphasis from Magwitch's appearance to what has happened to him; the use of the passive voice here – 'had been' – turns him more into victim than victimizer, the sufferer rather than the source of violence, even if the aggression, in an immediate sense, has come only from inanimate nature (water, mud, stones, flints, briars) rather than from man (in a longer perspective, however, the aggression has come from human beings, who have forced Magwitch to become a desperate fugitive and injure himself in the attempt to escape). After the semicolon, the focus changes to Magwitch's appearance and behaviour again, but this time it concentrates on his body and the sounds (growls) he emits; this focus continues after the next semicolon, in the clause which describes his chattering teeth; but in the last clause of the sentence he becomes the aggressor again, seizing Pip by the chin.

The final sentence of the extract is another longish one; it starts with a dependent clause indicating time – 'When' – and a moment when order is restored, 'when the church came to itself'; but this is then interrupted by an interpolated clause that, in its rhythm and diction – with phrases like 'sudden and strong', 'head over heels', 'steeple under my feet' – helps to convey the shock of having one's usual perceptions disrupted, as Pip's are when he is turned upside-down. The time clause is then repeated, followed by an insistent present-tense interjection, 'I say', that reminds us that we are reading a retrospective account. After this we move on to the main clause which states that Pip is perched on a high tombstone – as it were, sitting astride a grave but elevated above his usual level – and the sentence ends with a stress on two primal feelings: Pip's fear – he is still trembling – and Magwitch's ravenous hunger as he devours the bread.

The diction of the extract helps to convey and reinforce its meanings in a range of ways. There are many nouns: 'river'; 'sea' (both repeated twice); 'wilderness'; 'iron'; 'water'; 'mud'; and, in the plural, 'nettles'; 'dykes'; 'mounds'; 'gates'; 'cattle'; 'marshes'; 'stones'; 'flints';

'briars'; 'bread'; 'church'. Most of the nouns that are associated with the 'man' stress the extremity of his situation: 'iron' connotes hardness; 'rag' suggests poverty; and 'water', 'mud', 'stones' and 'briars' are all natural phenomena that can, in certain circumstances, harm human beings and, significantly in this case, impede their movements; they are further obstacles to Magwitch's liberty, already severely constrained by his leg-iron. The adjectives throughout the extract often have harsh and negative connotations: 'bleak' (used twice); 'dead'; 'buried'; 'dark'; 'flat'; 'low'; 'leaden'; 'savage'; 'terrible'; 'fearful'; 'coarse'; 'broken'. The past participles reinforce these connotations: 'soaked'; 'smothered'; 'lamed'; 'cut'; 'stung'; 'torn'; 'limped'; 'shivered'; 'glared'; 'growled'.

Magwitch's growls are the inarticulate edge of his dialogue with Pip. This dialogue takes the form of short, sharp exchanges, in which Magwitch issues imperatives – 'Hold your noise', 'Keep still', 'Tell us your name!', 'Tell us where you live' – and Pip's responses are confined to pleas and the utterance – three times – of his name, a repetition driven by fear but also reinforcing the awareness of his identity that he has just achieved. The man's utterances are characterized by some non-Standard-English usages: the vivid slang term, 'Give it mouth' for 'Say it', and the pronunciation of 'Point' as 'Pint'.

We can also see how elements of the passage take on symbolic dimensions. When the man with the 'terrible voice' starts up from among the graves, it is as if someone has risen from the dead – and given that it is a man, we could suggest that it might momentarily seem like Pip's late father. If we have read the rest of the novel, we know that the man who has risen up this afternoon will, in the later scene where he reveals himself as Pip's benefactor, call himself Pip's 'second father'. The 'great iron' on Magwitch's leg can be seen as a phallic symbol, which reinforces his patriarchal identity; but it could also be seen to indicate the burden of manhood that Pip will bear in the future as he experiences unrequited desire for Estella.

The extract includes four intertextual echoes – that is, points which recall some other text, not by Dickens. This kind of intertextual echo may be conscious on the author's part, but need not be; nor need it depend on the author having read the text that is echoed, since key elements drawn from that text may be circulating in the wider cultural ambience in which an author is writing. One intertextual link is with William Wordsworth's poem 'We are seven', first published in Wordsworth and Coleridge's *Lyrical Ballads* (1798; 1801; 1802). In 'We are seven', a small girl insists to an adult questioner that she has a family of seven, even though two of her siblings are dead and lie in the churchyard; Pip, in contrast, recognizes the reality of the death of his siblings and parents and the difference between them and himself, who still lives.

The three other intertextual links involve Magwitch. One is with the Oedipus legend from ancient Greek myth; Oedipus is lame – Oedipus literally means 'swollen-foot' – and Magwitch has been 'lamed by stones'. It might seem that the Oedipal role is more appropriate to Pip, whose own father is dead and who might feel, in fantasy, that he has been responsible, even if inadvertently, for his death, as Oedipus was inadvertently responsible for killing his own father. The matter is complicated by the fact that Pip's mother is also dead, whereas in the Oedipus myth the son, having killed the father, inadvertently possesses the mother, not knowing at first who she is; Oedipus's mother does, however, kill herself eventually, when she realizes that she has committed incest with her son, so in a sense her son is also responsible for her death in the longer term. But an intertextual echo in one text of another text does not entail a precise replication of that other text; the intertextual transfer may, and very probably will, alter and redistribute the other text being redeployed. This, we could argue, is what happens in the Dickens passage: Pip is the Oedipal figure in the sense that he may feel guilty at his father's death; but the lame foot has been transferred to the surrogate father who, like Hamlet's uncle, may seem to bear the guilt of killing the father. Another intertextual link involving Magwitch is with the Bible. As a man not only 'lamed by stones', but also 'cut by flints' and 'stung by briars', Magwitch has a biblical quality, as if he had undergone sufferings like those of Christ. A further intertextual link is with the generic figure whose identity Edgar, on the run because he is unjustly suspected of plotting to kill his father, assumes in Shakespeare's *King Lear*: Poor Tom, 'the basest and most poorest shape / That ever penury in contempt of man / Brought near to beast', one of those 'Bedlam beggars' who '[s]trike in their numbed and mortified arms / Pins, wooden pricks, nails, sprigs of rosemary' (*RSC* Shakespeare, 2:2:163–5, 170, 171–2).

In *Copperfield*, Murdstone, the surrogate father, lays violent hands on his substitute son but does not, at first, seem to have suffered physically as Magwitch has done. It is David, bullied and provoked, who does violence to Murdstone, as the next passage will show.

The Beater Bit: *David Copperfield*, pp. 108–9

He walked me up to my room slowly and gravely – I am certain he had a delight in that formal parade of executing justice – and when we got there, suddenly twisted my head under his arm.

'Mr Murdstone! Sir!' I cried to him. 'Don't! Pray don't beat me! I have tried to learn, sir, but I can't learn while you and Miss Murdstone are by. I can't indeed!'

'Can't you indeed, David?' he said. 'We'll try that.'

He had my head as in a vice, but I twined round him somehow, and stopped him for a moment, entreating him not to beat me. It was only a moment that I stopped him, for he cut me heavily an instant afterwards, and in the same instant I caught the hand with which he held me in my mouth, between my teeth, and bit it through. It sets my teeth on edge to think of it.

He beat me then, as if he would have beaten me to death. Above all the noise we made, I heard them running up the stairs, and crying out – I heard my mother crying out – and Peggotty. Then he was gone; and the door was locked outside; and I was lying fevered and hot, and torn, and sore, and raging in my puny way, upon the floor.

How well I recollect, when I became quiet, what an unnatural stillness seemed to reign through the whole house! How well I remember, when my heart and passion began to cool, how wicked I began to feel!

I sat listening for a long while, but there was not a sound. I crawled up from the floor, and saw my face in the glass, so swollen, red, and ugly that it almost frightened me. My stripes were sore and stiff, and made me cry afresh, when I moved; but they were nothing to the guilt I felt. It lay heavier on my breast than if I had been a most atrocious criminal, I dare say.

It had begun to grow dark, and I had shut the window (I had been lying, for the most part, with my head upon the sill, by turns crying, dozing, and looking listlessly out), when the key was turned, and Miss Murdstone came in with some bread and meat, and milk. These she put down upon the table without a word, glaring at me the while with exemplary firmness, and then retired, locking the door after her.

Long after it was dark I sat there, wondering whether anybody else would come. When this appeared improbable for that night, I undressed, and went to bed; and, there, I began to wonder fearfully what would be done to me. Whether it was a criminal act that I had committed? Whether I should be taken into custody and sent to prison? Whether I was at all in danger of being hanged?

I never shall forget the waking, next morning; the being cheerful and fresh for the first moment, and then the being weighed down by the stale and dismal oppression of remembrance. Miss Murdstone reappeared before I was out of bed; told me, in so many words, that I was free to walk in the garden for half an hour and no longer; and retired, leaving the door open, that I might avail myself of that permission.

I did so, and did so every morning of my imprisonment, which lasted five days. If I could have seen my mother alone, I should have gone down on my knees to her and besought her forgiveness; but I saw no one, Miss Murdstone excepted, during the whole time – except at evening prayers in the parlour; to which I was escorted by Miss Murdstone after everybody else was placed; where I was stationed, a young outlaw, all alone by myself near the door; and whence I was solemnly conducted by my jailer, before any one arose from the devotional posture. I only observed that my mother was as far off from me as she could be, and kept her face another way so that I never saw it; and that Mr Murdstone's hand was bound up in a large linen wrapper.

The one-sentence opening paragraph of the extract is at first dignified and decorous in its rhythm and vocabulary, but the interpolated clause indicates that Murdstone takes an inappropriate pleasure in the rituals of executing justice, and the conclusion of that sentence – 'suddenly twisted my head under his arm' – is startling and brutal. It is followed by the only example in this extract of direct-speech dialogue, and its shortness, in this context, signals the breakdown of dialogue between David and Murdstone, the prelude to the shift into physical violence. The first and second sentences of the following paragraph convey a strong sense of the physical struggle between man and boy. He has previously offered the wrong hand to Murdstone; now he bites Murdstone's hand. The sentence that ends the next paragraph shows a characteristic Dickensian progression over three clauses separated by semicolons: 'Then he was gone; and the door was locked outside; and I was lying fevered and hot, and torn, and sore, and raging in my puny way, upon the floor'. The first clause is short and direct and Murdstone is the subject; the second is slightly longer and the subject is the impersonal 'door'; the third is considerably longer and focuses on David and his desperate discontents, amplifying them by an accumulation of adjectives.

This sentence is also notable for its use of grammatical parallelism; each clause starts with a grammatical subject ('he'/'the door'/'I'), followed by 'was': 'he was'/ 'the door was'/'I was'. Across these parallel phrases, there is a shift from Murdstone ('he'), to the impersonal 'door', to David himself and his sufferings. A further example of parallelism occurs in the paired phrasing 'How well I recollect/How well I remember'. This emphasizes that David is remembering an earlier experience and shows his capacity, at least from this distance, to marshal and order that experience in words; but the parallel phrases also reinforce the persistence of his traumatic memories – in a sense, he remembers them all too well. The parallelism here is combined with another rhetorical device; the start of each sentence, 'How well I', is not simply parallel but identical; this kind of repetition, in which a word or phrase is repeated in, and particularly at the start of, a sentence, is known as anaphora and it was a favourite device of Dickens. Anaphora is also apparent in the thrice-repeated use, in the paragraph beginning 'Long after it was dark', of 'whether': 'Whether it was'; 'Whether I should'; 'Whether I was'. This repetition of 'whether' helps to convey David's sense of uncertainty about what is going to happen to him.

The present tense is used at two points in the extract, signalling David's perspective as an adult: 'I am certain he had a delight in that formal parade of executing justice' and 'It sets my teeth on edge to think of it'. The first sentence is analytical, with David articulating what he might have perceived at the time but could not have expressed in those words – that Murdstone takes a sadistic pleasure in the ritual that precedes administering physical punishment. The second vividly conveys the way in which his memory of biting Murdstone still disturbs him physically.

The diction includes verbs denoting struggle and violence: 'twisted'; 'twined'; 'stopped'; 'beat'; 'cut'; 'caught'; 'held'; 'bit'; 'locked'. Most of these are monosyllabic so that, in the context, they strike home like blows. Several adjectives indicate the painful after-effects of violence: 'fevered'; 'hot'; 'torn'; 'sore' (used twice); 'raging'; 'swollen'; 'red'; 'ugly'; 'stiff'. There is a significant body of vocabulary that refers to crime and punishment: 'executing justice' (where 'executing' in the sense of 'putting into effect' is shadowed by 'executing' in the sense of putting someone to death); 'wicked'; 'guilt'; 'criminal' (used twice); 'custody'; 'prison'; 'hanged'; 'imprisonment'; 'outlaw'. This vocabulary both demonstrates the acute sense of guilt that David suffered as a child and implies relationships between judicial and penal machinery and the intimate mechanisms of family life.

The extract contains four time-frames. The first is that of the beating itself, which lasts for a relatively short period and stays close to real time, the time such an event would actually take, though the account of the beating that followed the biting is compressed – it presumably went on for some time. This time-frame ends with David locked in his room, lying on the floor. The second covers, in summary form, a far longer time-stretch: the rest of the day and well into the evening. The third briefly evokes David waking the next morning, thinking momentarily that all is well, and then recalling what has happened and being made aware, by Miss Murdstone, that he is, in effect, a prisoner, a fact signalled by a restriction on his time: he is permitted to walk in the garden for no more than half an hour. The fourth time-frame is the most extensive, covering the five days of his imprisonment and summarizing repeated daily actions and David's persistent feelings, throughout that time, of guilt compounded by isolation. Pip experiences similar feelings in the next extract we analyse, from *Expectations*, when he has already secreted some food for Magwitch and feels he must rob the pantry for more.

Ask No Questions: *Great Expectations*, pp. 45–7

It was Christmas Eve, and I had to stir the pudding for next day, with the copper-stick, from seven to eight by the Dutch clock. I tried it with the load upon my leg (and that made me think afresh of the man with the load on *his* leg), and found the tendency of exercise to bring the bread-and-butter out at my ankle, quite unmanageable. Happily, I slipped away, and deposited that part of my conscience in my garret bedroom.

'Hark!' said I, when I had done my stirring, and was taking a final warm in the chimney corner before being sent up to bed; 'was that great guns, Joe?'

'Ah!' said Joe. 'There's another conwict off.'

'What does that mean, Joe?' said I.

Mrs Joe, who always took explanations upon herself, said, snappishly, 'Escaped. Escaped.' Administering the definition like Tar-water.

While Mrs Joe sat with her head bending over her needle-work, I put my mouth into the forms of saying to Joe, 'What's a convict?' Joe put *his* mouth into the forms of returning such a highly elaborate answer, that I could make out nothing of it but the single word 'Pip'.

'There was a conwict off last night,' said Joe, aloud, 'after sunset-gun. And they fired warning of him. And now, it appears they're firing warning of another.'

'*Who's* firing?' said I.

'Drat that boy,' interposed my sister, frowning at me over her work, 'what a questioner he is. Ask no questions, and you'll be told no lies.'

It was not very polite to herself, I thought, to imply that I should be told lies by her, even if I did ask questions. But she never was polite, unless there was company.

At this point, Joe greatly augmented my curiosity by taking the utmost pains to open his mouth very wide, and to put it into the form of a word that looked to me like 'sulks'. Therefore, I naturally pointed to Mrs Joe, and put my mouth into the form of saying, 'her?' But Joe wouldn't hear of that, at all, and again opened his mouth very wide, and shook the form of a most emphatic word out of it. But I could make nothing of the word.

'Mrs Joe,' said I, as a last resource, 'I should like to know – if you wouldn't much mind – where the firing comes from?'

'Lord bless the boy!' exclaimed my sister, as if she didn't quite mean that, but rather the contrary. 'From the Hulks!'

'Oh –h!' I said, looking at Joe. 'Hulks!'

Joe gave a reproachful cough, as much as to say, 'Well, I told you so.'

'And please what's Hulks?' said I.

'That's the way with this boy!' exclaimed my sister, pointing me out with her needle and thread, and shaking her head at me. 'Answer him one question, and he'll ask you a dozen directly. Hulks are prison-ships, right 'cross th' meshes.' We always used that name for marshes, in our country.

'I wonder who's put into prison-ships, and why they're put there?' said I, in a general way, and with quiet desperation.

It was too much for Mrs Joe, who immediately rose. 'I tell you what, young fellow,' said she, 'I didn't bring you up by hand to badger people's lives out. It would be blame to me, and not praise, if I had. People are put in Hulks because they murder, and because they rob, and forge, and do all sorts of bad; and they always begin by asking questions. Now, you get along to bed!'

I was never allowed a candle to light me to bed, and, as I went upstairs in the dark, with my head tingling – from Mrs Joe's thimble having played the tambourine upon it, to accompany her last words – I felt fearfully sensible of the great convenience that the Hulks were handy for me. I was clearly on my way there. I had begun by asking questions, and I was going to rob Mrs Joe.

Since that time, which is far enough away now, I have often thought that few people know what secrecy there is in the young, under terror. No matter how unreasonable the terror, so that it be terror. I was in mortal terror of the young man who so wanted my heart and liver; I was in mortal terror of my interlocutor with the ironed leg; I was in mortal terror of myself, from whom an awful promise had been extracted; I had no hope of deliverance through my all-powerful sister, who repulsed me at every turn; I am afraid to think of what I might have done, on requirement, in the secrecy of my terror.

If I slept at all that night, it was only to imagine myself drifting down the river on a strong spring-tide, to the Hulks; a ghostly pirate calling out to me through a speaking-trumpet, as I passed the gibbet-station, that I had better come ashore and be hanged there at once, and not put it off. I was afraid to sleep, even if I had been inclined, for I knew that at the first faint dawn of morning I must rob the pantry. There was no doing it in the night, for there was no getting a light by easy friction then; to have got one, I must have struck it out of flint and steel, and have made a noise like the very pirate himself rattling his chains.

As soon as the great black velvet pall outside my little window was shot with grey, I got up and went down stairs; every board upon the way, and every crack in every board, calling after me, 'Stop thief!' and 'Get up, Mrs Joe!'

In this extract, much of Pip's dialogue is in the interrogative mode, taking the form of questions: 'What does that mean'; 'What's a convict?'; 'Who's firing?'; 'where [does] the firing comes from?'; 'please what's Hulks?'; 'who's put into prison ships, and why they're put there?' These questions are given greater urgency by Pip's recent encounter in the churchyard with the fearful man. While some of the questions are relatively easy to answer by means of a factual reply – '*Who's* firing'; 'where [does] the firing come from?' – others, especially the double question, 'who's put into prison ships, and why they're put there?' – are more difficult, even for an adult willing to respond, since they involve both philosophical and practical issues relating to the definition of criminals and the system for dealing with them.

Joe's replies are mouthed rather than spoken and Mrs Joe answers abrasively, trying to cut short rather than participate in and develop the dialogue. The dialogue indicates the thwarted reciprocity inside the family group, with Joe too dominated by his wife to reply openly and Pip's sister unwilling to answer the boy's questions and turning the second reply that she makes into a threat that links asking questions with various kinds of law-breaking. There is a comic element in the passage – when Pip first assumes that Joe, when he mouths the word 'Hulks', is in fact indicating that Mrs Joe has the 'sulks'; but Pip's inner fears are too strong, and Mrs Joe too unpleasant, for comedy to prevail: this is, fundamentally, Dickens in serious mode.

The diction of the extract, as well as emphasizing extreme fear – the noun 'terror' recurs seven times – includes a range of words connected with crime and punishment: 'Hulks', repeated five times; 'convict' (or, in Joe's pronunciation, 'conwict') and 'rob', both repeated thrice; 'prison-ships', repeated twice; and, used once each, the associated terms 'murder', 'forge', 'gibbet-station'; 'pirate'; 'hanged'; 'chains'; 'thief'. These reinforce the sense that Pip's transgressions are not merely familial but enmeshed in a wider judicial and penal system. The verb 'forge' is especially significant; here, it means to make a fraudulent copy or imitation – the crime Magwitch and Compeyson have committed in counterfeiting money – but it is also a homophone (that is, it sounds the same but has a different meaning) – of the noun 'forge' in the sense of a blacksmith's workshop, the good place in *Expectations* which Pip had once believed in 'as the glowing road to manhood and independence' (*GE* 134) where Joe conducts his lawful business and demonstrates 'the virtue of industry' (*GE* 135). The identical spelling and sound of these two words, 'forge' and 'forge', suggests, along with other aspects of the novel such as Estella's real parentage, how crime may seep into, sap, taint the signifiers of respectability.

The narrative prose employs elaborate double and multiple sentences. The opening sentence begins 'It was Christmas Eve' and might arouse expectations of enjoyment and revelry; the action then described, stirring the pudding, might seem to be part of this revelry; but having to do so 'from seven to eight by the Dutch clock' suggests a more onerous duty, a sense of one's actions being regulated by time. This demanding task also threatens to reveal him as a thief by making the bread-and-butter likely to come out of his trousers at his ankle. A notably long sentence, of 78 words, links its five clauses with semicolons, and, in an example of one of Dickens's favourite devices, anaphora, its first three clauses begin 'I was in mortal terror of', the repetition driving home Pip's fear. The paragraph starting 'Since that time, which is far enough away now' explicitly indicates that the narrator is writing of an experience that is long past, and this sense of distance is strengthened when he offers a generalization about the terror that secrecy in the young can produce. But the extract can also plunge the reader strongly into Pip's experience, giving a vivid sense of immediacy. This movement between immediacy and partial detachment, between the perspective of the vulnerable child and that of the more distanced – though by no means indifferent – adult, is characteristic of Dickens's narrative technique.

The extract employs a range of imagery to reinforce its meanings. There is the metaphor of the 'load' on the leg of Pip and on the leg of the man who grabbed him in the churchyard; this denotes, literally, the bread-and-butter that Pip has hidden in his trousers and the leg-iron the fearful man wears; but it links up with the metaphor of a weight on one's conscience and with the image of the sinner bearing a heavy burden, as Christian does in John Bunyan's *The Pilgrim's Progress* (1678–84). Another metaphor is used to describe Mrs Joe's hitting Pip on the head as she speaks: 'playing the tambourine'. This is partly comic, with an ironic echo of enthusiastic religiosity, and partly euphemistic, evading the actuality of the physical assault; but the fundamental perhaps comes through more strongly for this attempt at evasion. The metaphor of a 'pall' for the darkness of night outside Pip's small window reinforces the sense of gloom: the primary literal meaning of a 'pall' is that of a cloth draped over a coffin, hearse or tomb. As well as these metaphors, a strong simile is used when Mrs Joe's definition is described as being administered 'like Tar-water', a disagreeable medicine consisting of pine tar and water that she often gives them. Again, this has a comic element, but connected with other evidence of Mrs Joe's behaviour, in this scene and elsewhere, it reinforces her tyranny. There is also a use of personification when the boards and cracks in the stairs Pip descends seem to call after him, as human beings might, 'Stop thief!' and 'Get up, Mrs Joe'. This strengthens the sense of Pip's fear and guilt.

This extract, like the previous one from *Copperfield*, contains four time-frames. There is, in summary form, the carefully regulated hour, timed by the clock, that Pip spends stirring the Christmas pudding, interrupted by the necessity of slipping away to his bedroom to remove the unruly bread-and-butter from his trousers. There is the time taken by the conversation about the hulks which concludes with Pip going off to bed. This is a dramatized, extended scene, with much direct-speech dialogue, that is closer to real time than to the compressed time of summary. The third time-frame returns to a summarizing mode to recount Pip's bad night and his dream, and the fourth time-frame brings him back to morning and to real time in which he acts while feeling a sense of menace. He must be about his surrogate father's business; but that business is of a felonious kind that could bring Pip to the gallows. From the moment of the recognition of his own identity and 'the identity of things' in the churchyard to the morning on which he wakes early, he has suffered, in accelerated form, a fall from innocence to experience.

Conclusions

Each extract combines dialogue and description to evoke vividly the isolated and threatened situations of its young protagonists and the way in which a new adult male figure enters threateningly into their worlds. In David's case, the figure does so in an apparently legitimate way, marrying David's mother and thus becoming his stepfather; but this turns out to be a cloak for controlling, bullying, sadistic behaviour.

In Pip's case, the figure is an outcast who leads Pip himself into theft and concealment; but he will later reveal himself as a benevolent figure, even if the gifts he bestows on Pip are ambivalent.

The dialogue in each extract aims to convey the actual way in which its characters might speak, using dialect terms and pronunciations where appropriate. All the dialogues are marked by a breakdown of reciprocity, of equal exchange between its participants: in *Copperfield*, between David and Peggotty, David and his mother and, above all, David and Murdstone; in *Expectations*, between Pip and the fearful man, Pip and Joe, Joe and Mrs Joe, and Mrs Joe and Pip. In the first extract from *Copperfield*, and the second from *Expectations*, the dialogue of the young protagonist is mainly in the interrogative mode; he asks questions about the rationale and nature of adult practices – marriage, crime and punishment – that adults who have unquestioningly accepted arbitrary customs find difficult to answer, and he receives only evasive and incomplete replies.

Three of the exchanges are marked by violent physical assault, of varying degrees of intensity: the fearful man grabs Pip and turns him upside-down; Murdstone beats David violently and David bites back; Mrs Joe plays on Pip's head like a tambourine with her thimbled finger. Magwitch's assault on Pip occurs outside the family hearth, in the open; but while it is a violent and frightening assault, it is driven by desperation more than malice aforethought; and the fact that it takes place on holy ground, and that some of Magwitch's injuries are akin to those of Christ, sets it in a larger spiritual dimension in which suffering violence may have a value. The violence of Murdstone and Mrs Joe is perpetrated in the family hearth, in what ought, conventionally, to be a place of peace and safety, and there are no mitigating circumstances; both Murdstone and Mrs Joe are driven by the desire for control and by a degree of sadism.

We can see, in each extract, how Dickens makes use, at key points, of long sentences punctuated by semicolons; of interpolations into sentences; of grammatical parallelism; and of anaphora, the repetition of words or phrases, especially at the start of sentences and clauses. All these contribute to an elaborate rhetorical style of a kind that is particularly associated with Dickens. We can also observe how each extract has a double vision, moving between the perspectives of a boy and of an adult, producing a mixture of immediacy and detachment: the vivid childhood experiences and the later reflection upon them in (relative) tranquillity – for the narrators still seem quite angry. Both books portray a child who is made to feel inappropriately guilty by a combination of adult oppression and negligence. Both show how that guilt is linked, in the child's imagination, with the existing penal system. Both are concerned with the interaction of painful and vivid individual experience with particular kinds of social order in which adults have largely unchecked power over children, children's feelings are not fully recognized, and the penal system, actually and imaginatively, penetrates into everyday life.

Methods of Analysis

- We assessed the respective proportions of narrative prose and dialogue in the extracts (e.g. there is considerable dialogue in the first extract, between David and Peggotty, though it is of an awkward kind because of Peggotty's discomfort, in the circumstances, with David's questions about marriage; but narrative prose dominates the opening of *Expectations*, with only a short dialogue between Magwitch and Pip because of Magwitch's desperation and Pip's fear).
- We drew attention to dialect terms and pronunciations in the direct-speech dialogue (e.g. David and Peggotty's use of the contracted form 'an't' for 'are not' or Magwitch's 'Give it mouth' for 'Say it' and 'Pint' for 'Point', and the way in which these help to convey the social location of characters).
- We pointed out the use of Standard English in dialogue (e.g. by David, his mother, and Murdstone, which also helps to convey the social location of characters and, in the case of David as a boy, shows the fluidity of his social position as he moves between dialect, with Peggotty, and Standard English, with his mother and Murdstone).
- We focused on the interrogative mode in dialogue, i.e. asking questions (e.g. David, when he asks Peggotty about marriage; Pip, when he asks his sister and Joe about the Hulks, and how their failure to get straight answers indicates a breakdown of reciprocity

between children and adults and an attempt to suppress children's curiosity).

- We underlined the imperative mode in dialogue (e.g. by Murdstone to David and by Magwitch to Pip on their first encounters, which marks the power relations of the encounters – both the adults are in a position to give orders to the child).

- We noted the use of indirect speech (e.g. in the unknown gentleman's first words to David, which, in the context, contributes to a sense of distance, in contrast to direct-speech dialogue).

- We examined the kind of sentences used (e.g. the long multiple sentence which takes David from the fear he may have annoyed Peggotty to the reassurance of her huge hug; the 124–word sentence that details the elements of Pip's new awareness of the identity of things and of himself).

- We observed the variation of tenses (e.g. in *Copperfield*, the two shifts into the present tense – 'my later understanding *comes* to my aid', 'At this minute I *see* him' – that signal the reader that David is looking back on his past experience from a later vantage-point; the present-tense interjection 'I say' in *Expectations* that gives a sense of a narrator speaking to the reader in the here-and-now as he recounts past events).

- We considered the use of grammatical parallelism (e.g. in the sentence from *Copperfield* in which each clause starts with a grammatical subject ('he'/'the door'/'I'), followed by 'was', and the way in which this produces a series of links between Murdstone's oppression, the impersonal door, and David's suffering, ending with emphasis on the last aspect).

- We identified examples of anaphora, the repetition of a word or phrase, especially at the start of sentences, to give pattern and emphasis (e.g. the twice-repeated 'How well I' in *Copperfield*, which reinforces the persistence of David's memories; the thrice-repeated 'I was in mortal terror of' in *Expectations*, which reinforces the sense of Pip's extreme fear).

- We detailed the diction or vocabulary (e.g. the way in which words such as 'curiously', 'so queer', 'unusually' and 'never' help to convey the unprecedented nature of the disturbance caused by Murdstone in *Copperfield*; how the harsh and negative adjectives used in the opening of *Expectations* contribute to our sense of the trauma of the events described there).

- We explored key examples of imagery (e.g. the metaphor of the 'load' on the leg of Pip and on the leg of the man who grabbed him in the churchyard to denote a weight on one's conscience and an impediment to one's freedom; the simile of Mrs Joe's 'Administering the definition like Tar-water' to indicate the unpleasant way she gives explanations).

- We discussed the combination of different time-frames (e.g. in *Copperfield*, the account, in something close to real time, of David's struggle with Murdstone that leads up to his biting him, the longer time-stretch when David is locked in his room, the description of waking the next morning, and the summary of the five days of his imprisonment; in *Expectations*, the summary of the hour spend stirring the pudding (with the interruption to relieve himself of the bread-and-butter), the conversation at cross-purposes in something close to real time, the summary of the near-sleepless night with its troubled dreams, and the description of waking the next morning to fear and action).

- We traced intertextual links (e.g. in *Expectations* with Wordsworth's 'We Are Seven', the Oedipus myth, the Bible, Shakespeare's *King Lear* and Bunyan's *Pilgrim's Progress*, which help to set the events in a broader literary, cultural and religious perspective and thus enrich their significance).

- We suggested possible relationships between the features analysed above and the broader themes of the novels (e.g. the vulnerability of children; the breakdown of reciprocity between people; the ways which the wider social system of crime and punishment may permeate family life).

Suggested Work

Analyse the two following passages, each of which describes a further painful experience in their protagonists' boyhood – David's arrival at school and Pip's being told that he must go to play at Miss Havisham's. Identify the key features of these passages and explore the kinds of characters, situations and emotions which these features help to evoke. Explore how they may be linked with wider cultural and social contexts.

[a] *Copperfield.* From 'I gazed upon the schoolroom into which he took me' to 'I positively began to have a dread of myself, as a kind of wild boy who did bite' (*DC* 129–31)

[b] *Expectations.* '"Now," said Mrs Joe, unwrapping herself' to 'what on earth I was expected to play at' (*GE* 81–3)

2

Ladies and Gentlemen

In *Copperfield* and *Expectations*, the aspiration to upward social mobility is primarily expressed in terms not of class, money or fame, but of the desire to become a lady or a gentleman. Given the mixed material, social, ethical and idealistic connotations of the terms 'lady' and 'gentleman', this can result in a confusion between social, material ascent and ethical elevation: between a desire to hold the status of lady or gentleman for the self-gratifying privileges it brings and the desire to behave in those ethically proper, self-abnegating ways which are associated with the ideals of being a lady or gentleman. In *Copperfield*, David is a gentleman born and remains one, despite his spells at Murdstone and Grinby's and as a vagabond. Little Em'ly, however, is a fisherman's daughter who wants to become a lady – and this is one of the characteristics that will later make her vulnerable to Steerforth's seductive powers. In *Expectations*, Pip, brought up in a blacksmith's household, becomes a gentleman in the social and material but not in the ethical and ideal sense and has to come close to losing everything in order to recognize that ethical and ideal gentlemanliness and social status are not necessarily commensurate – that a barely literate and semi-inarticulate skilled artisan with his own small business like Joe can be, in his way, the ethical and indeed religious incarnation of the gentlemanly ideal, a 'gentle Christian man'. We shall trace Dickens's portrayal of the desire for ladyhood and gentility, and its effects, in the extracts in this chapter. We begin with one from *Copperfield* in which Em'ly, as a girl, tells David that she would like to be a lady. The extract starts just after Em'ly has told David that she never saw her own father before he died – this is the 'coincidence' to which David refers.

Little Lady Bountiful: *David Copperfield*, pp. 84–6

Here was a coincidence! I immediately went into an explanation how I had never seen my own father; and how my mother and I had always lived by ourselves in the happiest state imaginable, and lived so then, and always meant to live so; and how my father's grave was in the churchyard near our house, and shaded by a tree, beneath the boughs of which I had walked and heard the birds sing many a pleasant morning. But there were some differences between Em'ly's orphanhood and mine, it appeared. She had lost her mother before her father; and where her father's grave was no one knew, except that it was somewhere in the depths of the sea.

'Besides,' said Em'ly, as she looked about for shells and pebbles, 'your father was a gentleman and your mother is a lady; and my father was a fisherman and my mother was a fisherman's daughter, and my uncle Dan is a fisherman.'

'Dan is Mr Peggotty, is he?' said I.

'Uncle Dan – yonder,' answered Em'ly, nodding at the boathouse.

'Yes. I mean him. He must be very good, I should think?'

'Good?' said Em'ly. 'If I was ever to be a lady, I'd give him a sky-blue coat with diamond buttons, nankeen trousers, a red velvet waistcoat, a cocked hat, a large gold watch, a silver pipe and a box of money.'

I said I had no doubt that Mr Peggotty well deserved those treasures. I must acknowledge that I felt it difficult to picture him quite at his ease in the raiment proposed for him by his grateful little niece, and that I was particularly doubtful of the policy of the cocked hat; but I kept these sentiments to myself.

Little Em'ly had stopped and looked up at the sky in her enumeration of these articles, as if they were a glorious vision. We went on again, picking up shells and pebbles.

'You would like to be a lady?' I said.

Emily looked at me, and laughed and nodded 'yes'.

'I should like it very much. We would all be gentlefolks together, then. Me, and uncle, and Ham, and Mrs Gummidge. We wouldn't

> mind then, when there comes stormy weather. – Not for our own sakes,
> I mean. We would for the poor fishermen's, to be sure, and we'd help
> 'em with money when they come to any hurt.'
>
> This seemed to me to be a very satisfactory and therefore not at all
> improbable picture. I expressed my pleasure in the contemplation of it,
> and little Em'ly was emboldened to say, shyly,
>
> 'Don't you think you are afraid of the sea, now?'
>
> It was quiet enough to reassure me, but I have no doubt if I had seen
> a moderately large wave come tumbling in, I should have taken to my
> heels, with an awful recollection of her drowned relations. However,
> I said 'No,' and I added, 'You don't seem to be either, though you say
> you are,' – for she was walking much too near the brink of a sort of old
> jetty or wooden causeway we had strolled upon, and I was afraid of her
> falling over.

Although this extract presents Em'ly as innocent, naïve and over-
imaginative in comparison to the knowing David, it is Em'ly rather than
David who shows a clear grasp of the difference in social status between
them as children: David's father was a gentleman and his mother a
lady, whereas her father and Uncle Dan were fishermen and her mother
a fisherman's daughter. When David suggests that Mr Peggotty –
Uncle Dan – 'must be very good', he seems to be stressing his ethical
disposition rather than his social status and Em'ly offers a rhetorical
question by way of agreement – 'Good?' – as if she were about to affirm
his goodness and perhaps provide examples of it. But she then turns the
conversation to matters of social and economic status. She starts with
a conditional clause – '*If* I was ever to be a lady' – which indicates that
the rewards she would like to give Mr Peggotty for his goodness are not
ones that she can immediately deliver but depend on a change in her
own social and financial position. She sees Mr Peggotty's virtue not as its
own reward but as meriting material forms of recompense. Six of these
are clearly specified commodities that seem to belong to some bizarre
polychromatic fashion system: a sky-blue coat with diamond buttons,
nankeen trousers (nankeen is a yellowish cotton cloth), a red velvet
waistcoat, a cocked hat, a large gold watch, a silver pipe. But one of
them features a precious stone – diamond buttons – and two are made
of precious metals: gold and silver. Em'ly would also give Mr Peggotty
the means of further expenditure: a box of money. In contrast to the

six earlier items, we are not told the colour of this box or the material of which it is made, as if to show that, with the mention of money, we are moving into a more abstract mode, a means of exchange rather than a specific item. Em'ly's vision is colourful, whimsical, fantastical and generous, but it is also strongly commodified and monetarized; it exemplifies the extent to which Em'ly's aspirations, even though they are for members of her family and household rather than for herself, take material form. It is almost as if Em'ly were a proto-consumer, drawing up a shopping list, a sense reinforced by the way in which the items simply accumulate and by the phrase 'her enumeration of these articles' – enumeration means to mention one by one, as in a list. The following simile, 'as if they were a glorious vision', points up the intermeshing and the potential ironic contradiction, of visionary and consumerist perspectives in Em'ly and raises the question of whether she is confusing the two.

There is a significant intratextual link with the scene later in the novel, in chapter 21, when David and Steerforth travel to Yarmouth and David, on the morning after their arrival, goes to Mr Omer's shop, now OMER AND JORAM, and learns that Em'ly is an apprentice there, that she has an 'elegant' taste in dresses (362) and that, due to her aloof behaviour, 'an ill-natured story got about, that Em'ly wanted to be a lady'. Omer's 'opinion is, that [this story] came into circulation principally on account of her sometimes saying, at the school, that if she was a lady she would like to do so-and-so for her uncle – don't you see? – and buy him such-and-such fine things'. David confirms that Em'ly 'has said so' to him when they 'were both children' (*DC* 363). Em'ly's desire to be a lady has clearly persisted. Soon afterwards he sees Em'ly herself, 'a most beautiful little creature', with an element of wilfulness and 'with much of the old capricious coyness lurking' in her face (*DC* 364). She has re-entered the narrative at a point that is bringing her close to her nemesis in the shape of Steerforth.

In their childhood exchange on the beach, Em'ly does not at first reply in words when David asks her directly if she would like to be a lady, but laughs and nods her assent – as if the ambition were too intimate, too delicate, to be openly acknowledged at once. But, perhaps reassured by David's interest, she then goes on to affirm directly that she would like it greatly – and, once more, translates the aspiration into terms of social status. But it is not solely her own status that she would like to improve, a point signalled by the switch from the first-person singular, 'I', to the first-person plural, 'We': she envisions the elevation of all those with whom she lives (though not of the wider society, since this would negate her own elevation). She sees the benefits of such an ascent first of all in terms of material safety, thus, in effect, stressing the danger of a fisherman's life, exemplified above all by her own father's death. But she also recognizes that there would still be fishermen who were in danger and she affirms that she would help them with money – the second time the term is used in this extract. The family would dispense charity, as prosperous people do and should: *noblesse oblige*. There is no questioning on Em'ly's part – or David's – of the social system which divides fishermen and their families from gentlemen and ladies. Indeed, Em'ly's aspiration to enhanced social status depends on that system, with its divisions, remaining intact in order to protect that status, rather than on some more general social enhancement that would remove such status.

The narrative prose fluctuates significantly throughout the passage. There is the exuberant exclamation: 'Here was a coincidence!', compressed into four words, but the sentence that follows is much longer (74 words), a rendering in indirect speech of how he wants his own situation to be understood by Em'ly. Like Em'ly's impending vision of herself as a lady, David's account is idealized, and in his case it encompasses a state that, supposedly, had existed in the past, still exists in the present, and will exist in the future. His account, as reported to us, signals the passage of time by its use of the pluperfect and past tenses – 'I had always lived', 'I had walked', '[we] lived so then'; but a desire to arrest time, a wish to continue in the same way as before, also characterizes it: he and his mother 'always meant to live so'. But this is already wishful thinking; he knows, even if he does not quite want to admit or articulate it, that Mr Murdstone has already invaded his life and come between him and his mother, changing the idealized configuration David projects when telling Em'ly about his family situation: David will return home from Yarmouth to find that he has a new father because his mother has married Murdstone.

When David hears Em'ly's vision of what she would do for her uncle if she ever became a lady, his polite reply is given in indirect speech, as if to distance it from his true attitude, which he shares with the reader through an elaborate sentence: 'I found it difficult to picture him quite at ease in the raiment proposed for him by his grateful little niece, and I was particularly doubtful of the policy of the cocked hat.' David employs polite circumlocutions here – 'I found it difficult to picture him quite at ease … I was particularly doubtful' – to suggest, in a way that is both gentle and patronising, that Em'ly's vision is touching but ludicrously funny and that it has a vulgar aspect that sits ill with her desire for ladyhood. But David's own propensity to improbable idealization, as revealed in his earlier vision of his idyllic life with his mother, subverts the superior stance he adopts here.

David can, however, concur with Em'ly's idea of herself and her fellow inhabitants of the boathouse being elevated to genteel status and becoming dispensers of charity: 'This seemed to me to be a very satisfactory and therefore not at all improbable picture.' His phrasing here suggests that the probability of the picture is a logical consequence of its satisfactoriness; in other words, because he finds the picture satisfying, it is therefore probable. We could ask what satisfies David about the picture, and suggest that it chimes with a wider Victorian vision in which social stratification is taken for granted, but where harmony can be achieved within a household whose benevolence overflows from its own members to benefit the less fortunate. It is a picture of domestic wellbeing and charity that is dependent on class division. So Em'ly and David, despite the latter's greater sophistication, converge in accepting society as it is.

'Differences', the word David uses in the first paragraph to refer to the dissimilarities between Em'ly's orphanhood and his own, is a key term in the extract. It refers both to social differences and to a more primal symbolic difference: an opposition between land and sea. David is linked with the land through such nouns as churchyard, house, tree, boughs. Em'ly is linked with the sea because her father's grave, her 'drowned relations', lie in its depths and she herself lives in a beached and converted boat. David and Em'ly meet on the shore, in the kind of space that is sometimes called 'liminal'; this adjective has its origin in *limen*, the Latin word for 'threshold', and means 'at a boundary or threshold'. The threshold position of David and Em'ly, between land and sea, is also shown by the way in which they pick up shells – those signs of the sea that can be found on land – and pebbles, which signify the land on the sea's margins (pebbles on the beach). To Em'ly, David denies that he fears the sea but he inwardly acknowledges that it would scare him if it became sufficiently turbulent; Em'ly does not seem to fear the sea and walks 'much too near the brink of a sort of old jetty or wooden causeway' – David's difficulty in precisely identifying the jetty or causeway marks both his unfamiliarity with features of the shoreline and the extent to which the sea can efface the distinguishing features of human artefacts. For Em'ly, the sea seems both attractive and dangerous; and in this respect it symbolizes the seductive force of Steerforth that will later steer her forth into the tumultuous ocean of sexual and social transgression. Her desire to be a lady, which seemed whimsical and harmless earlier in the extract, is now symbolically associated with potential destructiveness and transgression. David's fear of Em'ly 'falling over' anticipates the social and moral fall she will experience when she elopes with Steerforth and becomes a fallen woman. Steerforth will also perish in the sea, though tantalizingly near to the shore. David, by contrast, is linked with the land and, for all his vicissitudes and flights of fancy, stays close to earth.

The image of Em'ly as in danger of 'falling' provides an intertextual echo of the Bible, of the Fall of Man that follows Eve's yielding to temptation. Another biblical echo occurs in the references to 'fishermen', those humble folk from whom Christ drew four of his disciples, saying to the first two of them, the brothers Simon and Andrew, 'I will make you to become fishers of men' (Mark 1:17). A third biblical echo is the term 'raiment', which occurs several times in the Old and New Testaments; applying this term to Em'ly's commodified and partly comic vision of her uncle's transformation adds a religious nuance, a hint of a spiritual impulse in Em'ly's aspiration despite its elements of materialism and absurdity.

Other echoes in the passage are to genres rather than specific texts. David's idyll, with its grave, churchyard, shady tree and singing birds, calls to mind English pastoral poetry with its idealized rural settings. The image of the goods that Em'ly, if she became a lady, would bestow on Mr Peggotty, has, in addition to its material, comic and religious aspects, a fairy-tale quality in its combination of colourful, extravagant clothing and precious stones and metals, and the sense it gives of instant transformation: in the mind's eye, Mr Peggotty changes miraculously as Em'ly speaks. This metamorphosis links up with a significant strand in fairy stories that focuses on the sudden, magical acquisition of worldly goods and wealth – and the ills this may portend. Such metamorphosis is also a theme of *Expectations*; and the next passage shows the painful awareness of difference that occurs when Pip first visits Satis House and that stirs his desire to be a gentleman.

Jacks and Knaves: *Great Expectations*, pp. 89–92

'Call Estella,' she repeated, flashing a look at me. 'You can do that. Call Estella. At the door.'

To stand in the dark in a mysterious passage of an unknown house, bawling Estella to a scornful young lady neither visible nor responsive, and feeling it a dreadful liberty so to roar out her name, was almost as bad as playing to order. But, she answered at last, and her light came along the long dark passage like a star.

Miss Havisham beckoned her to come close, and took up a jewel from the table, and tried its effect upon her fair young bosom and against her pretty brown hair. 'Your own, one day, my dear, and you will use it well. Let me see you play cards with this boy.'

'With this boy! Why, he is a common labouring boy!'

I thought I overheard Miss Havisham answer – only it seemed so unlikely – 'Well? You can break his heart.'

'What do you play, boy?' asked Estella of myself, with the greatest disdain.

'Nothing but beggar my neighbour, miss.'

'Beggar him,' said Miss Havisham to Estella. So we sat down to cards.
[…]

'He calls the knaves, Jacks, this boy!' said Estella with disdain, before our first game was out. 'And what coarse hands he has. And what thick boots!'

I had never thought of being ashamed of my hands before; but I began to consider them a very indifferent pair. Her contempt was so strong that it became infectious, and I caught it.
[…]

'Estella, take him down. Let him have something to eat, and let him roam and look about him while he eats. Go, Pip.'

I followed the candle down, as I had followed the candle up, and she stood it in the place where we had found it. Until she opened the side entrance, I had fancied, without thinking about it, that it must necessarily be night-time. The rush of the daylight quite confounded me, and made me feel as if I had been in the candlelight of the strange room many hours.

'You are to wait here, you boy,' said Estella; and disappeared and closed the door.

I took the opportunity of being alone in the court-yard, to look at my coarse hands and my common boots. My opinion of these accessories was not favourable. They had never troubled me before, but they troubled me now, as vulgar appendages. I determined to ask Joe why he had ever taught me to call those picture-cards, Jacks, which ought to be called knaves. I wished Joe had been rather more genteelly brought up, and then I should have been so too.

She came back, with some bread and meat and a little mug of beer. She put the mug down on the stones of the yard, and gave me the bread and meat without looking at me, as insolently as if I were a dog in disgrace. I was so humiliated, hurt, spurned, offended, angry, sorry – I cannot hit upon the right word for the smart – God knows what its name was – that tears started to my eyes. The moment they sprang there, the girl looked at me with a quick delight in having been the cause of them. This gave me power to keep them back and to look at her: so, she gave a contemptuous toss – but with a sense, I thought, of having made too sure that I was so wounded – and left me.

But, when she was gone, I looked about me for a place to hide my face in, and got behind one of the gates in the brewery-lane, and leaned my sleeve against the wall there, and leaned my forehead on it and cried. As I cried, I kicked the wall, and took a hard twist at my hair; so bitter were my feelings, and so sharp was the smart without a name, that needed counteraction.

In this extract Pip is made sharply aware of the social difference that separates him from Estella. One of the signals of the unequal power relations that prevail in this situation is the prominence in the dialogue of the imperative mode, mostly used by Miss Havisham to Pip and to Estella and showing the hold she has over them: 'Call Estella' (repeated twice); 'Go, Pip'; 'Let me see you play cards with this boy'; 'Beggar him'; 'Estella, take him down'; 'Let him have something to eat.' Estella herself adopts the imperative mode when she tells Pip 'You are to wait here, you boy'; but almost all her other dialogue takes the form of indignant exclamations that show her disdain for Pip: 'Why, he is a common labouring boy!'; 'And what coarse hands he has. And what thick boots!' She employs the interrogative mode only once, when she asks Pip what card game he plays, but she does so in a hostile way. Pip himself speaks only in reply to Estella, and as if apologising for being able to play only beggar my neighbour; the name of the card game seems to allude to his own status as an already beggared neighbour. The dialogue has no reciprocity.

In the narrative prose, Pip's subordination to Miss Havisham is stressed by the omission of the first-person singular pronoun, 'I', from the paragraph that begins 'To stand in the dark' ('I stood in the dark' would be the more straightforward way of putting it). The absence of 'I' reinforces the idea that Pip is not initiating his own actions but performing reluctantly and under orders. The 'I' does return in later paragraphs, but Pip's subordination continues; in the presence of Miss Havisham and/or Estella, he does not initiate action himself, but is a passive observer and follower. When he is alone, he can only act in a way that indicates impotent humiliation and rage and turns back in anger upon inanimate objects and his own body: kicking the wall, twisting his hair.

The diction of the extract reinforces the sense of the social difference between Pip and Estella. In the dialogue this comes across especially in the distinction between the terms each uses to refer to one of the picture playing cards: Estella says 'knaves', Pip 'Jacks'. Pip's term marks him, in Estella's hearing, as uncouth, and he returns to the matter later in the extract, wondering why Joe had not taught him the correct term (this is the start of Pip's more negative evaluation of Joe, who despite his kindness lacks the vocabulary and comportment of a gentleman). Estella also uses the adjectives 'common', 'labouring', 'coarse' and 'thick' in relation to Pip, and these strike like hammers in his mind, especially 'coarse' and 'common', which he repeats in his account of his feelings when he is alone in the courtyard. Other diction drives home Estella's view of Pip as worthless. Estella is 'scornful'; asks Pip a question 'with the greatest disdain' and exclaims 'with disdain' at his solecisms; and shows a 'contempt' that is 'so strong that it became infectious'.

She 'insolently' avoids looking at him and gives 'a contemptuous toss' when he refuses to cry. Only once is she pleased, when tears start to Pip's eyes and she looks at him 'with a quick delight' in having provoked them. All these terms strengthen the sense of how Estella makes Pip suffer and of how Miss Havisham has taught her charge to behave sadistically towards the male sex, particularly when they come from a lower social order.

A variety of vocabulary conveys Pip's own feelings of embarrassment, shame, confusion and distress. He feels it 'a dreadful liberty' to 'roar out' Estella's name. Her contempt is 'infectious' and he starts to feel it himself. The rush of the daylight 'confounds' him. Satis House is 'dark', 'mysterious', 'unknown' and 'strange'. Most striking is the point at which Pip tries to find a precise term for his distress and generates six adjectives – 'humiliated, hurt, spurned, offended, angry, sorry' – but declares that none is correct. In a writer so eloquent as Dickens – or as Pip supposedly is, as the story's ostensible narrator – this inability to 'hit upon the right word' is itself eloquent, an index of the extremity and complexity of Pip's pain. He can only call it a 'smart', a sharp, stinging pain; the term, and the difficulty of identifying it, are later reiterated in the phrase 'a smart without a name'. This lack of a name, this inability to define the pain precisely in words, sharpens the smart, makes it less controllable.

At other points, Pip, as the adult narrator, is able to distance his experience, even give it a slightly comic aspect, by using the verbal device known as periphrasis, where several words are used rather than a shorter and more direct word or phrase: 'I began to consider [my hands] a very indifferent pair'; 'My opinion of these accessories [his 'coarse hands' and 'common boots'] was not favourable' and 'they troubled me now, as vulgar appendages'. But this seems like an attempt to evade the full force of his feelings, even in memory.

A key strand of imagery in the extract opposes light and dark. Pip stands 'in the dark' shouting Estella's name but her 'light' (that is, her candle) comes 'along the long dark passage like a star'. The 'star' simile here links up with Estella's name, which includes within itself *stella*, the Latin word for 'star'. After they have played cards, Pip follows Estella's candle down and then up, an obedient acolyte led by an unkindly light. Inside the house, he thinks it must be 'night-time' and the 'rush' of daylight, when Estella opens the side entrance, surprises and confuses him.

Other imagery is also significant: 'infectious', with its implication of disease, reflects on Estella as well as Pip; Pip catches her contempt for him. She refuses to look at him 'as insolently as if I were a dog in disgrace', reducing him to an errant domestic animal. The references to Pip's 'hands' and 'boots', first made contemptuously by Estella and soon afterwards inwardly echoed by Pip himself, are examples of the rhetorical device known as synecdoche, by which a part of something is made to stand for the whole; in this context, the use of such a device is reductive and fragmenting, focusing on the parts of a person rather than that person as a whole. Estella's use of synecdoche reduces Pip to his hands and boots. It is understandable that Pip should want to escape Estella's contempt by elevating himself socially – but ironically that will also involve reductiveness and self-fragmentation as he separates himself from his background.

The passage from *Copperfield* to which we turn next, in which Steerforth affirms that Em'ly was born to be a lady, also foreshadows the ill consequences that may befall the desire for social ascent. It is set in Steerforth's room at the inn in Yarmouth, and Miss Mowcher, the tiny hairdresser, is applying lotion to his profuse locks, with David looking on.

Elf and Fairy: *David Copperfield*, pp. 392–4

I never did in my days behold anything like Mowcher as she stood upon the dining table, intensely enjoying this refreshment, rubbing busily at Steerforth's head, and winking at me over it.

'Ah!' she said. 'Such things not much in demand hereabouts. That sets me off again! I haven't seen a pretty woman since I've been here, Jemmy.'

'No?' said Steerforth.

'Not the ghost of one,' replied Miss Mowcher.

'We could show her the substance of one, I think?' said Steerforth, addressing his eyes to mine. 'Eh, Daisy?'

'Yes, indeed,' said I.

'Aha?' cried the little creature, glancing sharply at my face, and then peeping round at Steerforth's. 'Umph?'

The first exclamation sounded like a question put to both of us, and the second like a question put to Steerforth only. She seemed to have found no answer to either, but continued to rub, with her head on one side and her eye turned up, as if she were looking for an answer in the air and were confident of its appearing presently.

'A sister of yours, Mr Copperfield?' she cried, after a pause, and still keeping the same look-out. 'Aye, aye?'

'No,' said Steerforth, before I could reply. 'Nothing of the sort. On the contrary, Mr Copperfield used – or I am much mistaken – to have a great admiration for her.'

'Why, hasn't he now?' returned Miss Mowcher. 'Is he fickle? oh, for shame! Did he sip every flower, and change every hour, until Polly his passion requited? – Is her name Polly?'

The Elfin suddenness with which she pounced upon me with this question, and a searching look, quite disconcerted me for a moment.

'No, Miss Mowcher,' I replied. 'Her name is Emily.'

'Aha?' she cried exactly as before. 'Umph? What a rattle I am! Mr Copperfield, ain't I volatile?'

Her tone and look implied something that was not agreeable to me in connexion with the subject. So I said, in a graver manner than any of us had yet assumed:

'She is as virtuous as she is pretty. She is engaged to be married to a most worthy and deserving man in her own station of life. I esteem her for her good sense, as much as I admire her for her good looks.'

'Well said!' cried Steerforth. 'Hear, hear, hear! Now I'll quench the curiosity of this little Fatima, my dear Daisy, by leaving her nothing to guess at. She is at present apprenticed, Miss Mowcher, or articled, or whatever it may be, to Omer and Joram, Haberdashers, Milliners, and so forth, in this town. Do you observe? Omer and Joram. The promise of which my friend has spoken, is made and entered into with her cousin; Christian name, Ham; surname, Peggotty; occupation, boat-builder; also of this town. She lives with a relative; Christian name, unknown; surname, Peggotty; occupation, seafaring; also of this town. She is the prettiest and most engaging little fairy in the world. I admire her – as my friend does – exceedingly. If it were not that I might appear to disparage her Intended, which I know my friend would not like, I would add, that to *me* she seems to be throwing herself away; that I am sure she might do better; and that I swear she was born to be a lady.'

Miss Mowcher listened to these words, which were very slowly and distinctly spoken, with her head on one side, and her eye in the air as if she were still looking for that answer. When he ceased she became brisk again in an instant, and rattled away with surprising volubility.

'Oh! And that's all about it, is it?' she exclaimed, trimming his whiskers with a little restless pair of scissors, that went glancing round his head in all directions. 'Very well: *very* well! Quite a long story. Ought to end "and they lived happily ever afterwards"; oughtn't it? Ah! What's that game at forfeits? I love my love with an E, because she's enticing; I hate her with an E, because she's engaged. I took her to the sign of the exquisite, and treated her with an elopement, her name's Emily, and she lives in the east? Ha! ha! ha! Mr Copperfield, ain't I volatile?'

Dialogue carries much of this extract and there are revealing contrasts between the speech styles of the three participants: Miss Mowcher, Steerforth and David. Miss Mowcher speaks in a lively way, her speech peppered with exclamations – 'Ah!' (twice); 'Aha?'; 'Aye, aye'; 'Very well: *very* well!'; 'Ha! ha! ha!' – and questions: 'Aha?'; 'Umph?' (twice). She can also ask more articulate questions, for example: 'A sister of yours, Mr Copperfield?'; 'Is her name Polly?' She draws attention to her own volubility – 'What a rattle I am!' – and to her own changeability, repeating, like a comedian's catchphrase, the rhetorical question 'Ain't I volatile?' A rich vein of allusion, which we will explore shortly, runs through her speech.

Steerforth's main contribution to the dialogue takes the form of a rhetorically accomplished oration that, rather like Dickens's own narrative prose, employs grammatical parallelism and sentences and phrases carefully punctuated by semicolons. Em'ly has entered into a promise 'with her cousin; Christian name, Ham; surname, Peggotty; occupation, boat-builder; also of this town. She lives with a relative; Christian name, unknown; surname, Peggotty; occupation, seafaring; also of this town'. David's speech, especially when he realizes where the conversation may be leading, is stiff and cautiously conventional, as when he says of Em'ly: 'She is as virtuous as she is pretty'.

The charged topic of the conversation is Little Em'ly. On its surface level, the issue is whether she should stay in 'her station in life' and marry Ham, or whether, as Steerforth asserts, 'she was born to be a lady' and should marry accordingly. The term 'lady' recalls the passage we discussed first in this chapter, in which Em'ly, as a girl, acknowledges to David that she would like to be a lady. On what we might call its subtextual level, reading beneath the words, the underlying topic of the conversation is whether Steerforth can seduce Em'ly, a question approached only indirectly, through hints and allusions – though quite strong ones in Miss Mowcher's case.

The narrative prose conveys Miss Mowcher's liveliness partly through the use of present participles: 'enjoying'; 'rubbing'; 'glancing'; 'peeping'; 'keeping'; 'looking'; 'trimming'. These help to impart a sense of constant motion, which is reinforced by the adjective 'restless', applied to her scissors; this is an example of an hypallage, or transferred epithet, in which an adjective is moved from the noun with which it would usually consort to another less expected one; it is in fact Miss Mowcher who is restless in her trimming of Steerforth's whiskers, but when the adjective is attached to her scissors, it animates them, gives them a life of their own, and increases the impression of Miss Mowcher's liveliness by suggesting that she is able to infuse a metallic tool with her own mobility.

There is also the gesture in which she has 'her head on one side and her eye turned up'; this recurs later, in almost identical phrasing, when she has 'her head on one side, and her eye in the air'. The gesture suggests she is waiting for an answer she does not hear and contributes to the sense of an uncomfortable undertone in her actions and words that David does not make explicit but indicates in a circumlocutory way: 'Her tone and look implied something that was not agreeable to me in the subject.' This 'something' is the idea of Em'ly as an object of desire and potential seduction.

The extract contains a specific intertextual reference that brings this unarticulated 'something' as near the surface as Dickens dares, or perhaps wishes, to bring it. When Miss Mowcher says 'Did he sip every flower, and change every hour, until Polly his passion requited' she is adapting her words from John Gay's *The Beggar's Opera* (1728), in which the highwayman MacHeath sings to Polly Peachum, whom he has married: 'My Heart was so free, / It rov'd like the Bee, / 'Till Polly my Passion requited; / I sipt each Flower, / I chang'd every Hour, / But here every Flower is united'. Miss Mowcher's reference conjures up a violent, predatory eighteenth-century world of promiscuity, seduction and crime that, with some modifications, still ran beneath the surface of Victorian gentility and respectability.

There is also the hint of an intertextual link to the Bible and ancient classical myth, in Miss Mowcher's cutting of Steerforth's hair. In biblical terms, the shearing of a man's hair by a woman calls to mind the story of Samson, shorn of his hair, the source of his great strength, by Delilah's stratagems, arrested by the Philistines, blinded and put to hard labour (Judges, 16:4–21). The shearing of Samson's hair is sometimes interpreted, in a psychoanalytic perspective, as a symbolic castration; but ironically, Steerforth's shearing by this diminutive Delilah does not emasculate him physically but blinds him morally; he will be fully capable, in a physical sense, of seducing Em'ly but will lack the ethical insight that would inhibit him from taking advantage of Em'ly's vulnerability to his class and charm. In terms of classical myth, Miss Mowcher is a miniature version of Atropos, the Fate who cuts the thread of life at death; her snipping now anticipates Steerforth's last moments in which, as David puts it, 'the life of the solitary man upon the mast hung by a thread' (865). We shall discuss this further in chapter 5.

In the current extract, there are also references, not to a specific text, but to a genre, that of fairy-tale. David's narrative describes Miss Mowcher as 'the little creature' who shows an 'Elfin suddenness'; Steerforth calls Miss Mowcher 'this little Fatima' and Little Em'ly a 'little fairy'. Miss Mowcher invokes a conventional fairy-tale conclusion when she says that Em'ly's story '[o]ught to end "and they lived happily afterwards"; oughtn't it?' But Miss Mowcher's question, which neither Steerforth nor herself answer, suggests a certain scepticism as to whether this happy ending will be fulfilled, and the reader familiar with the rest of *Copperfield* knows that it will not be.

Miss Mowcher then alludes to a genre of Victorian parlour-games called forfeits, in which each player had to deposit a small article or trinket that they could redeem if they successfully completed a task required by the game but that they would give up – forfeit – if they failed to fulfil this task. In this case, the game Miss Mowcher specifies seems to involve generating a narrative that includes key words starting with the letter 'E': 'enticing'; 'engaged'; 'exquisite'; 'elopement; 'Em'ly'; 'east'. The words provide an encapsulated summary of crucial stages of Em'ly's story; 'I took her to the sign of the exquisite' seems like a coded way of talking about a seduction that leads to intense sexual pleasure;

'elopement' anticipates Em'ly's elopement with Steerforth and suggests other words starting with 'e' that are not used but that would fulfil the rules of the game: 'estrangement' and 'exclusion'. Em'ly's elopement will result in her estrangement from her family and her exclusion from respectable British society; she once lived on the east coast of England but has now been sent to the east, a term suggestive of both the East End of London and the Orient, which were, to the Victorian middle-class mind, remote and little-known cultures, places of exile and excess. In this game of forfeits, the articles Em'ly will deposit and have to give up are no trinkets but physical and moral goods of inestimable value: her virginity and her virtue.

This extract suggests that Em'ly's desire to be a lady, Steerforth's belief that she was born to be a lady, his own status as a gentleman, and their mutual attraction, create a dangerous situation. Miss Mowcher is vividly alive to its possibilities but does not moralize; David is aware of the danger but does not bring it fully to consciousness, taking refuge in a formal declaration of Em'ly's virtue; Steerforth is driven by his sense that Em'ly is 'throwing herself away' socially rather than by an apprehension of how she might – with his help – throw herself away morally.

In the next extract, from *Expectations*, we see that Pip, now a young man living in London, has become a gentleman and that this also proves morally compromising, not with regard to sexual behaviour, but in his treatment of an old friend and quasi-parental figure: Joe Gargery.

Artisan and Gentleman: *Great Expectations*, pp. 244–8

'Have you seen anything of London, yet?'

'Why, yes, Sir,' said Joe, 'me and Wopsle went off straight to look at the Blacking Ware'us. But we didn't find that it come up to its likeness in the red bills at the shop doors;' which I meantersay,' added Joe, in an explanatory manner, 'as it is there drawd too architectooralooral.'

I really believe Joe would have prolonged this word (mightily expressive to my mind of some architecture that I know) into a perfect Chorus, but for his attention being providentially attracted by his hat, which was toppling. Indeed, it demanded from him a constant attention, and a quickness of eye and hand, very like that exacted by wicket-keeping. He made extraordinary play with it, and showed the greatest skill; now, rushing at it and catching it neatly as it dropped; now, merely stopping it midway, beating it up, and humouring it in various parts of the room and against a good deal of the pattern of the paper on the wall, before he felt it safe to close with it; finally, splashing it into the slop-basin, where I took the liberty of laying hands upon it.

As to his shirt-collar, and his coat-collar, they were perplexing to reflect upon – insoluble mysteries both. Why should a man scrape himself to that extent, before he could consider himself full dressed? Why should he suppose it necessary to be purified by suffering for his holiday clothes? Then he fell into such unaccountable fits of meditation, with his fork midway between his plate and his mouth; had his eyes attracted in such strange directions; was afflicted with such remarkable coughs; sat so far from the table, and dropped so much more than he ate, and pretended that he hadn't dropped it; that I was heartily glad when Herbert left us for the city.

I had neither the good sense nor the good feeling to know that this was all my fault, and that if I had been easier with Joe, Joe would have been easier with me. I felt impatient of him and out of temper with him; in which condition he heaped coals of fire on my head.

'Us two being now alone, Sir,' – began Joe.

'Joe,' I interrupted, pettishly, 'how can you call me, Sir?'

Joe looked at me for a single instant with something faintly like reproach. Utterly preposterous as his cravat was, and as his collars were, I was conscious of a sort of dignity in the look.

'Us two being now alone,' resumed Joe, 'and me having the intentions and abilities to stay not many minutes more, I will now conclude – leastways begin – to mention what have led to my having had the present honour. For was it not,' said Joe, with his old air of lucid exposition, 'that my only wish were to be useful to you, I should not have had the honour of breaking wittles in the company and abode of gentlemen.'

I was so unwilling to see the look again, that I made no remonstrance against this tone.

'Well, Sir,' pursued Joe, 'this is how it were. I were at the Bargemen t'other night, Pip;' whenever he subsided into affection, he called me Pip, and whenever he relapsed into politeness he called me Sir; 'when there come up in his shay-cart, Pumblechook. Which that same identical,' said Joe, going down a new track, 'do comb my 'air the wrong way sometimes, awful, by giving out up and down town as it were him which ever had your infant companionation and were looked upon as a playfellow by yourself.'

'Nonsense. It was you, Joe.'

'Which I fully believed it were, Pip,' said Joe, slightly tossing his head, 'though it signify little now, Sir. Well, Pip; this same identical, which his manners is given to blusterous, come to me at the Bargemen (wot a pipe and a pint of beer do give refreshment to the working-man, Sir, and do not over-stimulate), and his word were, "Joseph, Miss Havisham she wish to speak to you."'

'Miss Havisham, Joe?'

'"She wish," were Pumblechook's word, "to speak to you."' Joe sat and rolled his eyes at the ceiling.

'Yes, Joe? Go on, please.'

'Next day, Sir,' said Joe, looking at me as if I were a long way off, 'having cleaned myself, I go and see Miss A.'

'Miss A., Joe? Miss Havisham?'

'Which I say, Sir,' replied Joe, with an air of legal formality, as if he were making his will. 'Miss A., or otherways Havisham. Her expression air then as follering: "Mr. Gargery. You air in correspondence with Mr. Pip?" Having had a letter from you, I were able to say "I am". (When I married your sister, Sir, I said "I will;" and when I answered your friend, Pip, I said "I am.") "Would you tell him, then," said she, "that which Estella has come home and would be glad to see him."'

I felt my face fire up as I looked at Joe. I hope one remote cause of its firing, may have been my consciousness that if I had known his errand, I should have given him more encouragement.

'Biddy,' pursued Joe, 'when I got home and asked her fur to write the message to you, a little hung back. Biddy says, "I know he will be very glad to have it by word of mouth, it is holiday-time, you want to see him, go!" I have now concluded, Sir,' said Joe, rising from his chair, 'and, Pip, I wish you ever well and ever prospering to a greater and greater heighth.'

'But you are not going now, Joe?'

'Yes I am,' said Joe.

'But you are coming back to dinner, Joe?'

'No I am not,' said Joe.

Our eyes met, and all the 'Sir' melted out of that manly heart, as he gave me his hand.

This extract shows Joe, who has come to London with Mr Wopsle, visiting Pip in the lodgings he shares with Herbert Pocket, and the discomfort that both Joe and Pip suffer. The direct-speech dialogue marks the key difference between the 'working-man', as Joe calls himself, and the gentleman. Joe uses non-standard English, sometimes indicated by his grammar – for example, 'Us two' rather than 'we two' – and sometimes by a phonetic rendering of his pronunciation: 'Ware'us' for 'warehouse'; 'meantersay' for 'mean to say'; 'wot' for 'what'; 'fur' for 'for'; ''air' for 'are'; 'stimilate' for 'stimulate'; 'heighth' for 'height'. In Pip's presence, Joe is not a plain-speaking working man but seeks to employ elaborate vocabulary that he gets wrong – 'archtictooralooral' for 'architectural', 'companionation' for 'companion' – and to engage in elaborate, quasi-genteel circumlocution: 'this same identical, which his manners is given to blusterous, come to me at the Bargeman (wot a pipe and a pint of beer do give refreshment to the working-man, Sir, and do not over-stimulate)'.

It is only at the end of the dialogue that he engages in direct, plain speaking using simple declarative sentences composed of words of one syllable when he insists that he is going – 'Yes I am' – and that he is not returning for dinner: 'No I am not'; this is the point at which he regains his full dignity and autonomy, throwing off his servility to his notions of what constitutes genteel conduct. For the most part, the dialogue shows Joe in a comic light that slides towards the patronising, towards making fun of his manner of speaking from a position of superiority. But there is also a sense of Joe's underlying dignity that becomes uppermost at the end and makes Pip's unfortunate behaviour seem dubious.

This mixture of comedy, patronage and dignity also emerges in the way Pip's narrative prose presents Joe. The comic business with Joe's hat is prefaced by an awareness that it demands skills that in another context – such as keeping wicket at a cricket-match – might arouse admiration. The elaborate sentence that follows, punctuated by semicolons in a characteristic Dickensian manner, develops the comedy and shows it to be one of incongruity; Joe is behaving in a way that is inappropriate to the social situation he is in. The next paragraph similarly develops the comedy of Joe's inability, in that situation, to focus on eating. Comedy here comes close to cruelty, as if Joe were like a trained animal that cannot perform its tricks properly and is thus subject to fear and embarrassment because he cannot do so. But the element of cruelty reflects on Pip too, showing how much he feels the pressure of social embarrassment – the fact that Herbert is present to witness these spectacles contributes largely to Pip's discomfort, as his hearty gladness when Herbert leaves for the city demonstrates.

In the movement between immersion in his younger self and more detached reflection that occurs at various points in *Expectations*, Pip assumes, in retrospect, full responsibility for the discomfiture of the situation: 'I had neither the good sense nor the good feeling to know that this was all my fault'. This is an important moment of self-recognition, though we could suggest that Pip is too hard on himself: the idea that the discomfort might have been avoided if he 'had been easier with Joe' has its own naiveté, as if a different sort of behaviour on Pip's part could dissolve the distance between them. The gulf between them is a product of their individual differences, sharpened by separation – Pip has grown away from home – and of a particular society that marks social distinctions by the way people talk, dress and comport themselves.

When Joe does eventually deliver his message to Pip, it turns out to be erotically charged: 'Estella has come home and would be glad to see him'. To denote his response, Pip employs a primal metaphor, that of fire – 'I felt my face fire up'. In the larger symbolic structure of *Expectations*, this anticipates how Miss Havisham will die by fire, consumed, metaphorically, by the upsurge of the passions and sympathies that have been repressed for so long. Pip also suggests that embarrassment at his treatment of Joe may have contributed to his response. At the end of the extract, the metaphor of melting – like that of ice or snow – is used to denote the momentary but significant disappearance of deference in Joe, the thawing of that stiffness indicated by his earlier use of the term 'Sir', as the eyes of Joe and Pip 'met' – the visual and oral similarity between 'met' and 'melt' emphasizes the interrelation of melting and meeting – and Joe 'gave' Pip his hand. The verb 'gave' here carries an implication of friendship and generosity and the synecdoche of 'hand' indicates, not a reduction or fragmentation of Joe, but an extension of his whole being towards Pip; we shall later meet other key examples of the language of hands in *Expectations*. But the momentary meeting between them has not healed the sources of their estrangement.

Conclusions

All these passages demonstrate Dickens's concern with social division and his capacity to dramatize it through dialogue, description, character and incident. The two extracts from *Copperfield* invoke the idea of ladyhood explicitly; Em'ly would like to be a lady, Steerforth affirms she was born to be a lady. The two extracts from *Expectations* focus on gentility: the first on Pip's lack of it and the second on his possession of it. In the first *Copperfield* extract, Em'ly's desire to be lady is shown to be, all at once, generous, fantastic and materialistic; she imagines how she would help her family; her description of how she would kit out Mr Peggotty has a fantastical, whimsical, comic, fairy-tale aspect; but her idea of being a lady crucially involves the ability to buy consumer goods and to dispense money to her family and household and to those of the lower orders in need – and, while David implicitly deprecates her consumer choices, he acknowledges that Mr Peggotty is worthy of largesse and approves her charitable aspirations. In the first *Expectations* extract, Pip becomes painfully aware of his lack of genteel manners – evident in his hands, his boots and his use of the term 'Jacks' for 'knaves'. Em'ly's desire to be a lady, though compromised by its materialism and acceptance of social division, has a generous aspect; Pip's desire to be a gentleman is more self-centred, driven by the desire to overcome the humiliations he suffers with Estella. But as the third and fourth extracts show, both desires can have harmful consequences; Em'ly becomes a potential object of seduction for Steerforth; Pip becomes distanced from Joe and from an aspect of himself and his past.

Each passage combines dialogue and narrative prose in varying proportions: in the first extract, it is through dialogue that Em'ly's desire to be a lady is expressed, though her words are carefully, patronizingly placed by David's narrative prose. The proportion of dialogue is smaller in the second extract but crucial because it is the major means by which Estella expresses her contempt for Pip. The narrative prose registers no sense of superiority on Pip's part but focuses on his inferiority and the pain this causes him. Dialogue sustains much of the third extract and provides indirectly indications of sexual matters that Dickens would not have been able, and perhaps did not want, to mention openly.

In the fourth extract, Joe says much more than Pip, and Pip's main observations and reflections occur in the narrative prose, in which he castigates himself, retrospectively, for his attitude to Joe but still takes the opportunity to make Joe a figure of fun.

In his narrative prose and dialogue, Dickens draws on a rich repertoire of resources. The diction, the choice of words, is crucial in conveying the fanciful but material nature of Em'ly's desire to buy Mr Peggotty luxurious clothes and appurtenances; in showing how Estella makes Pip painfully aware of his subaltern status; in conveying the emotional blow Estella deals him. The tenses and forms of verbs play a significant role: the pluperfect and perfect tenses in David's account of his life with his mother indicate an idealized, long-standing condition that David would like to continue; the use of present participles to describe Miss Mowcher's actions increase the sense of her restlessness and liveliness. Pronouns, or their absence, can also be significant: the switch from 'I' to 'we' in Em'ly's vision of ladyhood; the absence of 'I' in Pip's account of standing in the dark corridor calling Estella.

Imagery helps to enhance the significance of the extracts at key points. As she enumerates the gifts she would bestow on Mr Peggotty, Em'ly looks into the sky 'as if they were a glorious vision', a simile that both acknowledges Em'ly's elevated generosity and casts it in an ironic light. Estella refuses to look at Pip 'as insolently as if he were a dog in disgrace', reducing him to a miscreant canine. There are also symbolic references in the first and second extracts that take on *intratextual* significance – they are echoed in other parts of the novel and contribute to its overall symbolic structure and its dramatization and exploration of its major themes. The first extract is set in a liminal space, on the border or threshold between land and sea; David is associated with the land, Em'ly with the sea, prefiguring their future fates. Em'ly will be steered forth into the sea of transgression, David will stay close to the earth. 'Falling' is also an important motif here, adumbrating Em'ly's later fate as a fallen woman. The second extract includes the opposition of light and dark: the dark of the Satis House corridor, Estella's candle, the sudden influx of daylight when she opens the side entrance: this series of references makes links between darkness, artificial light (the candle), the stars and daylight that find echoes at various points in the novel (the reading lamp that sheds a partial light on the mysterious stranger who visits Pip's London chambers at night; the flames that sear Miss Havisham). Intertextual echoes, both to genres and specific texts, play important roles in the extracts; the first extract includes allusions to the Bible and the third to John Gay's *Beggar's Opera*; the first extract alludes to English pastoral poetry; both *Copperfield* extracts allude to fairy-tale.

Methods of Analysis

- We explored the respective ways in which the extracts present the theme of gentility (e.g. the two *Copperfield* extracts invoke the idea of ladyhood explicitly; the first *Expectations* extract focuses on Pip's lack of gentility, the second on his possession of it).

- We assessed the respective contributions of narrative prose and dialogue (e.g. how dialogue is crucial to expressing Em'ly's desire to be a lady and how the narrative prose acknowledges but ironizes this; how Joe says much more than Pip at their London meeting while Pip pursues his own self-criticism, and his uneasily comic portrayal of Joe, in the narrative prose).

- We examined the diction and its effects (e.g. how it conveys the fanciful, generous and materialistic aspects of Em'ly's desire to buy Mr Peggotty luxurious clothes and appurtenances; how it brings home the blow to Pip's feelings that Estella's disdain delivers).

- We highlighted the tenses and forms of verbs (e.g. the pluperfect and perfect tenses in David's account of his life with his mother that place that relationship in time; the present participles that enhance the sense of Miss Mowcher's liveliness).

- We drew attention to imagery (e.g. Em'ly's 'glorious vision' of the gifts she imagines bestowing on Mr Peggotty; Estella's refusal to look at Pip, as if he were 'a dog in disgrace').

- We explored the broader symbolic references that take on *intratextual* significance through their echoes in other parts of the respective novels (e.g. the linking of Em'ly with the sea and the danger of falling, and of David with the land; the mixture of darkness, candlelight, starlight (through Estella's name) and daylight).

- We identified *intertextual* echoes to both specific texts and genres (e.g. to the Bible and Gay's *Beggar's Opera*; to fairy-tale and English pastoral poetry).

Suggested Work

Analyse the two following passages, each of which evokes a further significant moment in each novel in which the issue of the division between gentlemen and ladies and ordinary folk arises. The first is when David, at Murdstone and Grinby's, feels conscious of himself as a 'little gent' among 'common men and boys'. The second is when Pip confides his desire to be a gentleman, and his reason for it, to Biddy and discusses the matter with her. Analyse how each passage presents the issue and explore the attitudes to gentility which it depicts.

[a] *Copperfield*. From 'I know I do not exaggerate' to 'never in any letter (though many passed between us) revealed the truth' (*DC* 216–17)
[b] *Expectations*. From '"Biddy," said I, after binding her to secrecy' to 'as a punishment for belonging to such an idiot' (*GE* 154–6)

3

Obsessives and Eccentrics

One of the best-known aspects of Dickens is his gallery of obsessive and eccentric characters (the boundary between the two is often blurred). These characters can seem to take on an independent existence – life is perhaps not quite the right word, given their exaggerated and caricatural aspects – and some of them have become detached from the texts in which they first appeared to function, even with those who have never read Dickens, as shorthand ways of denoting certain kinds of behaviour, as when we call a miserly person a Scrooge or a financially careless one a Micawber. But these characters are originally constructed of words and set within plots and narratives that help to animate them, turn them into figures who act even if only (like Miss Havisham) through stasis and repetition. It is fascinating to analyse how the text constructs these characters and it increases the understanding of Dickens's art to do so. Our sense of the reach and depth of that art deepens when we explore how these characters and their situations, and the responses of other characters to them, embody and dramatize wider social concerns such as women and marriage, attitudes to psychological disorder and the division between public and private life. We begin with the figure of Rosa Dartle in *Copperfield* and consider how Dickens portrays David's first meeting with her at Mrs Steerforth's, with Steerforth himself also present.

Lady to Let: *David Copperfield*, pp. 350–1

There was a second lady in the dining-room, of a slight short figure, dark, and not agreeable to look at, but with some appearance of good looks too, who attracted my attention: perhaps because I had not expected to see her; perhaps because I found myself sitting opposite to her; perhaps because of something really remarkable in her. She had black hair and eager black eyes, and was thin, and had a scar upon her lip. It was an old scar – I should rather call it seam, for it was not discoloured, and had healed years ago – which had once cut through her mouth, downward towards the chin, but was now barely visible across the table, except above and on her upper lip, the shape of which it had altered. I concluded in my own mind that she was about thirty years of age, and that she wished to be married. She was a little dilapidated – like a house – with having been so long to let; yet had, as I have said, an appearance of good looks. Her thinness seemed to be the effect of some wasting fire within her, which found a vent in her gaunt eyes.

She was introduced as Miss Dartle, and both Steerforth and his mother called her Rosa. I found that she lived there, and had been for a long time Mrs Steerforth's companion. It appeared to me that she never said anything she wanted to say, outright; but hinted it, and made a great deal more of it by this practice. For example, when Mrs Steerforth observed, more in jest than earnest, that she feared her son led a wild life at college, Miss Dartle put in thus:

'Oh, really? You know how ignorant I am, and that I only ask for information, but isn't it always so? I thought that kind of life was on all hands understood to be – eh?'

'It is education for a very grave profession, if you mean that, Rosa,' Mrs Steerforth answered with some coldness.

Oh! Yes! That's very true,' returned Miss Dartle. 'But isn't it, though? – I want to be put right, if I am wrong – isn't it, really?'

'Really what?' said Mrs Steerforth.

'Oh! You mean it's *not*!' returned Miss Dartle. 'Well, I'm very glad to hear it! Now, I know what to do! That's the advantage of asking. I shall never allow people to talk before me about wastefulness and profligacy, and so forth, in connexion with that life, any more.'

' And you will be right,' said Mrs Steerforth. 'My son's tutor is a conscientious gentleman; and if I had not implicit reliance on my son, I should have reliance on him.'

X | Should you?' said Miss Dartle. 'Dear me! Conscientious, is he? Really conscientious, now?'

| Yes, I am convinced of it,' said Mrs Steerforth.

| How very nice!' exclaimed Miss Dartle. 'What a comfort! Really conscientious? Then he's not – but of course he can't be, if he's really conscientious. Well, I shall be quite happy in my opinion of him, from this time. You can't think how it elevates him in my opinion, to know for certain that he's really conscientious!'

Her own views of every question, and her correction of everything that was said to which she was opposed, Miss Dartle insinuated in the same way: sometimes, I could not conceal from myself, with great power, though in contradiction even of Steerforth.

This is David's first encounter with Rosa Dartle, and the movement of the prose conveys his uncertainty about how to interpret, how to 'read' her. A whole paragraph passes before we learn her name or her position in Mrs Steerforth's household. The first sentence bristles with partial contradictions and with uncertainties. David first says that Rosa is 'not agreeable to look at', but this is not quite the same as saying that she is 'disagreeable' to look at; he then goes on to observe that she has 'some appearance of good looks too', thus modifying his original claim that she is not agreeable to look at and suggesting that there might be something agreeable about her. David makes a stereotypical, sexist summation of Rosa, as a 'dilapidated' spinster, but she exceeds his stereotype and clearly intrigues him; he repeats the phrase 'appearance of good looks' in the penultimate sentence of the first paragraph, as if he himself might feel a hint of attraction to her. The phrase 'appearance of good looks' is awkward, as if to reinforce the sense that David is finding it difficult to assess Miss Dartle, to see her for what she is. The term 'appearance' suggests that her 'good looks' may be nothing more than an appearance, an apparition, a kind of illusion and perhaps hints at David's fear of any attraction she might arouse in him.

The next three clauses provide an example of anaphora, which, as we mentioned in chapter 1, is a favourite device of Dickens. Here the repeated phrase 'perhaps because' marks David's uncertainty as he attempts to assign reasons for the fact that Miss Dartle attracts his attention. He offers two relatively innocuous possible reasons – that he had not expected to see her, that he found himself sitting opposite her – but his third reason, separated from its two predecessors by a semicolon and gaining weight because it falls at the end of the sentence, suggests that the attention-attracting factor may be 'something really remarkable in her'. It is significant that David is unable precisely to identify this 'remarkable' quality but that he stresses its authenticity in the alliterative phrase 'really remarkable' (rather than simply 'remarkable').

There follows an elaborate description of what is initially called a scar, but which an interpolated clause then modifies to a 'seam' – again there is a sense of second thoughts, as if David cannot make up his mind even about this more specific aspect of her physical features. 'Seam' and 'seem' are homophones – that is, both words sound the same despite their different spelling and meaning – and to hear the echo of 'seem' in 'seam' links the latter word with the earlier phrase 'appearance of good looks' and with David's difficulty in distinguishing the apparent from the real in his perception of Rosa, his uncertainty as to whether she is what she seems. The 'seam' is a mark of some old injury now barely visible but altering the shape of her upper lip; this gives her an aspect of subdued grotesqueness and also makes the first-time reader of *Copperfield* who does not know the source of the scar wonder how she got it and expect the novel to reveal this later – as indeed happens soon afterwards.

The adjectives applied to Rosa convey a sense of both frailty ('slight', 'short', 'gaunt') and intensity ('dark', 'black', 'eager'). A simile likens her, as a woman still unmarried at the age of about 30, to a house that has been to let for a long time, awaiting a tenant. It is a patronising, slightly comic and subtly poignant image from a writer who often uses houses to symbolize human states (Satis House in *Expectations*, Bleak House in the novel of that title). Dickens also uses the metaphor of 'some wasting fire within her' to suggest that an inward passion is consuming her and making her physically thin. The full extent of this passion is only revealed later in the novel, as we shall discuss in chapter 4.

The extract also portrays Rosa Dartle's style of speaking: her avoidance of outright statement and her deployment of hints that make what she might have said outright more significant. Mrs Steerforth partly acknowledges that her son leads a wild life at college but she does so 'more in jest than earnest' and asserts her 'implicit reliance' on her son and, if that were lacking, on his tutor. Rosa does not directly contradict her but suggests otherwise. Rosa's speech is in the interrogative and exclamatory modes, punctuated with question marks and exclamation marks, and also by dashes that give a jerky, staccato effect and sometimes indicate a stopping short – what is called an aposiopesis, a breaking-off. For example: 'But isn't it, though? – I want to be put right, if I am wrong – isn't it really?' Or: 'What a comfort! Really conscientious. Then he's not – but of course he can't be, if he's really conscientious.' She repeatedly uses the term 'isn't it': 'isn't it always so?'; 'isn't it, though?', rather like a lawyer putting pressure on a witness by asking 'Isn't it so?', with the implication that the witness should acknowledge that something is so – that Steerforth is indeed leading a wild life at college and that his tutor is not aiming to prevent this. Rosa is obliquely indicating Mrs Steerforth's denial of reality. When she says, 'You can't think how it elevates him in my opinion, to know for certain that he's really conscientious!', the exclamation has an ironic dimension, as if she were echoing what Mrs Steerforth says but undermining it by her tone. David recognizes her forensic skill and acknowledges that she exercises it 'with great power'. The extract we shall examine in chapter 4 shows her throwing off this style of speaking and adopting another, more direct mode of great power.

We turn now to Pip's encounter, as a boy, with another remarkable woman, Miss Havisham, whom he also finds very difficult to 'read'.

Broken Bride: *Great Expectations*, pp. 86–8

I entered, therefore, and found myself in a pretty large room, well lighted with wax candles. No glimpse of daylight was to be seen in it. It was a dressing-room, as I supposed from the furniture, though much of it was of forms and uses then quite unknown to me. But prominent in it was a draped table with a gilded looking-glass, and that I made out at first sight to be a fine lady's dressing-table.

Whether I should have made out this object so soon, if there had been no fine lady sitting at it, I cannot say. In an armchair, with an elbow resting on the table and her head leaning on that hand, sat the strangest lady I have ever seen, or shall ever see.

She was dressed in rich materials – satins, and lace, and silks – all of white. Her shoes were white. And she had a long white veil dependent from her hair, and she had bridal flowers in her hair, but her hair was white. Some bright jewels sparkled on her neck and on her hands, and some other jewels lay sparkling on the table. Dresses, less splendid than the dress she wore, and half-packed trunks, were scattered about. She had not quite finished dressing, for she had but one shoe on – the other was on the table near her hand – her veil was but half arranged, her watch and chain were not put on, and some lace for her bosom lay with those trinkets, and with her handkerchief, and gloves, and some flowers, and a prayer-book, all confusedly heaped about the looking-glass.

It was not in the first moments that I saw all these things, though I saw more of them in the first moments than might be supposed. But, I saw that everything within my view which ought to be white, had been white long ago, and had lost its lustre, and was faded and yellow. I saw that the bride within the bridal dress had withered like the dress, and like the flowers, and had no brightness left but the brightness of her sunken eyes. I saw that the dress had been put upon the rounded figure of a young woman, and that the figure upon which it now hung loose, had shrunk to skin and bone. Once, I had been taken to see some ghastly waxwork at the Fair, representing I know not what impossible personage lying in state. Once, I had been taken to one of our old marsh churches to see a skeleton in the ashes of a rich dress, that had been dug out of a vault under the church pavement. Now, waxwork and skeleton seemed to have dark eyes that moved and looked at me. I should have cried out, if I could.

'Who is it?' said the lady at the table.

'Pip, ma'am.'

'Pip?'

'Mr. Pumblechook's boy, ma'am. Come – to play.'

'Come nearer; let me look at you. Come close.'

It was when I stood before her, avoiding her eyes, that I took note of the surrounding objects in detail, and saw that her watch had stopped at twenty minutes to nine, and that a clock in the room had stopped at twenty minutes to nine.

'Look at me,' said Miss Havisham. 'You are not afraid of a woman who has never seen the sun since you were born?'

I regret to state that I was not afraid of telling the enormous lie comprehended in the answer 'No.'

'Do you know what I touch here?' she said, laying her hands, one upon the other, on her left side.

'Yes, ma'am.' (It made me think of the young man.)

'What do I touch?'
'Your heart.'
'Broken!'

This is Pip's first encounter with Miss Havisham. It shows a movement between immediacy and distance that is characteristic of the narrative technique of *Expectations*. It plunges the reader into Pip's situation, but draws back from time to time to indicate Pip is writing from a later perspective. Indications of this later perspective occur when he says that the dressing-room furniture is 'of forms and uses then quite unknown to me' – but, implicitly, known to him now, as an experienced adult – and when he remarks that '[i]t was not in the first moments that I saw all these things', an acknowledgement that he has retrospectively revised his experiences.

The extract includes single straightforward sentences: 'No glimpse of daylight was to be seen in it [the room]'; 'Her shoes were white'; double sentences: 'Some bright jewels sparkled on her neck and on her hands, and some other jewels lay sparkling on the table'; and multiple sentences, most notably the last sentence of paragraph three, which gives a strong sense of interrupted action, amplified by the interpolated clause and by the use of commas rather than semicolons. Miss Havisham was in the process of dressing for her marriage ceremony but this was never completed; she has been frozen in time but there is a sense of arrested, unfinished movement, rather than composed stasis. The frozen scene also ironically anticipates what might have been the scene after the wedding, in the privacy of the bridal chamber, with the half-arranged veil, the watch and chain, the bosom-lace, the handkerchiefs and gloves and flowers and prayer book being taken off or put down rather than picked up and put on, as the newlyweds moved towards the consummation of their marriage.

If we examine the diction of the passage, we find finite and infinitive verbs that stress the act of seeing: 'to be seen'; 'I have ever seen, or shall ever see'; 'to see' (repeated twice); 'I saw' (repeated five times). 'White' is a key adjective – applied to satins, lace, silks, veil and then, with surprising incongruity in the context of the bridal apparel, hair. But the adjective is qualified when Pip says that all the whites had become 'faded and yellow'; this makes us readjust our imaginative envisioning of the interior and gives a sense of the time that must have passed to change the brightness and colour of these once-white items. Another important adjective/noun is 'bright'/'brightness' (with an intertextual echo, perhaps, of the line 'Brightness falls from the (h)air' in the song 'Adieu, farewell, earth's bliss' from Thomas Nashe's *Summer's Last Will and Testament* (1592). 'Bright' and 'brightness' alliterate with another key noun and adjective: 'bride' and 'bridal'.

Rather than being woven into other sentences, the symbols of the waxwork and skeleton are elaborated in stand-alone sentences, each of which opens in an identical way, providing another example of Dickens's use of anaphora: 'Once, I had been taken': the passive form here shows Pip being subjected to experiences rather than choosing them freely, as he is now subjected to Miss Havisham; it stresses the powerlessness of the child. The sentences thus stand out and highlight the symbolic links between Miss Havisham, artificiality and death. There is also an opposition between natural and artificial light that relates to the broader symbolic structure of the novel that pits spontaneity against artifice: Miss Havisham's room is well lit, but with candles, and any hint of daylight is shut out. She defines herself as 'a woman who has never seen the sun since Pip's birth'. This reference to Pip's birth implies that he might have inadvertently played some part in Miss Havisham's sequestration from the sunlight and, it may be, increases the sense of guilt he might already feel at having survived his parents and his five siblings who died in infancy. The image of Miss Havisham having 'withered' like her bridal dress strengthens the sense that she has been cut off from natural processes of recuperation.

Miss Havisham's dialogue and body language have a theatrical, melodramatic quality that is another key aspect of Dickens's work. In contrast to the scene we discussed in chapter 1, in which the firing of the guns, following on from Pip's encounter with the fearful man, sparks off a series of questions on Pip's part, even if they receive little or no answer, it is now Pip who is being questioned. Miss Havisham adopts the interrogative mode from a position of power that forces Pip to respond, even if untruthfully. Her dialogue also takes on imperative forms – 'Come nearer'; 'Come close'; 'Look at me' – and a one-word exclamation: 'Broken!': an adjective that refers first of all to Miss Havisham's heart, employing the melodramatic cliché of the 'broken' heart, but refers more widely to the broken reciprocity between her and other people. Pip's part in the dialogue is confined to brief responses made up of monosyllables (apart from Pumblechook's name).

From this disturbing meeting between the young boy and the frozen old lady, we now move to a more endearing though not unshadowed encounter when David Copperfield meets Mr Dick.

Mr Dick's Head: *David Copperfield*, pp. 257–9

'I wish you'd go upstairs,' said my aunt, as she threaded her needle, 'and give my compliments to Mr Dick, and I'll be glad to hear how he gets on with his Memorial.'

I rose with all alacrity, to acquit myself of this commission.

'I suppose,' said my aunt, eyeing me as narrowly as she had eyed the needle in threading it, 'you think Mr Dick a short name, eh?'

'I thought it was rather a short name, yesterday,' I confessed.

'You are not to suppose that he hasn't got a longer name, if he chose to use it,' said my aunt, with a loftier air. 'Babley – Mr Richard Babley – that's the gentleman's true name.'

I was going to suggest, with a modest sense of my youth and familiarity I had been already guilty of, that I had better give him the full benefit of that name, when my aunt went on to say:

'But don't you call him by it, whatever you do. He can't bear his name. That's a peculiarity of his. Though I don't know that it's much of a peculiarity, either; for he has been ill-used enough, by some that bear it, to have a mortal antipathy for it, Heaven knows. Mr Dick is his name here, and everywhere else, now – if he ever went anywhere else, which he don't. So take care, child, you don't call him anything *but* Mr Dick.'

I promised to obey, and went upstairs with my message; thinking, as I went, that if Mr Dick had been working at his Memorial long, at the same rate as I had seen him working at it, through the open door, when I came down, he was probably getting on very well indeed. I found him still driving at it with a long pen, and his head almost laid upon the paper. He was so intent upon it, that I had ample leisure to observe the large paper kite in a corner, the confusion of bundles of manuscript, the number of pens, and, above all, the quantity of ink (which he seemed to have in, in half-gallon jars by the dozen), before he observed my being present.

'Ha! Phoebus!' said Mr Dick, laying down his pen. 'How does the world go? I'll tell you what,' he added, in a lower tone, 'I shouldn't wish it to be mentioned, but it's a – ' – here he beckoned to me, and put his lips close to my ear – 'it's a mad world. Mad as Bedlam, boy!' said Mr Dick, taking snuff from a round box on the table, and laughing heartily.

Without presuming to give my opinion on this question, I delivered my message.

'Well" said Mr Dick, in answer, 'my compliments to her, and I – I believe I have made a start. I think I have made a start,' said Mr Dick, passing his hand among his grey hair, and casting anything but a confident look at his manuscript. 'You have been to school?'

'Yes, sir,' I answered; 'for a short time.'

'Do you recollect the date,' said Mr Dick, looking earnestly at me, and taking up his pen to note it down, 'when King Charles the First had his head cut off?'

I said I believed it happened in the year sixteen hundred and forty-nine.

'Well,' returned Mr Dick, scratching his ear with his pen, and looking dubiously at me. 'So the books say; but I don't see how that can be. Because, if it was so long ago, how could the people about him have made that mistake of putting some of the trouble out of *his* head, after it was taken off, into *mine*?'

I was very much surprised by the inquiry; but could give no information on this point.

'It's very strange,' said Mr Dick, with a despondent look upon his papers, and with his hand among his hair again, 'that I never can get that quite right. I never can make that perfectly clear. But no matter, no matter!' he said cheerfully, and rousing himself, 'there's time enough! My compliments to Miss Trotwood, I am getting on very well indeed.'

I was going away, when he directed my attention to the kite.

'What do you think of that for a kite?' he said.

I answered that it was a beautiful one. I should think it must have been as much as seven feet high.

'I made it. We'll go and fly it, you and I,' said Mr Dick. 'Do you see this?'

He showed me that it was covered with manuscript, very closely and laboriously written; but so plainly, that as I looked along the lines, I thought I saw some allusion to King Charles the First's head again, in one or two places.

'There's plenty of string,' said Mr Dick, 'and when it flies high, it takes the facts a long way. That's my manner of diffusing 'em. I don't know where they may come down. It's according to circumstances, and the wind, and so forth; but I take my chance of that.'

His face was so very mild and pleasant, and had something so reverend in it, though it was hale and hearty, that I was not sure but that he was having a good-humoured jest with me. So I laughed, and he laughed, and we parted the best friends possible.

This extract describes David's first direct encounter with Mr Dick. Before David meets him, Mr Dick's name is the main topic of the dialogue between David and his aunt. It is a name that dissociates him from a full social and familial identity of a conventional kind. Aunt Betsey makes his social status clear – he is a 'gentleman', a key term in *Copperfield*, as it is in *Expectations* – and tells David his full name, Richard Babley, but warns David not to use it and makes it clear that this is because some members of his family have treated him badly and aroused in him very strong feelings against the name. He has thus placed himself outside the usual conditions of nomenclature and outside the biological family. Betsey's remark that he does not go anywhere else further emphasizes his social oddity.

There is a vivid and concise description of David's sight of Mr Dick writing – 'I found him still driving at it [the Memorial] with a long pen, and his head almost laid upon the paper.' But there is already a sense of obsession and distortion here – in the term 'driving' and in the position of the head which seems to be nearly merging with the paper. Writing is a key activity in *Copperfield* – a novel whose protagonist becomes a successful writer – and Mr Dick performs a bizarre parody of writing in which he never gets anywhere, though this could also be an intertextual reference back to Laurence Sterne's *Tristram Shandy* (1760–67) and an anticipation of certain kinds of Samuel Beckett's texts. The longer sentence that follows the description of Mr Dick at work enumerates other key objects in the room – the paper kite, the manuscript bundles, the multiplicity of pens and amount of ink – all of which adds to a sense of tension between movement and stasis, of equipment being assembled for a task of writing that never makes progress. The delay before Mr Dick actually speaks to David – a delay enacted in the length of the sentence itself before the final clause – emphasizes his absorption in his task.

When Mr Dick does acknowledge David's presence and speaks, he does not address him by his actual, mundane name, a further example of how he has withdrawn from the conventional processes of naming. Instead, he designates David by a classical reference, 'Phoebus', which turns him, momentarily, into a young sun-god and creates an intertextual link with ancient Greek myth. Mr Dick goes on to make further intertextual links when, like a comic King Lear, he offers a general observation on global insanity, 'it's a mad world', partly echoing the proverbial phrase, 'it's a mad world, my masters', which was used as the title of a 1603 pamphlet by Nicholas Breton and Thomas Middleton's play of about 1608. The mention of Bedlam takes on a deeper and more specific significance when we learn soon afterwards that Mr Dick's brother wanted to confine him for life to an asylum – a specific example of how family members may misuse each other and a reason for Mr Dick's renunciation of his family name. It is, however, also possible to hear, in the family name 'Babley', the word 'babble', in the sense of foolish, excited or confused talk, and this links up with Mr. Dick's manner of speaking and writing – although he has already shown himself capable of delivering concise and commonsensical advice at a key moment, when Betsey is wondering what to do with David soon after his arrival and Mr Dick declares: 'I should wash him!' (249).

After David has delivered the message from Betsey, asking Mr Dick how he is getting on with his Memorial, Mr Dick's repeated assertion that he has 'made a start' is rendered questionable by his unconfident look at his manuscript and then by his return to the topic that obsesses him, King Charles I's head – or more exactly the troubles that seem to have survived the king's decapitation and obsessively persist in his own head. Mr Dick then shifts the focus to his kite that – again bizarrely – is covered in manuscript. This contributes to a parodic image of the writer at work, sending out his words to the world, and links up with the images of writing that recur throughout the extract. But the positive adjectives in the penultimate sentence of the extract – 'mild', 'pleasant', 'reverend', 'hale', 'hearty' – emphasize that Mr Dick is likeable rather than alarming. He is an endearing eccentric but the references to the way his family has treated him, to the idea of putting him into an asylum, and to the force of his obsession creates a penumbra of darkness around him.

In *Expectations*, Wemmick's eccentricities are also endearing and his caring treatment of his Aged Parent contrasts with the familial abuse that Mr Dick fears; but Wemmick is careful to confine his eccentricities, and his protectiveness, to his home. Our next extract is from Pip's account of his first visit there.

Wemmick's Castle: *Great Expectations*, pp. 229–31

Wemmick's house was a little wooden cottage in the midst of plots of garden, and the top of it was cut out and painted like a battery mounted with guns.

'My own doing,' said Wemmick. 'Looks pretty; don't it?'

I highly commended it. I think it was the smallest house I ever saw; with the queerest gothic windows (by far the greater part of them sham), and a gothic door, almost too small to get in at.

'That's a real flagstaff, you see,' said Wemmick, 'and on Sundays I run up a real flag. Then look here. After I have crossed this bridge, I hoist it up – so – and cut off the communication.'

The bridge was a plank, and it crossed a chasm about four feet wide and two deep. But it was very pleasant to see the pride with which he hoisted it up and made it fast; smiling as he did so, with a relish and not merely mechanically.

'At nine o'clock every night, Greenwich time,' said Wemmick, 'the gun fires. There he is, you see! And when you hear him go, I think you'll say he's a Stinger.'

The piece of ordnance referred to, was mounted in a separate fortress, constructed of lattice-work. It was protected from the weather by an ingenious little tarpaulin contrivance in the nature of an umbrella.

'Then, at the back,' said Wemmick, 'out of sight, so as not to impede the idea of fortifications – for it's a principle with me, if you have an idea, carry it out and keep it up – I don't know whether that's your opinion – ' I said, decidedly.

' – At the back, there's a pig, and there are fowls and rabbits; then, I knock together my own little frame, you see, and grow cucumbers; and you'll judge at supper what sort of a salad I can raise. So, sir,' said Wemmick, smiling again, but seriously too, as he shook his head, 'if you can suppose the little place besieged, it would hold out a devil of a time in point of provisions.'

Then, he conducted me to a bower about a dozen yards off, but which was approached by such ingenious twists of path that it took quite a long time to get at; and in this retreat our glasses were already set forth. Our punch was cooling in an ornamental lake, on whose margin the bower was raised. This piece of water (with an island in the middle which might have been the salad for supper) was of a circular form, and he had constructed a fountain in it, which, when you set a little mill going and took a cork out of a pipe, played to that powerful extent that it made the back of your hand quite wet.

'I am my own engineer, and my own plumber, and my own gardener, and my own Jack of all Trades,' said Wemmick, in acknowledging my compliments. 'Well; it's a good thing, you know. It brushes the Newgate cobwebs away, and pleases the Aged. You wouldn't mind being at once introduced to the Aged, would you? It wouldn't put you out?'

I expressed the readiness I felt, and we went into the castle. There, we found, sitting by a fire, a very old man in a flannel coat: clean, cheerful, comfortable, and well cared for, but intensely deaf.

'Well aged parent,' said Wemmick, shaking hands with him in a cordial and jocose way, 'how am you?'

'All right, John; all right!' replied the old man.

'Here's Mr. Pip, aged parent,' said Wemmick, 'and I wish you could hear his name. Nod away at him, Mr. Pip; that's what he likes. Nod away at him, if you please, like winking!'

'This is a fine place of my son's, sir,' cried the old man, while I nodded as hard as I possibly could. 'This is a pretty pleasure-ground, sir. This spot and these beautiful works upon it ought to be kept together by the Nation, after my son's time, for the people's enjoyment.'

'You're as proud of it as Punch; ain't you, Aged?' said Wemmick, contemplating the old man, with his hard face really softened; '*there's* a nod for you;' giving him a tremendous one; '*there's* another for you;' giving him a still more tremendous one; 'you like that, don't you? If you're not tired, Mr. Pip – though I know it's tiring to strangers – will you tip him one more? You can't think how it pleases him.'

I tipped him several more, and he was in great spirits. We left him bestirring himself to feed the fowls, and we sat down to our punch in the arbour; where Wemmick told me as he smoked a pipe that it had taken him a good many years to bring the property up to its present pitch of perfection.

'Is it your own, Mr. Wemmick?'

'O yes,' said Wemmick, 'I have got hold of it, a bit at a time. It's a freehold, by George!'

'Is it, indeed? I hope Mr. Jaggers admires it?'

'Never seen it,' said Wemmick. 'Never heard of it. Never seen the Aged. Never heard of him. No; the office is one thing, and private life is another. When I go into the office, I leave the Castle behind me, and when I come into the Castle, I leave the office behind me. If it's not in any way disagreeable to you, you'll oblige me by doing the same. I don't wish it professionally spoken about.'

This description of John Wemmick's Walworth house is shared between Pip as narrator and Wemmick's remarks in direct speech. Pip's narrative prose brings out the oddity, the unusual quality, of Wemmick's cottage. He uses two superlatives, 'smallest' and 'queerest', which help to convey an exceptional degree of smallness and unusualness. The description of the door as 'almost too small to get into' and the thrice-repeated adjective 'little' also contribute to the sense of exceptional smallness. The house has a miniaturized aspect, as if it were a doll's house, as if to enter it were to return, with some difficulty, to childhood. The adjective 'gothic', used twice, conjures up gothic architecture and the gothic novel, but there is an irony in the application of the adjective to such a small cottage rather than to the castles that feature in such founding texts of Gothic fiction as Horace Walpole's *The Castle of Otranto* (1764) and Ann Radcliffe's *Mysteries of Udolpho* (1794). But we can relate this downscaling to the fact that by the time *Expectations* was published, Gothic fiction had mutated into Victorian sensation fiction, for example Wilkie Collins's *The Woman in White* (1860) and Mary Elizabeth Braddon's *Lady Audley's Secret* (1862), which transferred Gothic elements to domestic English settings. The adjective 'sham' suggests the inauthenticity of most of the 'gothic' elements of Wemmick's castle. The word 'chasm', for a ditch about four feet wide and two deep, is a domesticated intertextual echo of Coleridge's 'deep romantic chasm' in '*Kubla Khan* (1816), while the mundane mensuration recalls Wordsworth's 'The Thorn' (1798): 'I've measured it from side to side / 'Tis three feet long and two feet wide'. But the elements of irony and the recognition of inauthenticity, while indicating that Pip, as narrator, has the taste and discernment of a gentleman, do not set up the cottage and its garden as an object of mockery. The extract also indicates that its features are the result of human inventiveness and practical application, and Pip's diction stresses this: 'ingenious' and 'constructed' (both used twice); 'contrivance'; and 'painted'. Although the narrative prose sometimes uses the passive case ('was cut out', 'was mounted'), Wemmick's direct-speech contributions make it clear that he was the active agent: 'My own doing'; 'I knock together my own little frame'; and, most comprehensively, 'I am my own engineer, and my own plumber, and my own gardener, and my own Jack of All Trades.'

Wemmick's cottage is also a microcosm – the term is especially appropriate, given its miniaturized, small-scale quality – of four key aspects of nineteenth-century Britain: the country house, agriculture, technology and war. The gothic windows and doors of the house, the bower, the ornamental lake with island and fountain, are all features that might be found, on a much larger scale, in an English country house with extensive, landscaped grounds. Indeed, Wemmick's Aged Parent sees his son's house and garden as worthy of being conserved as a national treasure, like a country house, for popular pleasure and edification: 'This spot and these beautiful works upon it ought to be kept together by the Nation, after my son's time, for the people's enjoyment.' The bridge that can be hoisted up and down, the umbrella-like 'contrivance' that protects the gun, the fountain that sprays out water when a little mill is set going, are all examples of technology – not the forbidding technology of the Victorian factory but technology on a human and domestic scale. Wemmick's display of technological ingenuity calls to mind the Great Exhibition of 1851. Wemmick's garden is also a small-scale farm, with a pig, fowls, rabbits and a cucumber frame. The military appurtenances and analogies – the painting of the top of the cottage to resemble 'a battery mounted with guns', the flag, the drawbridge, the cannon – make the house a literal version of the axiom 'An Englishman's home is his castle' but also relate to the battles and sieges of the Crimean War (1854–56) and the 'Indian Mutiny' (1857–58) that were still vividly in the British public consciousness while Dickens was writing and publishing *Expectations*.

Within this microcosm, Wemmick is able partly to recover the humanity set aside when he is at work – to brush away 'the Newgate cobwebs', as he puts it, even though his purchase of the freehold of his house and the cost of its fixtures, fittings, furniture and garden features have probably been obtained, at least partly, from his dealings with the 'portable property' of Newgate prisoners condemned to death. Wemmick's kindly treatment of his Aged Parent is signalled by the alliterative accumulation of positive adjectives when Pip first meets him – 'clean, cheerful, comfortable, and well cared for'. It contrasts with those relationships in *Expectations* where reciprocal kindness between parents (or their surrogates) and children is absent due to callousness or neglect: Mrs Joe and Pip; Miss Havisham and Estella; even Joe and Pip, as the latter becomes a gentleman and grows increasingly distant from Joe. But Wemmick cannot bring together the two aspects of his life in any sustained and continuous way: kindness is largely confined to his private life but its material embodiment in the shape of his house and garden depends on the dubious proceeds of his working life: and in this respect he stands for a wider division between a private life where the affections can flow but which is supported by a public life where benevolent feelings are suppressed.

Conclusions

Our analysis of each of these extracts has shown how Dickens portrays obsessive and/or eccentric characters through a mixture of description, dialogue, sentence structure, diction and imagery. Each character presents a puzzle to the narrator. In the case of Rosa Dartle and David, and Miss Havisham and Pip, they are meeting for the first time and the two ladies are difficult for the protagonist to 'read', to interpret. In the case of Mr Dick, David has already seen him but this is the first time he has spoken to him; in the case of John Wemmick, Pip has already met him, but only at work, in Little Britain and Newgate, so he encounters a new aspect of him at Walworth. Each character is differentiated: Rosa Dartle is presented as an intriguing, ambiguous figure who hovers between seeming attractive and off-putting and who gives a sense of blocked energy; Miss Havisham is shown as frozen in time but not as a case of simple inertia; her stasis entails a repeated, sustained performance, a ritualistic re-enactment of the moment of heartbreak that gives a sense of arrested action and, as with Rosa, of blocked energy; Mr Dick is portrayed as an amiable, engaging figure whose obsession gives him pain and has estranged him from his threatening family and made him drop his original surname. John Wemmick confines his inventiveness and affection to a separate sphere and lives a divided life.

Dickens's diction helps to convey Rosa's mixture of frailty and intensity and the whiteness-turned-yellow, fusing youth and age, virginity and decay, in Miss Havisham's appearance and ambience. In the account of Miss Havisham, the words 'bright/brightness/bride/ bridal' form an alliterative linking and stress the contrast between the promise of brightness as Miss Havisham prepared to be a bride with the faded repetition of her current existence. The positive adjectives applied to Mr Dick help to make him agreeable rather than alarming. The terms applied to Wemmick's house convey its oddity and its miniature, childlike quality.

Anaphora, the repetition of a word or phrase, especially at the start of a sentence, is employed to good effect in the first extract, where the repeated use of 'perhaps because' stresses David's ambivalent response to Rosa Dartle, and in the second extract, where repeating the passive form 'Once I had been taken' reinforces the sense that Pip is being subjected to experiences rather than initiating them himself.

Imagery helps to vivify and deepen the portrayals of the obsessives and eccentrics. The simile of the unmarried Rosa as a dilapidated house that has been to let for a long time signifies the passive position in which she is placed, while the metaphor of the 'wasting fire within her' conveys the destructive effects of her repressed energies. The opposition between artificial and natural light, evident in the second *Expectations* extract discussed in chapter 2, also occurs in Pip's first encounter with Miss Havisham and feeds into a broader theme of the novel, and indeed of all Dickens's fiction: the conflict between spontaneity and artifice.

Dialogue is important in all four extracts. It is not only Rosa Dartle's appearance that is intriguing, but her way of speaking, which makes uses of aposiopesis (a sudden breaking-off), indirection and irony to convey the points she wishes to uphold. Miss Havisham adopts interrogative and imperative modes of speech that signify her power over Pip and sums up her emotional trauma in a one-word exclamation: 'Broken!', while

Pip responds almost entirely in monosyllables. Mr Dick offers David recondite allusions, repeatedly asserts that he has 'made a start' when he seems to be getting nowhere, and returns obsessively to the matter of King Charles I's head. Wemmick, through his dialogue, displays his pride in his home, his practical skills, his filial affection and the divisions of his life into two spheres.

There are significant intratextual links in each extract. The first meeting with Miss Havisham anticipates later meetings and that final encounter in which flames will envelop her. Rosa Dartle's way of speaking when David first meets her contrasts with her frank outburst after Steerforth's death, which we discuss in chapter 4. We can also suggest intriguing intertextual links. Some of these are with other Dickens novels. The image of Rosa as a dilapidated house links with Satis House in *Expectations* and with Bleak House in the novel of that title. The use of the terms 'bright' and 'brightness' may echo Thomas Nashe's line 'Brightness falls from the (h)air' in his 'Adieu, farewell earth's bliss', a celebrated and haunting Elizabethan lament for decay and mortality. Mr Dick alludes to ancient Greek myth when he dubs David 'Phoebus' and to Shakespeare, Nicholas Breton and Thomas Middleton when he declares 'it's a mad world'. The 'gothic' element of Wemmick's house relates to Gothic fiction and its Victorian successor, sensation fiction, and its account of Wemmick's moat and bridge echo Coleridge's *Kubla Khan* and Wordsworth's 'The Thorn'.

Rosa, Miss Havisham, Mr Dick and Wemmick are examples of deviant psychology – in the sense that their mental processes, in their respective ways, do not accord with the norms of their society – but they also exemplify key aspects of that society by exaggerating and caricaturing them. Rosa Dartle is unmarried at the age of 30 and can find or construct no alternative to marriage in a society in which matrimony is the crucial defining state for a woman. Her energies therefore have no direct outlet; but this makes her fascinating to David in ways not shared by the other women he meets. Miss Havisham has been jilted at the moment at which she was about to enter into the crucial defining state of marriage and has remained trapped in a compulsive repetition of the moment of jilting that can also be seen, in reverse as it were, as an ironic re-enactment of the postmarital divestment of her clothes and accessories that would have taken place in the intimacy of the bridal chamber as the marriage moved towards consummation. Again, she is unable to find or make any alternative to marriage, and her energies have no outlet other than in repetition and the emotional abuse of Estella, who is being trained to procure Miss Havisham's revenge on men. Mr Dick is locked into obsessions which link him with the act of writing and with the King who lost his head in an epochal moment of British and European history. Sheltered by Betsey Trotwood, he becomes an amiable eccentric rather than a threatening obsessive, but a penumbra of dark possibilities nevertheless distantly shadows him in a society in which the mental asylum is becoming a more prominent way of dealing with psychological distress and deviance. John Wemmick finds a kind of solution to the problem of how to have a heart – and a decent habitation – in a heartless world; but his house and garden reproduce, in miniature, four aspects of that world – the country house, agriculture, technology and war – and his division of his days involves a self-suppression that is indicative of a wider and developing split in modern society between a working life that involves, to a greater or lesser extent, the repression of conscience and feeling, and a private life which is asked to carry the weight of the scruples and emotions largely excluded from the workaday world while also depending on the money earned in that world. Although the force and skill of Dickens's portrayal can make each of these characters seem to take on an existence independent both of the texts in which they appear and the society to which those texts refer, they are the products of those texts and they do relate to the wider society.

Methods of Analysis

- We highlighted how each extract shows an obsessive or eccentric figure whom the narrator finds difficult to interpret (e.g. Rosa Dartle both attracts and disturbs David; John Wemmick reveals a wholly different side of himself to Pip).
- We discussed the diction and its effects (e.g. the way words such as 'slight', 'short', 'dark', 'black' and 'eager' convey a mixture of frailty and intensity in Rosa; how terms such as 'mild', 'pleasant' and 'hale' emphasize Mr Dick's amiability).

- We observed examples of anaphora (e.g. the thrice-repeated phrase 'perhaps because', which contributes to the sense of David's ambivalent response to Rosa Dartle; the double reiteration of 'Once I had been taken' which indicates, through the passive verb, that Pip is being subjected to experiences rather than initiating them).

- We explored how imagery helps to vivify and deepen the portrayals of the obsessives and eccentrics (e.g. the simile of the unmarried Rosa as a dilapidated house that has been to let for a long time, which signifies the passive position in which she is placed as a single woman, and the metaphor of the 'wasting fire within her', which conveys the destructive effects of her repressed energies).

- We identified symbolic patterns that feature more widely in Dickens (e.g. the opposition between artificial and natural light in Pip's first encounter with Miss Havisham, which feeds into a broader theme of *Expectations*, and indeed of all Dickens's fiction, the conflict between spontaneity and artifice).

- We examined the dialogue (e.g. how Rosa Dartle's style of speaking makes use of aposiopesis (a sudden breaking-off), indirection and irony; how Miss Havisham adopts interrogative and imperative modes of speech that signify her power over Pip, and sums up her emotional trauma in a one-word exclamation: 'Broken!').

- We indicated significant intratextual links in each extract (e.g. how Pip's first meeting with Miss Havisham links up with later meetings and with that final encounter in which flames will envelop her; how Rosa Dartle's way of speaking when David first meets her contrasts with her frank outburst after Steerforth's death).

- We traced possible intertextual links with Dickens's other novels and with texts by other writers (e.g. the image of Rosa as a dilapidated house may link with Satis House in *Expectations* and with the titular dwelling of *Bleak House*; the 'gothic' element of Wemmick's house may relate to Gothic fiction and its Victorian successor, sensation fiction, and the account of Wemmick's moat and bridge to Coleridge's *Kubla Khan* and Wordsworth's 'The Thorn'.

- We considered these four figures – Rosa Dartle, Miss Havisham, Mr Dick, John Wemmick – as examples of deviant psychology that also represent key aspects of that society by exaggerating and caricaturing them (e.g. Rosa is a 30-year-old spinster who can find or construct no alternative to marriage in a society in which matrimony is the crucial defining state for a woman; John Wemmick's self-division exemplifies a widening split in modern society between working and private life but also implies the continued dependence of private life on working life).

Suggested Work

Analyse the two following passages. The first focuses on Uriah Heep and offers a glimpse of the culture that helped to shape him. The second portrays Mr Wopsle's attempts to conquer the London stage with his version of *Hamlet*. Consider how these obsessive and eccentric figures are portrayed and relate them to wider cultural and social phenomena.

[a] *Copperfield*. From "'Ah! But you know we're so very umble'" to "'but I've got a little power!'" (*DC* 637–9)
[b] *Expectations*. From 'On our arrival in Denmark' to "'or perhaps we shall meet him'" (*GE* 274–6)

4

Moments of Truth

Key strands in both *Copperfield* and *Expectations* lead up to moments of truth in which masks are shed and relationships reconfigured, often radically. In these novels, as elsewhere in Dickens, such moments mix psychological and social realism with melodrama and sometimes melodrama dominates. The priority is not realism in the sense of verisimilitude or probability, but the shock of recognition that rhetorically accomplished melodrama can achieve. Dickens's fondness for melodrama has sometimes been seen as a flaw, a lapse from the convincingness and complexity of realism into a simplified kind of writing that draws on a repertoire of stereotyped phrases and poses, and solicits stock responses; but in another perspective, which seems more fruitful in Dickens's case, we can see melodrama as a particular literary convention that, once we accept its terms sympathetically, provides a stylized and heightened means of truth-telling that is as effective as realism in its own way, and sometimes more so, partly because it highlights the essentials of a situation and partly because it provides a means of obliquely saying more than realism, constrained by the dominant discourses of its day, can encompass (in Dickens's work, for example, it can provide ways of talking about sexuality that were not available in the public language of the time). Dickens is prepared for his style, and his characters, to strike poses and to adopt an evidently rhetorical rather than apparently natural mode of utterance. He works in a theatrical way in staging these moments, not only in the dialogue but also in the narrative prose which dramatizes the movements of minds forced to confront – or sometimes still evading – unpleasant realities.

The first extract we consider, from *Copperfield*, is the moment of truth in which Uriah Heep fully reveals his malevolence – a profoundly disturbing experience for David:

Dark Double: *David Copperfield*, pp. 816–19

'I am the agent and friend of Mr Wickfield, sir,' said Traddles, in a composed and business-like way. 'And I have a power of attorney from him in my pocket, to act for him in all matters.'

'The old ass has drunk himself into a state of dotage,' said Uriah, turning uglier than before, 'and it has been got from him by fraud!'

'Something has been got from him by fraud, I know,' returned Traddles quietly; 'and so do you, Mr Heep. We will refer that question, if you please, to Mr Micawber.'

'Ury – ! ' Mrs Heep began, with an anxious gesture.

'You hold your tongue, mother,' he returned; 'least said, soonest mended.'

'But, my Ury – '

'Will you hold your tongue, mother, and leave it to me?'

Though I had long known that his servility was false, and all his pretences knavish and hollow, I had had no adequate conception of the extent of his hypocrisy, until I now saw him with his mask off. The suddenness with which he dropped it, when he perceived that it was useless to him; the malice, insolence, and hatred, he revealed; the leer with which he exulted, even at this moment, in the evil he had done – all this time being desperate too, and at his wits' end for the means of getting the better of us – though perfectly consistent with the experience I had of him, at first took even me by surprise, who had known him so long, and disliked him so heartily.

I say nothing of the look he conferred on me, as he stood eyeing us, one after another; for I had always understood that he hated me, and I remembered the marks of my hand upon his cheek. But when his eyes passed on to Agnes, and I saw the rage with which he felt his power over her slipping away, and the exhibition, in their disappointment, of the odious passions that had led him to aspire to one whose virtues he could never appreciate or care for, I was shocked by the mere thought of her having lived, an hour, within sight of such a man.

After some rubbing of the lower part of his face, and some looking at us with those bad eyes, over his grisly fingers, he made one more address to me, half whining, and half abusive.

'You think it is justifiable, do you, Copperfield, you who pride yourself so much on your honour and all the rest of it, to sneak about my place, eaves-dropping with my clerk? If it had been *me*, I shouldn't have wondered; for I don't make myself out a gentleman (though I never was in the streets either, as you were, according to Micawber), but being *you*! – And you're not afraid of doing this, either? You don't think at all of what I shall do, in return; or of getting yourself into trouble for conspiracy and so forth? Very well. We shall see! Mr What's-your-name, you were going to refer some question to Micawber. There's your referee. Why don't you make him speak? He has learnt his lesson, I see.'

Seeing that what he said had no effect on me or any of us, he sat on the edge of his table with his hands in his pockets, and one of his splay feet twisted round the other leg, waiting doggedly for what might follow.

Mr Micawber, whose impetuosity I had restrained thus far with the greatest difficulty, and who had repeatedly interposed with the first syllable of SCOUN-drel! without getting to the second, now burst forward, drew the ruler from his breast (apparently as a defensive weapon), and produced from his pocket a foolscap document, folded in the form of a large letter. Opening this packet, with his old flourish, and glancing at the contents, as if he cherished an artistic admiration of their style of composition, he began to read as follows:

'"Dear Miss Trotwood and gentlemen – "'

'Bless and save the man!' exclaimed my aunt in a low voice. 'He'd write letters by the ream, if it was a capital offence!'

Mr Micawber, without hearing her, went on.

'"In appearing before you to denounce probably the most consummate Villain that has ever existed,"' Mr Micawber, without looking off the letter, pointed the ruler, like a ghostly truncheon, at Uriah Heep, '"I ask no consideration for myself. The victim, from my cradle, of pecuniary liabilities to which I have been unable to respond, I have ever been the sport and toy of debasing circumstances. Ignominy, Want, Despair, and Madness, have, collectively or separately, been the attendants of my career."'

The relish with which Mr Micawber described himself as a prey to these dismal calamities, was only to be equalled by the emphasis with which he read his letter; and the kind of homage he rendered to it with a roll of his head, when he thought he had hit a sentence very hard indeed.

"'In an accumulation of Ignominy, Want, Despair, and Madness, I entered the office – or, as our lively neighbour the Gaul would term it, the Bureau – of the Firm, nominally conducted under the appellation of Wickfield and – HEEP, but in reality, wielded by – HEEP alone. HEEP, and only HEEP, is the mainspring of that machine, HEEP, and only HEEP, is the Forger and the Cheat.'"

In this confrontation with Uriah Heep, three people speak: Traddles, who states his position in an efficient, collected and concise manner; Heep, who shows his own eloquence; and Micawber, who adopts his customary style but strengthens it with denunciatory invective. David himself stays silent; no direct speech is attributed to him; it is in his narrative prose that he registers his own responses, piling pejorative terms on Heep: nouns such as 'servility', 'pretences', 'hypocrisy', 'malice', 'insolence', 'hatred', 'leer', 'evil', 'rage'; adjectives like 'false', 'knavish', 'hollow', 'desperate', 'bad', 'grisly'; 'whining'; 'abusive'. These terms accumulate with particular force in the long sentence starting 'The suddenness', which is, in a characteristically Dickensian way, is marked by semicolons and an interpolation that help to make the sentence seem a deliberate, elaborate, carefully considered and weighty judgement.

David especially stresses the effect of the revelation of the true Heep, whose existence David had already discerned and who is 'perfectly consistent' with David's previous 'experience' of him but who nonetheless, fully and suddenly revealed, surprises and shocks him, particularly when David sees Heep looking at Agnes and registers Heep's matrimonial and sexual designs on her – his 'odious passions'. But it is worth noting that two of those passions – the desire to marry Agnes and to possess her sexually – are not in themselves 'odious'; indeed, towards the end of *Copperfield*, they will become David's own. The extremity of David's response to Heep, the vehemence of his repudiation, might suggest that Heep is, in part, a projection of all David's bad impulses, a kind of repulsive double. But, if this is the case, David does not fully acknowledge it; the moment of truth for Heep is also a moment of self-evasion for David.

At one notable moment, the narrative prose employs a device known as apophasis – from the Greek verb meaning 'to speak off', or deny. This entails announcing that one will say or do nothing and then, in effect, saying or doing it with particular emphasis (the initial announcement is part of the extra emphasis because it implies that the withheld statement is one of particular enormity that exceeds adequate or decorous articulation). Thus David begins '*I say nothing* of the look [Heep] conferred on me' but goes on, in the clause, 'I had always understood that he hated me', to make it clear that it was a look of hatred and then, in the final clause, to suggest that it was particularly exacerbated by the blow David had once dealt him. The mention of 'the marks of my hand upon his cheek' makes an intratextual link with the earlier passage in chapter 42 in which David, provoked by Heep's attempt to entrap him in his scheming, strikes Heep's 'invitingly' lank cheek with his open hand with such force that his 'fingers tingled as if [he] had burnt them' (686). The subsequent paragraph is worth quoting in full at this point since it reinforces the sense of a strange 'connexion' between David and Uriah.

> He caught the hand in his, and we stood in that connexion, looking at each other. We stood so, a long time; long enough for me to see the white marks of my fingers die out of the deep red of his cheek, and leave it a deeper red.   (*DC* 686)

The look Heep and David give each other here feeds into the look that Heep gives David in the extract and each passage reinforces the import of the other.

Heep's utterances exhibit a marked change from his earlier professions of humility; he insults Mr Wickfield and chides and silences his own mother; he tries to hit back verbally at David and, for himself, repudiates the title of 'gentleman', that key word in *Copperfield* – though he insinuates that David himself had at one time fallen below gentlemanly status and been 'in the streets'. But it is Micawber, rather than David, who delivers the public denunciation of Heep and he does so by reading aloud from a large document – in other words, by reading a piece of writing, another example of the importance of writing, written documents and reading aloud and silently, in this novel whose protagonist becomes a writer.

The document shows Micawber's usual capacity for circumlocution and self-dramatization as a 'victim' of 'pecuniary liabilities' from babyhood and as the perennial 'sport and toy of debasing circumstances'. He presents himself as what could almost be a figure in an allegorical drama or painting in which the personified forces of 'Ignominy, Want, Despair, and Madness' attend him. David's narrative commentary suggests that Micawber relishes this role, that he takes a pleasure from it that is both masochistic and egotistic, both self-abasing and self-aggrandizing. But if the document is, in part, a further episode in Micawber's self-dramatization, it is also, and primarily, a denunciation of Heep as 'probably the most consummate Villain that has ever existed'. Heep's humiliation is emphasized not only by Micawber's well-turned sentences but also by the typographical use of capital letters for the first syllable of 'SCOUND-drel!' and for HEEP's surname. Micawber clearly identifies Heep as a forger and cheat. But his rigorous condemnation should not disguise the extent to which Micawber, while by no means as bad as Heep, is nonetheless manipulative and irresponsible, using and excusing his financial improvidence to cast himself as an object of pity. As with Heep and David, a moment of truth for Heep serves as a moment of self-evasion for Micawber.

This is a moment of truth for which we have been prepared and which David has expected. We now consider a moment of truth in *Expectations* that Pip has not expected at all and that throws his whole world into confusion.

Shock of Recognition: *Great Expectations*, pp. 332–4

I stood with my lamp held out over the stair-rail, and he came slowly within its light. It was a shaded lamp, to shine upon a book, and its circle of light was very contracted; so that he was in it for a mere instant, and then out of it. In the instant, I had seen a face that was strange to me, looking up with an incomprehensible air of being touched and pleased by the sight of me.

Moving the lamp as the man moved, I made out that he was substantially dressed, but roughly; like a voyager by sea. That he had long iron-grey hair. That his age was about sixty. That he was a muscular man, strong on his legs, and that he was browned and hardened by exposure to weather. As he ascended the last stair or two, and the light of my lamp included us both, I saw, with a stupid kind of amazement, that he was holding out both his hands to me.

'Pray what is your business?' I asked him.

'My business?' he repeated, pausing. 'Ah! Yes. I will explain my business, by your leave.'

'Do you wish to come in?'

'Yes,' he replied; 'I wish to come in, Master.'

I had asked him the question inhospitably enough, for I resented the sort of bright and gratified recognition that still shone in his face. I resented it, because it seemed to imply that he expected me to respond to it. But, I took him into the room I had just left, and, having set the lamp on the table, asked him as civilly as I could, to explain himself.

He looked about him with the strangest air – an air of wondering pleasure, as if he had some part in the things he admired – and he pulled off a rough outer coat, and his hat. Then, I saw that his head was furrowed and bald, and that the long iron-grey hair grew only on its sides. But, I saw nothing that in the least explained him. On the contrary, I saw him next moment, once more holding out both his hands to me.

'What do you mean?' said I, half suspecting him to be mad.

He stopped in his looking at me, and slowly rubbed his right hand over his head. 'It's disapinting to a man,' he said, in a coarse broken voice, 'arter having looked for'ard so distant, and come so fur; but you're not to blame for that – neither on us is to blame for that. I'll speak in half a minute. Give me half a minute, please.'

He sat down on a chair that stood before the fire, and covered his forehead with his large brown veinous hands. I looked at him attentively then, and recoiled a little from him; but I did not know him.

'There's no one nigh,' said he, looking over his shoulder; 'is there?'

'Why do you, a stranger coming into my rooms at this time of the night, ask that question?' said I.

'You're a game one,' he returned, shaking his head at me with a deliberate affection, at once most unintelligible and most exasperating; 'I'm glad you've grow'd up, a game one! But don't catch hold of me. You'd be sorry arterwards to have done it.'

I relinquished the intention he had detected, for I knew him! Even yet, I could not recall a single feature, but I knew him! If the wind and the rain had driven away the intervening years, had scattered all the intervening objects, had swept us to the churchyard where we first stood face to face on such different levels, I could not have known my convict more distinctly than I knew him now, as he sat in the chair before the fire. No need to take a file from his pocket and show it to me; no need to take the handkerchief from his neck and twist it round his head; no need to hug himself with both his arms, and take a shivering turn across the room, looking back at me for recognition. I knew him before he gave me one of those aids, though, a moment before, I had not been conscious of remotely suspecting his identity.

This extract provides a series of carefully graded stages that lead up to Pip's sudden and complete recognition of Magwitch. The extract is notable for its chiaroscuro, its play of light and shadow, which, in its mobility, anticipates cinematic effects. The chiaroscuro also serves a symbolic function. In the first paragraph, the light that comes from the lamp, partly and fitfully illuminating the stranger, is a metaphor for Pip's limited understanding of the situation. The circle of light, like the circle of Pip's perception and cognition at this point, is very limited, meant to fall upon a book rather than to illuminate an immediate reality. At first, the stranger comes within the light only momentarily so that Pip is unable to see him for even a briefly sustained length of time. Pip then moves the lamp so that it continues to illuminate the man and, as the man comes to the top of the stairs, the light of the lamp includes both of them, suggesting that they are linked together in some larger way, as yet unknown to Pip. Inside the room, once the lamp is placed on the table, the scene is set for Pip's illumination to occur.

Three partially parallel sentences, each starting with 'That', enumerate the characteristics of the as yet unnamed and unrecognized man as Pip moves the light over him. Pip grasps him metonymically, by parts rather than as a whole, almost as if he were giving the kind of enumerative description that might feature in a police report or a description of a wanted man, or that would later occur in the Sherlock Holmes stories. Each of the stranger's characteristics separates him from the gentlemanly world Pip now inhabits. Although his substantial rather than shoddy clothes signify a certain degree of prosperity, they are rough – not the clothes of a gentleman – and make him resemble a sea voyager; there is an implication of the wider, wilder world beyond the confines of middle-class London life, the world of the sea beyond the marshes, the sea that leads out to the far countries of the British Empire and the globe. His hair is long and iron-grey, indicating age, and marking him as a potential paternal figure to the fatherless Pip. He is muscular, a characteristic he shares with Joe Gargery, and the weather has browned and hardened him, indicating that he works out of doors and labours with his body.

But the characteristics Pip identifies in the light of the lamp do not explain the stranger. A range of phrases and terms indicates Pip's ongoing bafflement: 'strange to me'; 'incomprehensible'; 'a stupid kind of amazement'; 'nothing that in the least explained him'; 'half suspecting him to be mad'; 'but I did not know him'. Pip is particularly perturbed by the stranger's shows of emotion: that he is touched and pleased to see Pip; that he holds out both his hands to him; that he appears to recognize him and is pleased to do so; that he looks around Pip's quarters with 'an air of wondering pleasure, as if he had some part in the things he admired'; that he is disappointed when Pip does not reciprocate his feelings.

It is only when Magwitch warns Pip not to lay hands on him – an indication, along with his muscularity, that he is a physically dangerous man – that the shock of recognition comes. Two relatively short sentences, each ending 'I knew him' with an exclamation mark, drive home the fact – and surprise – of recognition. A long conditional sentence, starting with 'If', then assembles a list of vivid possibilities in a series of grammatically parallel phrases containing verbs which, though in the pluperfect tense, punch home, in the forward drive of the sentence, with force, energy and immediacy: 'had driven away'; 'had scattered'; 'had swept'. None of these hypothetical events has actually happened, but they are so vividly described that we may, in the moment of reading, almost believe that they have. They serve as vivid analogies to Pip's actual experience of recognition. It is as if, within the same sentence, a time machine had zoomed him into the past then sped him back to the present, reminding him both of the powerful originary moment and the present one and signalling the distance, the difference, between them as well as their intimate interconnection. In the churchyard, the boy Pip and the adult Magwitch stood face to face on different levels; now the adult Pip stands while the older Magwitch sits. Although Magwitch, muscular and hardened, with a history of violence, might, as he warns, be able to subdue Pip physically, their respective positions signify that the shift in power between surrogate father and son has begun and anticipate Magwitch's later feebleness as he lies dying in the prison hospital, in a passage we shall consider in chapter 5.

Three parallel clauses follow, each starting with 'No need to', which indicate what Magwitch actually does at this point to prompt Pip to a recognition which he has, in fact, already, in an instant, attained, after his initial puzzlement. It is significant that Magwitch does not use words but employs gestures, like a mime artist, to identify himself, as if referring to some more primal realm, beyond language (though it will soon become starkly clear that there is no escape from language and law). Each clause makes an intratextual link with Pip's encounters with Magwitch in the first and third chapters of *Expectations*: the file that Pip brings him; the handkerchief round Magwitch's head, like the 'old rag tied round [the] head' of the 'fearful man' (*GE* 4); the figure hugging himself and shivering. These details would have also served as a prompt to Dickens's original readers, particularly of the serial version of *Expectations*, who might not immediately recall the early chapters of the book, and they have probably performed the same function for subsequent first-time readers unfamiliar with the plot of the novel. But it is made clear that Pip himself does not need these details: in contrast to his earlier enumeration of Magwitch in metonymic fashion by identifying various parts of him – an enumeration that does not provide the vital clue to who he is – Pip's recognition here is holistic, grasping the identity of his visitor as a whole even though he cannot remember one individual feature. It is a moment of major reconfiguration in Pip's identity; he will never be the same again; all his bearings must be recalibrated and the rest of the novel will show him endeavouring to recover from the effects of this life-changing revelation.

We will now consider a different kind of revelation in *Copperfield*; the moment of truth at which, after Steerforth's death, Rosa Dartle drops her mask before Mrs Steerforth and emerges in the full vehemence of her passion and anger.

Rosa's Revenge: *David Copperfield*, pp. 870–2

'Rosa!' said Mrs Steerforth, 'come to me!'

She came, but with no sympathy or gentleness. Her eyes gleamed like fire as she confronted his mother, and broke into a frightful laugh.

'Now,' she said, 'is your pride appeased, you madwoman? *Now* he has made atonement to you – with his life! Do you hear? – His life!'

Mrs Steerforth, fallen back stiffly in her chair, and making no sound but a moan, cast her eyes upon her with a wide stare.

'Aye!' cried Rosa, smiting herself passionately on the breast, 'look at me! Moan, and groan, and look at me! Look here!' striking the scar, 'at your dead child's handiwork!'

The moan the mother uttered, from time to time, went to my heart. Always the same. Always inarticulate and stifled. Always accompanied with an incapable motion of the head, but with no change of face. Always proceeding from a rigid mouth and closed teeth, as if the jaw were locked and the face frozen up in pain.

'Do you remember when he did this?' she proceeded. 'Do you remember when, in his inheritance of your nature, and in your pampering of his pride and passion, he did this, and disfigured me for life? Look at me, marked until I die with his high displeasure; and moan and groan for what you made him!'

'Miss Dartle,' I entreated her. 'For Heaven's sake – '

'I *will* speak!' she said, turning on me with her lightning eyes. 'Be silent, you! Look at me, I say, proud mother of a proud false son! Moan for your nurture of him, moan for your corruption of him, moan for your loss of him, moan for mine!'

She clenched her hand, and trembled through her spare, worn figure, as if her passion were killing her by inches.

'YOU, resent his self-will!' she exclaimed. 'YOU, injured by his haughty temper! YOU, who opposed to both, when your hair was grey, the qualities which made both when you gave him birth! YOU, who from his cradle reared him to be what he was, and stunted what he should have been! Are you rewarded, *now*, for your years of trouble?'

'Oh, Miss Dartle, shame! Oh cruel!'

'I tell you,' she returned, 'I *will* speak to her. No power on earth should stop me, while I was standing here! Have I been silent all these years, and shall I not speak now? I loved him better than you ever loved him!' turning on her fiercely. 'I could have loved him, and asked no return. If I had been his wife, I could have been the slave of his caprices

for a word of love a year. I should have been. Who knows it better than
I? You were exacting, proud, punctilious, selfish. My love would have
been devoted – would have trod your paltry whimpering under foot!'

With flashing eyes, she stamped upon the ground as if she actually
did it.

'Look here!' she said, striking the scar again, with a relentless hand.
'When he grew into the better understanding of what he had done, he
saw it, and repented of it! I could sing to him, and talk to him, and show
him the ardour that I felt in all he did, and attain with labour to such
knowledge as most interested him; and I attracted him. When he was
freshest and truest, he loved *me*. Yes, he did! Many a time, when you
were put off with a slight word, he has taken Me to his heart!'

She said it with a taunting pride in the midst of her frenzy – for
it was little less – yet with an eager remembrance of it, in which the
smouldering embers of a gentler feeling kindled for the moment.

'I descended – as I might have known I should, but that he fascinated
me with his boyish courtship – into a doll, a trifle for the occupation
of an idle hour, to be dropped, and taken up, and trifled with, as the
inconstant humour took him. When he grew weary, I grew weary.
As his fancy died out, I would no more have tried to strengthen any
power I had, than I would have married him on his being forced to
take me for his wife. We fell away from one another without a word.
Perhaps you saw it, and were not sorry. Since then, I have been a mere
disfigured piece of furniture between you both; having no eyes, no ears,
no feelings, no remembrances. Moan? Moan for what you made him;
not for your love. I tell you that the time was, when I loved him better
than you ever did!'

She stood with her bright angry eyes confronting the wide stare, and
the set face; and softened no more, when the moaning was repeated,
than if the face had been a picture.

This is a highly melodramatic scene but – once we accept we are
dealing with melodrama rather than realism – a strong and effective
one that conveys psychological truths about passion and repression.
At first, dialogue and narrative prose alternate, but the balance then
shifts to what is almost a monologue on Rosa's part. The extract starts
with Mrs Steerforth uttering an imperative that is also an appeal; Rosa
at first appears to respond but it is clear almost at once that she is not
going to provide the consolation Mrs Steerforth wants. This marks a

shift in the balance of power between the two women that is confirmed when Rosa speaks and instantly dominates the situation.

It is not the first time in *Copperfield* that Rosa vehemently articulates her feelings rather than speaking in the indirect way of which we saw an example in the previous chapter. We can make an intratextual link between this extract and the scene in chapter 50 where Rosa, with David looking on, ruthlessly berates Em'ly for leading Steerforth astray, calling the young fallen woman, among other things, '[t]his piece of pollution, picked up from the water-side' (788) and declaring: 'If I could order it to be done, I would have this girl whipped to death' (789). But it is the first time that Rosa speaks out in the presence of Mrs Steerforth. Her passionate denunciation of Mrs Steerforth and her affirmation of her own love for Steerforth hold the stage. At this moment of truth, Rosa is, like Dickens himself, a master of rhetoric, employing vivid phrasing, anaphora, repetition and grammatical parallelism: 'Moan' occurs eight times in Rosa's discourse. Seven of its occurrences are at the start of her sentences or clauses, in the form of what might be called a rhetorical imperative, in that it commands Mrs Steerforth to do what she is doing already. It features most notably in the parallel locution of 'Moan for', repeated four times, in the sentence 'Moan for your nurture of him, moan for your corruption of him, moan for your loss of him, moan for mine', and this phrasing recurs in the later clause 'Moan for what you made him'. 'Moan' also features once in Rosa's discourse as a one-word rhetorical question ('Moan?'). The pronoun 'YOU', in block capitals, recurs, with accusatory emphasis, in four successive sentences, while 'Do you remember' and 'Look here!' are both repeated twice, and 'His life!' twice occurs at the end of sentences.

Rosa also employs some striking imagery: that, in relation to Steerforth, she descended into a 'doll' – an image that evokes the Victorian nursery and has connotations, ironic in the context, of childhood innocence; in one sense, of course, we can infer that Rosa may be innocent in that she could still be a virgin; it is unclear whether her earlier relationship with Steerforth was physically consummated and, if so, who seduced whom. But whatever the nature of that relationship, her strong but thwarted adult passions make her a person embittered by experience. There is an intertextual link between the 'doll' metaphor and the image Bella Rokesmith, *née* Wilfer, uses in discussion with her new husband in Book the Fourth, chapter five, of Dickens's last completed novel *Our Mutual Friend* (1865): 'I want to be something so much worthier than the doll in the doll's house' (Penguin Classics edn (1985) 746). The 'doll' image also links intertextually with the central image of the play *A Doll's House* [*Et Dukkeheim*] (1879) by the Norwegian dramatist Henrik Ibsen. Although Rosa never becomes a wife and mother like Bella and Ibsen's Nora Helmer, the 'doll' image is bound up with a moment at which Rosa rejects her subordinate status; though, as it turns out, she never escapes from Mrs Steerforth but remains bound to her as soother and accuser into old age, when Mrs Steerforth, sunk in senility, keeps reliving the shock of Steerforth's death and Rosa, 'a sharp, dark, withered woman, with a white scar on her lip', acting as her 'impatient attendant', by turns caresses her, and quarrels with her; now fiercely telling her, 'I loved him better than you ever did!', replaying the moment of truth scene, and 'now soothing her to sleep, like a sick child' (947, 948).

In a second image, Rosa uses the metaphor of 'a mere disfigured piece of furniture' to describe her status in relation to Steerforth and his mother after Steerforth's 'fancy' for Rosa died out. We can make an intratextual link between this metaphor and the simile David employed in the account of his first meeting with Rosa, in the passage that we discussed in the previous chapter, when he called her 'a little dilapidated – like a house – with having been so long to let'. Rosa's own account of herself is more derogatory than David's, making herself 'disfigured' rather than simply 'dilapidated' and shrinking herself from a house to a generic 'piece of furniture'. She does not even endow herself with the degree of particularity of a specific type of furniture, a wardrobe, say, or an armchair. As well as these specific images, there is a further image that emerges from the references, in this and other passages, to Rosa's scar – and it has become a scar now, rather than a seam, as if its scar-status were renewed and confirmed by Rosa's open acknowledgement of her painful feelings. The physical scar becomes a sign of emotional trauma, of the way in which wounded affections and blocked energies can persist and, as in this case, explode.

Rosa's rhetoric combines indictment and narrative. With the forensic skills she had displayed in David's first meeting with her, she speaks partly as if she were a prosecuting counsel attacking the accused in a court of law, but the assault is now open rather than oblique and clearly displays her own deep emotional investment. She makes two main claims: that Mrs Steerforth was, in effect, responsible for her son's death because she had encouraged his bad and suppressed his good qualities; and that she herself, Rosa, loved Steerforth more than his mother did. Rosa's eloquence contrasts with the inarticulacy of the object of Rosa's attack, Mrs Steerforth, and with the comparative silence of David, who attempts only two feeble interjections. Clearly it would detract from the dramatic focus of this scene if David intervened too much or too strongly; but his relative muteness indicates the force of Rosa's personality at this point – she has reduced others to silence – and also suggests David's partial identification with Rosa in her fondness for Steerforth and her indictment of Mrs Steerforth for over-indulging him and thus contributing to his destruction.

David's eloquence in this extract emerges not in direct speech but in his narrative prose, which intensifies the sense of Rosa's obsessive, manic power. She shows 'no sympathy or gentleness'; her laugh is 'frightful'; her eyes are 'flashing', 'bright' and 'angry'; she is close to being in a 'frenzy'; her hand is 'relentless'. Imagery helps to reinforce the portrayal of Rosa at this point: a simile likens the gleam of her eyes to fire and this links up with the fire imagery in the description of how 'the smouldering embers of a gentle feeling kindled' momentarily in her remembrance of how Steerforth would take her to his heart. The strand of fire imagery associates itself with the metaphor of 'lightning' that is applied to Rosa's eyes in this extract.

We can also make an intratextual link between the fire imagery here and the extract we discussed in the previous chapter, where David, meeting Rosa for the first time, observes that her thinness 'seemed to be the effect of some wasting fire within her'. The sense of being consumed by strong feelings in the earlier extract also links intratextually with the comparison, in this extract, between her feelings for Steerforth and a mortal disease, when she clenches her hand and trembles 'as if her passion were killing her by inches'. In the earlier extract, however, the inner energies showed themselves in her thinness rather than in any bodily gesture; here they show themselves through gestures and poses which are both theatrical and informed by intense feeling – smiting herself on the breast, striking her scar, clenching her hand, trembling, stamping.

In David's narrative prose, Rosa's intensity contrasts with the speechlessness and immobility of Mrs Steerforth, but the techniques David uses to describe her state are similar to the techniques he uses in describing Rosa and to those Rosa herself uses in her denunciation of Mrs Steerforth – for example, the anaphora, the reiterated 'Always', that begins four successive sentences. The term 'moan' that, as we saw, recurs eight times in Rosa's indictment, twice occurs in the narrative prose as a noun ('a/the moan'), and once as a gerund, a verb form functioning as a noun ('the moaning'). This reinforces the sense of Mrs Steerforth's distress which can only be expressed in primal sounds rather than words. Adjectives such as 'inarticulate', 'stifled', 'incapable', 'rigid', 'closed', 'locked', 'frozen up' and 'set' powerfully convey Mrs Steerforth's verbal and bodily paralysis in the face of Rosa's onslaught.

The next passage we explore, from *Expectations*, also shows a thwarted woman dramatically changed, but this time from vengefulness to penitence, when Pip visits Satis House after Estella's marriage.

The Old Bride's Tears: *Great Expectations*, pp. 410–12

[Miss Havisham] turned her face to me for the first time since she had averted it, and, to my amazement, I may even add to my terror, dropped on her knees at my feet; with her folded hands raised to me in the manner in which, when her poor heart was young and fresh and whole, they must often have been raised to heaven from her mother's side.

To see her with her white hair and her worn face kneeling at my feet, gave me a shock all through all my frame. I entreated her to rise, and got my arms about her to help her up; but she only pressed that hand of mine which was nearest to her grasp, and hung her head over it and wept. I had never seen her shed a tear before, and, in the hope that the relief might do her good, I bent over her without speaking. She was not kneeling now, but was down upon the ground.

'O!' she cried, despairingly. 'What have I done! What have I done!'

'If you mean, Miss Havisham, what have you done to injure me, let me answer. Very little. I should have loved her under any circumstances. – Is she married?'

'Yes.'

It was a needless question, for a new desolation in the desolate house had told me so.

'What have I done! What have I done!' She wrung her hands, and crushed her white hair, and returned to this cry over and over again. 'What have I done!'

I knew not how to answer, or how to comfort her. That she had done a grievous thing in taking an impressionable child to mould into the form that her wild resentment, spurned affection, and wounded pride, found vengeance in, I knew full well. But that, in shutting out the light of day, she had shut out infinitely more; that, in seclusion, she had secluded herself from a thousand natural and healing influences; that, her mind, brooding solitary, had grown diseased, as all minds do and must and will that reverse the appointed order of their Maker; I knew equally well. And could I look upon her without compassion, seeing her punishment in the ruin she was, in her profound unfitness for this earth on which she was placed, in the vanity of sorrow which had become a master mania, like the vanity of penitence, the vanity of remorse, the vanity of unworthiness, and other monstrous vanities that have been curses in this world?

'Until you spoke to her the other day, and until I saw in you a looking-glass that showed me what I once felt myself, I did not know what I had done. What have I done! What have I done!' And so again, twenty, fifty times over, What had she done!

'Miss Havisham,' I said, when her cry had died away, 'you may dismiss me from your mind and conscience. But Estella is a different case, and if you can ever undo any scrap of what you have done in keeping a part of her right nature away from her, it will be better to do that, than to bemoan the past through a hundred years.'

'Yes, yes, I know it. But, Pip – my Dear!' There was an earnest womanly compassion for me in her new affection. 'My Dear! Believe this: when she first came to me, I meant to save her from misery like my own. At first I meant no more.'

'Well, well!' said I. 'I hope so.'

'But as she grew, and promised to be very beautiful, I gradually did worse, and with my praises, and with my jewels, and with my teachings, and with this figure of myself always before her a warning to back and point my lessons, I stole her heart away and put ice in its place.'

'Better,' I could not help saying, 'to have left her a natural heart, even to be bruised or broken.'

> With that, Miss Havisham looked distractedly at me for a while, and then burst out again. What had she done!

Like the previous extract, this one is highly melodramatic but, once the melodrama is allowed for, very effective. Pip's discovery that his benefactor was Magwitch rather than Miss Havisham, discussed earlier in this chapter, was the most profound reversal of his expectations in the course of the novel, and it made a great change in his idea of Miss Havisham and his relationship with her. But Miss Havisham's behaviour here is a further reversal of expectations which, while not as upsetting as the revelation of his benefactor's true identity, makes a deep impact on him, as the narrative stresses in the use of the terms 'amazement', 'terror' and 'shock through all my frame'.

The scene reverses the power relations between Pip and Miss Havisham that were established even before Pip's visit to Satis House, and confirmed on his first meeting with its chief resident. Miss Havisham subordinates herself to Pip, kneeling at his feet and then prostrating herself on the ground. Although her behaviour, especially given Pip's previous experience of her, is bizarre, her overall physical appearance is described simply, in monosyllables – 'her white hair and her worn face' – that convey her age and the extent to which she has been damaged by life. Pip offers a diagnosis of Miss Havisham that has four key elements: she has emotionally abused 'an impressionable child', Estella; she has become the victim of 'a master mania'; she has gone against 'nature', seen as the source of healing influences, by secluding herself and by keeping part of Estella's 'right nature' away from her; and she has gone against God. Religious references are important in the passage: her folded hands suggest to Pip how she must have looked praying as a child; her self-seclusion and emotional abuse of Estella have 'reverse[d] the appointed order of their Maker'. Pip also turns her into an example of a more general tendency that exhibits itself in several kinds of vanity: of sorrow, of penitence, of remorse, of unworthiness. There is an intertextual reference to the Old Testament Book of Ecclesiastes, with its lament that 'All is vanity'. But Pip does not say that all is vanity, but rather that certain kinds of self-seclusion and self-denigration are.

Despite his diagnosis, Pip feels compassion for Miss Havisham, and, reciprocally, Miss Havisham starts to feel compassion for him, but hers is of a gendered kind: 'an earnest *womanly* compassion'. While her actions are unprecedented and unexpected, they do show an underlying continuity with her previous comportment in that they are self-dramatizing. Just as she dramatized herself as broken-hearted in her first meeting with Pip, so she now dramatizes herself as consumed by remorse. Looked at one way, she has undergone a kind of catharsis, a sort of psychological equivalent of Magwitch escaping from the Hulks, breaking out of the mental prison in which she has been immured for so long even if it is only into a desolate region of remorse and despair. But her repeated declaration of regret – 'What have I done!' – threatens to lock her into another frozen state of repetition. Along with this reiterated declaration, however, goes a narrative account, a story, of what she has done in which she starts to acknowledge her actions – 'as [Estella] grew, and promised to be very beautiful'. There is an implication here that regret is better dealt with by narrative, by telling a story, rather than formulaic lamentation – an implication that Pip, it could be argued, puts into practice through the writing of his story and the living of his life.

Conclusions

All these extracts dramatize moments of truth and each mixes melodrama with psychological and sociological realism in varying degrees. They demonstrate the capacity of melodrama to convey intense psychological states whose force and nature may evade representation in a realistic mode that eschews melodrama. Melodrama offers a heightened, stylized, focused means of staging moments of revelation and of discovering the truth about others and about oneself – though the latter truths may be evaded or unacknowledged.

The extracts all have strong theatrical elements, giving the sense we could adapt them to the stage by retaining the original dialogue and changing narrative prose into stage directions (although a full-scale adaptation would need to make further changes). The extracts also evince a proto-cinematic imagination and seem easily rewritable in filmic terms such as lighting effects, reaction shots, and, in the case of Pip's recognition scene with Magwitch, flashbacks. Dialogue is important in all of them and almost becomes monologue in the scene of Rosa's denunciation of Mrs Steerforth. As always with dialogue, silence, or sparse speech can also be significant: that of Mrs Steerforth, reduced to inarticulacy in the scene with Rosa; or that of David, silent in the scene with Uriah and sparing of speech in the scene with Rosa.

Both Micawber's indictment of Heep and Rosa's of Mrs Steerforth call to mind a somewhat irregular courtroom in which a prosecuting counsel with an intense emotional investment in the indictment holds the floor. In both cases, the prosecution case also reflects, to some extent, on the prosecutor. If Mrs Steerforth had been so neglectful of her son's moral welfare and Rosa had perceived it so clearly, why did she not try, in some way, to intervene more forcefully before? If Heep's manipulations are odious, are not Micawber's, though not as bad, also dislikeable and potentially harmful in some respects? In the scene between Pip and Miss Havisham, the courtroom changes to a private chamber that remains the theatre it has always been for Miss Havisham since her jilting, but that has now also become, with her penitence, a kind of personal temple, a quasi-religious space of prostration in which Miss Havisham accuses herself, with Pip as the firm but kindly priest. But Pip knows that he also has much to reproach himself for.

Narrative prose complements dialogue and adds elements dialogue cannot provide, for example in David's descriptions of the responses of Heep and Mrs Steerforth and in Pip's account of his moment of recognition, with its replay of the opening scene of the novel, and his moral verdict on Miss Havisham. They show how narrative prose may deepen the portrayal of moments of truth by registering the observations of the narrator, by capturing the reactions, in terms of facial expressions and body language, of other characters, and by offering diagnostic judgements. But just as the indictments delivered by Micawber and Rosa reflect on those who make them, so the judgements made by David on Heep and Pip on Miss Havisham reflect on the indicters as well as on those they indict.

Diction makes an important contribution to each passage. David heaps abuse on Heep in a way that both intensifies the villain's perfidy and also, by its very insistence, reflects on David himself, raising the question of whether, and if so to what extent, Heep is his dark double. A variety of vocabulary brings home Pip's initial incomprehension of the identity of his nocturnal visitor. Vivid nouns and adjectives sharpen the sense of Rosa's near-frenzy. Words and phrases such as 'amazement', 'terror' and 'shock' drive home the impact of Miss Havisham's changed behaviour on Pip, while simple monosyllables convey her age and frailty.

Grammatical parallelism is used to good effect in the long conditional sentence, in the recognition scene from *Expectations*, which evokes a series of hypothetical events with such force that they can seem, momentarily, to have actually happened. Parallelism and anaphora reinforce Rosa's outburst against Mrs Steerforth. Anaphora also emphasises the extremity of Mrs Steerforth's distress when David describes her moans in response to Rosa's onslaught.

Imagery figures vividly in Rosa's description of herself as a 'doll' and 'a mere disfigured piece of furniture'. Her disfigurement, now firmly a scar rather than a seam, serves both as a physical reminder of bodily injury and a metaphor of the emotional wounds she has suffered. David uses images of fire and embers to suggest both Rosa's incandescent rage and her repressed tenderness, while her passionate feelings are compared to a mortal disease. The chiaroscuro, the play of light and shadow, is important in the recognition scene from *Expectations*; it adds to the dramatic effect and also serves to symbolize the fluctuations of Pip's own understanding, as he moves, partially and fitfully, towards the moment of full comprehension of his mysterious visitor's identity.

There are major intratextual links between these extracts and earlier parts of *Copperfield* and *Expectations*, as we would expect in scenes that depict moments of truth in the later stages of a novel, where their impact, what they reveal, confirm or reconfigure, depends significantly on what has gone before. There is David's memory, as he registers the hatred in Heep's look, of the time he struck Heep and saw the stripes on Heep's cheek. There are the links between the recognition scene in *Expectations* and the first chapter of the novel, conveyed through metonymy and mime: the file; the old rag round Magwitch's head; the self-hugging and shivering. There is the link between the scene evoking Rosa's denunciation of Mrs Steerforth, in which Rosa likens herself to a piece of furniture, and the extract we discussed in chapter 3, in which David compares her to a house that has been too long to let. There is also an association between David's remark in the earlier extract that Rosa's thinness 'seemed to be the effect of some wasting fire within her' and his comparison of her, in the extract considered in this chapter, to the effect of a mortal disease. As well as these intratextual links, there is an intertextual reference to the Old Testament Book of Ecclesiastes, with its lament that 'all is vanity' (1:2).

These moments of truth, experienced by the narrator or by others with whom he is closely involved, reconfigure lives and perceptions. For the narrator, they are key stages in his education by life, and he will emerge a sadder but perhaps wiser man. His education is not over yet, however; he must encounter one of the greatest truths of all, that of death, and try to come to terms with it. This is the subject of the next chapter.

Methods of Analysis

- We highlighted the theatrical elements of the extracts (e.g. the poses struck by Rosa and Miss Havisham).
- We underlined their proto-cinematic elements (e.g. the movement between Rosa's denunciation and Mrs Steerforth's reaction; the play of light and shadow when Magwitch visits Pip).
- We considered their melodramatic aspects (e.g. the villain's unmasking in the confrontation between Micawber and Heep; the sinner's penitence in the scene between Pip and Miss Havisham).
- We discussed their diction (e.g. the accumulation of abusive terms in David's description of Heep; the words and phrases emphasizing Pip's bafflement about the identity and intentions of his nocturnal visitor).
- We assessed the significance of dialogue, of who does and does not speak (e.g. Rosa's indictment, which becomes almost a monologue; David's relative silence during this indictment and his complete silence during the denunciation of Heep).
- We highlighted examples of grammatical parallelism (e.g. in the sentence in the second extract that evokes a series of hypothetical events with such force that they seem, momentarily, actual; in Rosa's outburst against Mrs Steerforth in the third extract).

- We identified uses of anaphora (e.g. in Rosa's denunciation of Mrs Steerforth; in David's description of Mrs Steerforth's moans in response to Rosa's onslaught).

- We explored the imagery and symbolism of the passage (e.g. Rosa's self-description as a doll and disfigured item of furniture; the play of light and shadow, symbolizing Pip's fitful and fluctuating perception of his mysterious visitor).

- We traced intratextual links between these extracts and earlier parts of *Copperfield* and *Expectations* (e.g. David's memory of the time he struck Heep; the links between Magwitch's file, rag and self-hugging in the recognition scene and in the first chapter of *Expectations*).

- We noted the intertextual reference, in the final extract, to the Old Testament Book of Ecclesiastes, with its lament that 'All is vanity'.

- We suggested how these moments of truth may relate to wider psychological and social phenomena (e.g. the projection of one's own disavowed feelings on to others, in the case of David and Heep; the position of women in Victorian society in the case of Rosa and Miss Havisham).

Suggested Work

Analyse the two following passages. The first shows David discovering the truth about the strange man who has been stalking Aunt Betsey. The second portrays Jaggers letting Pip know – by means of a hypothetical case rather than a direct acknowledgement – the truth about Estella's parentage and his reasons for concealing it. Discuss how the features of the passages work to convey these moments of truth and consider what they reveal about the characters who disclose the truth and how they contribute to the development and significance of the narrative.

[a] *Copperfield*. From 'It was midnight when I arrived home' to '"We'll keep it to ourselves, Trot"' (*DC* 755–7)

[b] *Expectations*. From 'Mr Jaggers nodded his head retrospectively' to '"what item was it you were at, when Mr Pip came in?"' (*GE* 424–6)

5

Dying in Style

In *Copperfield*, Dora dies at home and Ham and Steerforth in a shipwreck. In *Expectations*, Magwitch receives the death sentence, along with others, in a courtroom and then dies in prison. But wherever and however key characters meet their end in Dickens, they do so in style – that is, Dickens provides a memorable verbal orchestration of their passing. Such orchestration has sometimes provoked mockery and rejection, as in Oscar Wilde's famous comment on *The Old Curiosity Shop* (1840–41), that 'one must have a heart of stone to read the death of Little Nell without laughing'. But analysis of Dickens's scenes of dying reveals a more various, complex and robust treatment of the approach and arrival of death than Wilde's quip allows, in which sentimentality and religiosity are mixed with real pathos and an unsparing sense of loss. We shall look first at David's conversation with Dora as she nears death.

Dora's Departure: *David Copperfield*, pp. 836–8

It is night; and I am with her still. Agnes has arrived; has been among us for a whole day and an evening. She, my aunt, and I, have sat with Dora since the morning, all together. We have not talked much, but Dora has been perfectly contented and cheerful. We are now alone.

Do I know, now, that my child-wife will soon leave me? They have told me so; they have told me nothing new to my thoughts; but I am far from sure that I have taken that truth to heart. I cannot master it. I have withdrawn by myself, many times today, to weep. I have remembered Who wept for a parting between the living and the dead. I have bethought me of all that gracious and compassionate history. I have tried to resign myself, and to console myself; and that, I hope, I may have done imperfectly; but what I cannot firmly settle in my mind is, that the end will absolutely come. I hold her hand in mine, I hold her heart in mine, I see her love for me, alive in all its strength. I cannot shut out a pale lingering shadow of belief that she will be spared.

'I am going to speak to you, Doady. I am going to say something I have often thought of saying lately. You won't mind?' with a gentle look.

'Mind, my darling?'

'Because I don't know what you will think, or what you may have thought sometimes. Perhaps you have often thought the same. Doady, dear, I am afraid I was too young.'

I lay my face upon the pillow by her, and she looks into my eyes, and speaks very softly. Gradually, as she goes on, I feel, with a stricken heart, that she is speaking of herself as past.

'I am afraid, dear, I was too young. I don't mean in years only, but in experience, and thoughts, and everything. I was such a silly little creature! I am afraid it would have been better, if we had only loved each other as a boy and girl, and forgotten it. I have begun to think I was not fit to be a wife.'

I try to stay my tears, and to reply, 'Oh, Dora, love, as fit as I to be a husband!'

'I don't know,' with the old shake of her curls. 'Perhaps! But if I had been more fit to be married I might have made you more so, too. Besides, you are very clever, and I never was.'

'We have been very happy, my sweet Dora.'

'I was very happy, very. But, as years went on, my dear boy would have wearied of his child-wife. She would have been less and less a companion for him. He would have been more and more sensible of what was wanting in his home. She wouldn't have improved. It is better as it is.'

'Oh, Dora, dearest, dearest, do not speak to me so. Every word seems a reproach!'

'No, not a syllable!' she answers, kissing me. 'Oh, my dear, you never deserved it, and I loved you far too well to say a reproachful word to you, in earnest – it was all the merit I had, except being pretty – or you thought me so. Is it lonely, downstairs, Doady?'

'Very! Very!'

'Don't cry! Is my chair there?'

 'In its old place.'

'Oh, how my poor boy cries! Hush, hush! Now, make me one promise. I want to speak to Agnes. When you go downstairs, tell Agnes so, and send her up to me; and while I speak to her, let no one come – not even aunt. I want to speak to Agnes by herself. I want to speak to Agnes, quite alone.'

I promise that she shall, immediately; but I cannot leave her, for my grief.

'I said that it was better as it is!' she whispers, as she holds me in her arms. 'Oh, Doady, after more years, you never could have loved your child-wife better than you do; and, after more years, she would so have tried and disappointed you, that you might not have been able to love her half so well! I know I was too young and foolish. It is much better as it is!'

The narrative prose here is notable, especially in Dickens, for its directness. 'We are now alone' and 'I cannot master it' are simple four-word sentences. 'It is night; and I am with her still' is a double sentence but consists only of common monosyllables. The sentence starting 'I hold her hand in mine' is a multiple sentence but its first three clauses again consist of common monosyllables and are grammatically parallel; the first and second clauses are almost identical, with only the object changed – in a kind of progression from the physical to the emotional, 'heart' replaces 'hand'. The spare prose sensitively conveys the combination, in David's thoughts, of a knowledge that Dora will soon die and a tenuous belief that she will live; he is partly, to use a modern idiom, in denial.

In accordance with the comparatively simple diction and sentence structure of the narrative prose, the imagery is also sparing. Thinking of Dora's impending death, David uses a common metaphor that serves as a euphemism, a substitution of a milder word for a harsher one: 'leave' for 'die'. The common metaphor of 'heart' occurs three times: once as an image of accepting a truth emotionally and not just intellectually – taking it 'to heart'; once as a metaphor for love – 'I hold her heart in mine'; and once, as a metaphor for the pain of anticipated bereavement when David feels, 'with a stricken heart', that Dora is applying the past tense to herself. The belief that Dora may still survive is imaged as 'a pale lingering shadow', almost, we might say, the ghost of a belief, and in this respect it stands, not only for the tenuous state of David's belief, but for Dora's present existential state; she too could be seen as 'a pale lingering shadow', almost a ghost.

The use of tenses is important in this extract. It is predominantly in the present tense, which gives a sense of immediacy. The past tense is used to refer both to the immediate past, in the narrative prose (Agnes's arrival, sitting with Dora, David's withdrawals to weep) and, in Dora's dialogue, to the more distant past, to her relationship with and marriage to David. David is acutely and painfully aware that Dora is using the past tense about herself and here a grammatical fact takes on an existential weight: Dora will indeed soon be in the past, the inevitable fate of the dead. The future tense takes on a poignant and ominous significance: Dora 'will soon' leave David but a faint belief that 'she will be spared' lingers. The perfect conditional tense, consisting of 'would' and a verb in the perfect tense, features significantly in Dora's dialogue. This tense often serves as a tense of regret or consolation, since it is used to express a hypothesis about what could have been the case in the past or future, if certain conditions had been fulfilled; thus Dora employs it regretfully when she says 'it *would have been* better, if we had only loved each other as a boy and girl'; but she tries to use it consolingly when she says 'my dear boy *would have wearied* of his child-wife' and 'She *wouldn't have improved*' ' 'she *would so have tried and disappointed* [David]' if she had survived and stayed married to him. This attempt at consolation, however, drives home the inevitability of her death.

There is a significant intertextual allusion to the New Testament when David states that he has 'remembered Who wept for a parting between the living and the dead'. The figure who wept here is Jesus – his spiritual eminence signified by the capital 'W' of the pronoun – and the reference is to the death and raising of Lazarus in the Gospel of St John (11:33–5): 'When Jesus therefore saw her [Mary, the sister of Lazarus] weeping, and the Jews also weeping which came with her, he groaned in the spirit and was troubled, / And said, Where have ye laid him? They said unto him, Lord, come and see. / Jesus wept.' But this allusion has two ironies in relation to Dora's death: one is that, in the Gospel story, Lazarus is raised up soon after his death in the body, but there is no sense that this will happen to Dora, at least before the Day of Judgement; the second is that, if Dora were raised up as Lazarus was, 'bound hand and foot with graveclothes: and his face was bound about with a napkin' (St John 11:44), it would partake more of the macabre than the miraculous, seem closer to a scene from a Gothic novel than a Gospel. The ghoulish element of the Lazarus story becomes stronger if we make an intratextual link between its invocation here and a passage near the start of *Copperfield* that recounts an incident from David's early childhood:

> One Sunday night my mother reads to Peggotty and me in there [the best parlour, kept for Sunday use], how Lazarus was raised up from the dead. And I am so frightened that they are afterwards obliged to take me out of bed, and shew me the quiet churchyard, with all the dead lying in their graves at rest, below the solemn moon. (*DC* 62)

This vividly shows how the idea of being raised from the dead, even when expressed in a Gospel story, may be frightening rather than comforting; and as seeing the dead at rest, rather than resurrected like Lazarus, calmed the young David, so the prospect of Dora reposing in death, rather than risen from the grave, might soothe the adult David; at the same time that prospect would drive home the finality of her earthly extinction. When David goes on to say 'I have bethought me of all that gracious and compassionate history', he is probably referring, not only to the tale of Lazarus but more broadly to the narrative of the Gospels as a whole, and he grants it a true rather than fictional status by calling it a history, a spiritual status by applying the adjective 'gracious', which in a Christian context means 'showing divine grace', and a status that is, all at once, spiritual, ethical and emotional by using the adjective 'compassionate', a key religious, moral and affective virtue for Dickens. But he acknowledges that this 'history' has been insufficient, due to his own imperfection, to provide him with the consolation, and the acceptance of Dora's death, that he seeks.

A dialogue between Dora and David ensues in which Dora does most of the talking, in a more thoughtful way than has previously been the case, but still in a manner that is continuous with her previous speech style and that invokes the childhood references which have been so much a part of their conversation and relationship. It is a painful irony that Dora starts to mature as she is dying. She articulates what David has been partly aware of for some time but has not allowed to emerge fully into his consciousness: that, 'as years went by, my dear boy would have wearied of his child-wife'. Dying in Dickens is also a time for explicit or implicit judgement on lives and relationships. In the case of Dora and David, the situation makes both partners reflect on their marriage and portrays a growth of moral awareness in Dora and a moment of heightened self-awareness in David himself.

A key aspect of the passage is the way in which it prefigures and prepares for Dora's eventual replacement by Agnes. Agnes has 'arrived' and Dora 'will soon leave'; in linking these two events, we can see that 'leave' functions not only as a euphemism but also creates a contrast between two actions: an arrival that has already occurred, indicated by the past tense, and a departure that is likely to occur soon, indicated by the future tense. In the dialogue, as the scene nears its end, Dora repeats, three times, 'I want to speak to Agnes', and the narrative signals clearly that a transfer of David's affection from Dora to Agnes, approved by Dora herself, is in the offing.

The scene also makes possible a moment of metafictional awareness on the reader's part: in a sense, Dora has been sacrificed to the narrative demand for an ultimately happy ending which – as she recognizes, as David as writer and husband must also recognize – would have been impossible had she lived, would have turned *Copperfield* into another kind of story, one of disappointed hopes, of unfulfilled expectations. We find this other kind of story in *Expectations*, but there too there is a death that ultimately seems to presage a happy ending – which does not quite arrive as expected. The death is that of Magwitch, and it is in two phases. The first phase is staged, not in the privacy of the bedchamber, but in a public arena that has some likeness to a theatre: the courtroom.

Death Sentences: *Great Expectations*, pp. 466–8

The trial was very short and very clear. Such things as could be said for him, were said – how he had taken to industrous habits, and had thriven lawfully and reputably. But, nothing could unsay the fact that he had returned, and was there in presence of the Judge and Jury. It was impossible to try him for that, and do otherwise than find him guilty.

At that time, it was the custom (as I learnt from my terrible experience of that Sessions) to devote a concluding day to the passing of Sentences, and to make a finishing effect with the Sentence of Death. But for the indelible picture that my remembrance now holds before me, I could scarcely believe, even as I write these words, that I saw two-and-thirty men and women put before the Judge to receive that sentence together. Foremost among the two-and-thirty, was he; seated, that he might get breath enough to keep life in him.

The whole scene starts out again in the vivid colours of the moment, down to the drops of April rain on the windows of the court, glittering in the rays of April sun. Penned in the dock, as I again stood outside it at the corner with his hand in mind, were the two-and-thirty men and women; some defiant, some stricken with terror, some sobbing and weeping, some covering their faces, some staring gloomily about. There had been shrieks from among the women convicts, but they had been stilled, and a hush had succeeded. The sheriffs with their great chains and nosegays, other civic gewgaws and monsters, criers, ushers, a great gallery full of people – a large theatrical audience – looked on, as the two-and-thirty and the Judge were solemnly confronted. Then, the Judge addressed them. Among the wretched creatures before him whom he must single out for special address, was one who almost from his infancy had been an offender against the laws; who, after repeated imprisonments and punishments, had been at length sentenced to exile for a term of years; and who, under circumstances of great violence and daring had made his escape and been re-sentenced to exile for life. That miserable man would seem for a time to have become convinced of his errors, when far removed from the scenes of his old offences, and to have lived a peaceable and honest life. But in a fatal moment, yielding to those propensities and passions, the indulgence of which had so long rendered him a scourge to society, he had quitted his haven of rest and repentance, and had come back to the country where he was proscribed. Being here presently denounced, he had for a time succeeded in evading the officers of Justice, but being at length seized

while in the act of flight, he had resisted them, and had – he best knew
whether by express design, or in the blindness of his hardihood – caused
the death of his denouncer, to whom his whole career was known. The
appointed punishment for his return to the land that had cast him out,
being Death, and his case being this aggravated case, he must prepare
himself to Die.

The sun was striking in at the great windows of the court, through
the glittering drops of rain upon the glass, and it made a broad shaft
of light between the two-and-thirty and the Judge, linking both
together, and perhaps reminding some among the audience, how both
were passing on, with absolute equality, to the greater Judgement that
knoweth all things and cannot err. Rising for a moment, a distinct speck
of face in this way of light, the prisoner said, 'My Lord, I have received
my sentence of Death from the Almighty, but I bow to yours," and
sat down again. There was some hushing, and the Judge went on with
what he had to say to the rest. Then, they were all formally doomed,
and some of them were supported out, and some of them sauntered out
with a haggard look of bravery, and a few nodded to the gallery, and
two or three shook hands, and others went out chewing the fragments
of herb they had taken from the sweet herbs lying about. He went last of
all, because of having to be helped from his chair and to go very slowly;
and he held my hand while all the others were removed, and while the
audience got up (putting their dresses right, as they might at church or
elsewhere) and pointed down at this criminal or at that, and most of all
at him and me.

No proper names are used in this extract. Magwitch is mainly
referred to as 'he' and otherwise as 'That miserable man' and 'the
prisoner'. The 'Judge' is referred to only by his office. This anonymity
contributes to the sense of an inexorable process in which individuals are
fungible – that is, they could be replaced by others who could perform
the same functions, as prisoner, Judge, juror, court officer or audience
member. There is only one instance of direct speech, from Magwitch,
but otherwise the extract employs indirect speech to recount what was
said at Magwitch's trial and, at greater length, what the Judge said to
the convicted on sentencing day. This strengthens the impression of an
impersonal process unfolding, in which human agency is diminished.

The extract starts with a short, summarizing paragraph on Magwitch's
trial. This paragraph begins with a short sentence – 'The trial was very

short and very clear' – which sets the pattern for the concision and clarity of the whole paragraph. The report of what has been said of Magwitch in mitigation is given in the passive voice, without being attributed to any specific person, as if it were an inevitable part of a legal proceeding rather than the result of any individual initiative: 'Such things as could be said for him, were said.' It is then stated, in an echo and reversal of the verb 'said', that 'nothing could unsay' the fact that he had returned and that, according to the letter of the law, he must be found guilty. Again there is the sense that this is an inevitable legal procedure and that whoever took part in it, the same decision would necessarily be reached.

The next paragraph starts with a clear reminder that the narrator is looking back – 'At that time, it was the custom' – and this initial phrasing has a detached tone, as if he were an historian, recalling the customary behaviour of a past era; but the tone is disrupted by a personalized parenthesis indicating that he is drawing on 'terrible' experience. He continues to emphasize that he is looking back, at 'the indelible picture that my remembrance now holds'; the adjective 'indelible' stresses the unforgettability of the memory, the fact that it cannot be erased; 'picture' shows its pictorial quality (and, anticipatorily, points to its quality as cinema, as a moving picture in both senses, in motion and arousing emotion); and 'remembrance', a favourite Dickens word, underlines that Pip is engaged in recollecting as he writes. Pip also stresses the barely credible quality of what he witnessed, engaging in that familiar rhetorical technique that aims to sharpen a reader or hearer's conviction by saying, in effect: Unbelievable though this may seem, it's true. The number of people involved is also stressed: two-and-thirty men and women: this is a collective experience. If it is the case, in the famous phrase from Blaise Pascal's *Les Pensées* (written 1657–58), that 'On mourra seul' – one dies alone – it is also the case that all men and women are mortal: thus dying is both the ultimately isolating and ultimately universal experience and the collective courtroom condemnation could be seen to symbolize the human condition. At the end of the sentence, however, one figure is placed in the foreground.

The first sentence of the next paragraph moves into the present tense – 'starts out again' – giving the sense of a scene coming to life vividly in the memory, beginning to move; but the wording also indicates that this is a repeated experience, as a traumatic memory might be: it is 'starting out *again*'. Pip conveys the sense of a personal relationship to Magwitch, in which he is not quite one of the convicted though close to being so – 'I stood outside [the dock] at the corner with his hand in mine' – and this joining of hands can be linked, intratextually, with the earlier and later scenes in which Pip and Magwitch make or fail to make physical contact: Magwitch's violent handling of Pip in the churchyard at the start of the novel; Pip's bewilderment at the outheld hands of the strange nocturnal visitor; Pip's intention of laying hands on the visitor, which the latter warns him against. But the personal relationship with Magwitch is located here within a collective event in which grammatically parallel phrases, starting with 'some', portray the varied responses of the prisoners: defiant, terror-stricken, sobbing, weeping, covering their faces, gloomily staring. The paragraph moves into a focus on Magwitch – still unnamed – as the Judge comments on him, draws out again to describe a collective scene rich in religious significance, homes in on Magwitch once more when he speaks, returns to the response of the convicted to the death sentences and finally comes back to Magwitch at the end.

The passage recognizes the rigorous and inexorable nature of justice and does not suggest that it can be interfered with; but there are also ironies at the expense of justice. When Pip remarks that Magwitch is allowed to sit down in the dock 'that he might get breath enough to keep life in him', there is an irony in the fact that he is being kept alive in order that he may be judicially killed. There is also an ironic disjunction between the judge's interpretation of Magwitch's reasons for returning from Australia – that he had yielded again to those inclinations and strong emotions in which he had indulged when he was a criminal outcast – and what Pip, and the reader, know his true motives to be.

The adjective 'theatrical' is applied to the audience in the large public gallery and a sense of theatre runs through the whole scene. It is a kind of public performance of the administration of justice, in which judge, jury and convicted play their appointed roles and the audience, itself part of the total spectacle, watches. As in a theatre, lighting effects play a crucial part but here the source of light – the sun – is a product of nature (and perhaps implicitly, in Dickens's perspective, of God) rather than artifice. The sun helps to give the scene a religious dimension when it shines through the windows of the court and its broad shaft of light links the thirty-two convicts and the judge together (making a total of 33, the same as the number of years in the life of Christ). Pip observes that this visual spectacle could serve as a reminder and symbol that, in a Christian perspective, all people, whatever their worldly positions, will be 'absolutely equal' before an omniscient, infallible divine judgement. Dickens gives the law its due but sets it in a larger context. Nonetheless, he casts a faintly ironic note on the social niceties of formal religious observance when he remarks, in parenthesis, on the audience 'putting their dresses right, as they might at church or elsewhere'. Sensory, judicial and religious discourses come together to deepen the import of the scene in which 32 people, Magwitch among them, face imminent death.

The next extract we shall consider shows death, not in bedchamber or courtroom, but in the open air and on the margin of land and sea, as Ham sacrifices himself vainly to rescue Steerforth from the shipwreck.

Dead Men's Shore: *David Copperfield*, pp. 864–6

I ran to him [Ham] – as well as I know, to repeat my appeal for help. But, distracted though I was, by a sight so new to me and terrible, the determination in his face, and his look out to sea – exactly the same look as I remembered in connexion with the morning after Em'ly's flight – awoke me to a knowledge of his danger. I held him back with both arms; and implored the men with whom I had been speaking, not to listen to him, not to do murder, not to let him stir from off that sand!

Another cry arose on shore; and looking to the wreck, we saw the cruel sail, with blow on blow, beat off the lower of the two men, and fly up in triumph round the active figure left alone upon the mast.

Against such a sight, and against such determination as that of the calmly desperate man who was already accustomed to lead half the people present, I might as hopefully have entreated the wind. 'Mas'r Davy,' he said, cheerily grasping me by both hands, 'if my time is come, 'tis come. If 'tan't, I'll bide it. Lord above bless you, and bless all! Mates, make me ready! I'm a-going off!'

I was swept away, but not unkindly, to some distance, where the people around me made me stay; urging, as I confusedly perceived, that he was bent on going, with help or without, and that I should endanger the precautions for his safety by troubling those with whom they rested. I don't know what I answered, or what they rejoined; but, I saw hurry on the beach, and men running with ropes from a capstan that was there, and penetrating into a circle of figures that hid him from me. Then, I saw him standing alone, in a seaman's frock and trousers: a rope in his hand, or slung to his wrist: another round his body: and several of the best men holding, at a little distance, to the latter, which he laid out himself, slack upon the shore, at his feet.

The wreck, even to my unpractised eye, was breaking up. I saw that she was parting in the middle, and that the life of the solitary man upon the mast hung by a thread. Still, he clung to it. He had a singular red cap on, – not like a sailor's cap, but of a finer colour; and as the few yielding planks between him and destruction rolled and bulged, and his anticipative death-knell rung, he was seen by all of us to wave it. I saw him do it now, and thought I was going distracted, when his action brought an old remembrance to my mind of a once dear friend.

Ham watched the sea, standing alone, with the silence of suspended breath behind him, and the storm before, until there was a great retiring wave, when, with a backward glance at those who held the rope which was made fast round his body, he dashed in after it, and in a moment was buffeting with the water; rising with the hills, falling with the valleys, lost beneath the foam; then drawn again to land. They hauled in hastily.

He was hurt. I saw blood on his face, from where I stood; but he took no thought of that. He seemed hurriedly to give them some directions for leaving him more free – or so I judged from the motion of his arm – and was gone as before.

And now he made for the wreck, rising with the hills, falling with the valleys, lost beneath the rugged foam, borne in towards the shore, borne on towards the ship, striving hard and valiantly. The distance was nothing, but the power of the sea and wind made the strife deadly. At length he neared the wreck. He was so near, that with one more of his vigorous strokes he would be clinging to it, – when a high, green, vast hill-side of water, moving on shoreward, from beyond the ship, he seemed to leap up into it with a mighty bound, and the ship was gone!

Some eddying fragments I saw in the sea, as if a mere cask had been broken, in running to the spot where they were hauling in. Consternation was in every face. They drew him to my very feet – insensible – dead.

He was carried to the nearest house; and, no one preventing me now, I remained near him, busy, while every means of restoration were tried; but he had been beaten to death by the great wave, and his generous heart was stilled for ever.

As I sat beside the bed, when hope was abandoned and all was done, a fisherman, who had known me when Emily and I were children, and ever since, whispered my name at the door.

'Sir,' said he, with tears starting to his weather-beaten face, which, with his trembling lips, was ashy pale, 'will you come over yonder?'

The old remembrance that had been recalled to me, was in his look. I asked him, terror-stricken, leaning on the arm he held out to support me:

'Has a body come ashore?'

He said, 'Yes.'

'Do I know it?' I asked then.

He answered nothing.

But, he led me to the shore. And on that part of it where she and I had looked for shells, two children – on that part of it where some lighter fragments of the old boat, blown down last night, had been scattered by the wind – among the ruins of the home he had wronged – I saw him lying with his head upon his arm, as I had often seen him lie at school.

This extract employs a variety of techniques to convey the turmoil and menace of Ham's doomed attempt to rescue Steerforth from the shipwreck – though Ham is only directly named once and Steerforth not at all. There are extended sentences that give a sense of the tumultuous flow of the action, as in the 74-word sentence starting 'Ham watched the sea' that occupies nearly a whole paragraph. Longer sentences are varied with much more concise ones: 'They hauled in hastily'; 'He was hurt'; 'He answered nothing'; 'But, he led me to the shore.' A slightly longer sentence, of nine words, ends with two successive adjectives, introduced by dashes, creating a kind of staccato effect that jerks the reader from bad to the worst, the stress falling on the final monosyllable: 'They drew him to my very feet – insensible – dead.'

Present participles help to give a sense of ongoing, restless, exhausting activity, occasionally punctuated by moments of stasis: 'breaking up', 'parting', 'buffeting' and, in a lull as Ham waits for the wave to retire, 'standing'. Present participles are combined with metaphor in the twice-repeated phrase 'rising with the hills, falling with the valleys'. Personification is used for the 'cruel' sail which 'beat[s] off' a man who tries to cling to it and for the huge wave that has 'beaten [Ham] to death'. The sea metaphorically becomes a sublime Wordsworthian landscape with hills and valleys which has metamorphosed into turbulent motion and inspires awe and terror ('a high, green, vast hill-side of water'). Natural imagery is also applied to Ham: David compares the futility of his attempts to stop Ham trying to rescue Steerforth to entreating the wind to stop blowing. Metaphor is employed in the description of Steerforth clinging to the mast: we are told that 'the life of the solitary man upon the mast hung by a thread. Still, he clung to it'. The image of the 'thread' makes an intertextual link with ancient Greek and Roman mythology in which three fates (*Moirai* in Greek, *Parcae* in Latin) control life, with Clothos spinning the thread of life and Atropos cutting it at death. There is also an intratextual link in the 'thread' image with Miss Mowcher cutting Steerforth's hair, in the passage we discussed in chapter 3. The mast to which Steerforth clings symbolizes both life and the phallic prowess that enabled Steerforth to possess Em'ly; he is now about to lose his grip on both. In the sentence 'Still, he clung to it', the referent of 'it' is ambiguous; it could mean 'the mast' or 'life'; and the ambiguity is appropriate since, in clinging to the one, Steerforth is clinging to the other. Steerforth's 'singular red cap' also functions symbolically; its difference from an ordinary sailor's cap, its 'finer colour', suggests Steerforth's higher-class status; but it also calls to mind the *bonnet rouge*, the red Phrygian cap (so-called because of its ancient association with the region of Phrygia) that came to signify liberty, first in the western provinces of the Roman Empire, and, centuries later, in the French Revolution; in this respect, the red cap suggests the subversive aspect of Steerforth. It could also signify the blood that might have flowed when Steerforth took Little Em'ly's virginity. The metaphor of Steerforth's 'anticipative death-knell' is used to describe the sound of the few remaining planks rolling and bulging and makes explicit Steerforth's closeness to his end.

The extract makes seven clear intratextual links with earlier parts of *Copperfield*, which set the events it describes in a longer temporal perspective. The first link is interpolated into the second sentence, where the look on Ham's face is 'exactly the same look as I remembered in connexion with the morning after Little Em'ly's flight'. This refers back to chapter 32, when David, having seen that Ham's face, looking out to sea, was 'not angry' but sternly determined, had the 'frightful thought' that 'if ever [Ham] encountered Steerforth, he would kill him' (*DC* 517). The reference back has an ironic dimension: for Ham will now try, not to kill Steerforth, but to save Steerforth's life and will, perhaps willingly, lose his own life in the vain attempt. It is ambiguous as to whether Ham knows that it is Steerforth he is trying to rescue; if he does, his determination to make the attempt may be increased by his awareness of the murderous intentions towards Steerforth he once harboured, and perhaps still does; it is a reaction against them. Whether or not he knows who he is trying to rescue, there is probably a self-destructive element in his efforts, a desire to die because he has never recovered from the loss of Em'ly.

The second reference back occurs when the man on the mast waves his red cap and brings 'an old remembrance to [David's] mind of a once dear friend'. The third occurs in the clause describing the fisherman who asks for David after Ham's death as having 'known me when Em'ly and I were children'. The fourth, repeating a word used earlier in the passage, observes that the 'old remembrance that had been recalled to me, was in his look'. The fifth identifies the part of the shore on which Em'ly and David, as children, 'had looked for shells', the sixth refers to 'the ruins of the home [Steerforth] had wronged'; and the seventh and final, which concludes the extract (and the chapter), is when David sees the man on the mast, now dead on the shore, lying 'with his head upon his arm, as I had often seen him lie at school', a simple and poignant touch that recalls the end of chapter 6 which describes the day of his first meeting with Steerforth at Mr Creakle's school: 'I thought of him very much after I went to bed, and raised myself, I recollect, to look at him where he lay in the moonlight, with his handsome face turned up, and his head reclining easily on his arm' (*DC* 140).

David is not the main actor in this extract; in a state of distraction – he uses the adjective 'distracted' twice of himself – he tries to stop Ham risking his life in the attempt to rescue Steerforth but others restrain him; and he later keeps 'busy', in an unspecified way, near Ham as attempts are made to revive him, but it is too late. For the most part, David is the agonized, terrified spectator and, as befits his profession, the recorder, the writer. It is Ham who is the romantic hero, determined, 'calmly desperate', 'standing alone', accepting that he may die, perhaps wanting to die, going back into the waves even after he is injured. Steerforth also takes what action he can in the extreme circumstances: shortly before this extract starts, he has twice been described as the 'active figure' and the phrase is used again when he is called 'the active figure left alone upon the mast'. The solitude suggested here by 'alone' is further emphasized when he is described as 'the solitary man upon the mast' and this isolation gives him an heroic dimension and links him with Ham, 'standing alone' before he makes his first foray into the sea. Perhaps here in contrast to Ham, who, in his very attempt to secure Steerforth's survival, may be actively courting his own death, Steerforth actively tries to survive, even though he is no longer in a position to initiate action or control events, as he has so often been before. Steerforth and Ham are already linked together by their desire for Little Em'ly and now they are further conjoined, first by the proximity of death, and then its reality as a result of the power of the sea; both are engulfed by powerful forces they cannot control. David, the survivor, lives on.

David has no chance to say goodbye to Steerforth in *Copperfield*, but in *Expectations*, Pip is able to say goodbye to Magwitch, and to try to make final amends to him, as the next extract shows.

Deathbed Daughter: *Great Expectations*, pp. 468–70

The daily visits I could make him were shortened now, and he was more strictly kept. Seeing, or fancying, that I was suspected of an intention of carrying poison to him, I asked to be searched before I sat down at his bedside, and told the officer who was always there, that I was willing to do anything that would assure him of the singleness of my designs. Nobody was hard with him, or with me. There was duty to be done, and it was done, but not harshly. The officer always gave me the assurance that he was worse, and some other sick prisoners in the room, and some other prisoners who attended on them as sick nurses (malefactors, but not incapable of kindness, GOD be thanked!), always joined in the same report.

As the days went on, I noticed more and more that he would lie placidly looking at the white ceiling, with an absence of light in his face, until some word of mine brightened it for an instant, and then it would subside again. Sometimes he was almost, or quite, unable to speak; then, he would answer me with slight pressures on my hand, and I grew to understand his meaning very well.

The number of the days had risen to ten, when I saw a greater change in him than I had seen yet. His eyes were turned towards the door, and lighted up as I entered.

'Dear boy,' he said, as I sat down by his bed. I thought you was late. But I knowed you couldn't be that.'

'It is just the time,' said I. 'I waited for it at the gate.'

'You always waits at the gate; don't you, dear boy?'

'Yes. Not to lose a moment of the time.'

'Thank'ee, dear boy, thank'ee. God bless you! You've never deserted me, dear boy.'

I pressed his hand in silence, for I could not forget that I had once meant to desert him.

'And what's the best of all,' he said, 'you've been more comfortable alonger me, since I was under a dark cloud, than when the sun shone. That's best of all.'

He lay on his back, breathing with great difficulty. Do what he would, and love me though he did, the light left his face ever and again, and a film came over the placid look at the white ceiling.

'Are you in much pain to-day?'

'I don't complain of none, dear boy.'

'You never do complain.'

He had spoken his last words. He smiled, and I understood his touch to mean that he wished to lift my hand, and lay it on his breast. I laid it there, and he smiled again, and put both his hands upon it.

The allotted time ran out, while we were thus; but, looking round, I found the governor of the prison standing near me, and he whispered, 'You needn't go yet.' I thanked him gratefully, and asked, 'Might I speak to him, if he can hear me?'

The governor stepped aside, and beckoned the officer away. The change, though it was made without noise, drew back the film from the placid look at the white ceiling, and he looked most affectionately at me.

'Dear Magwitch, I must tell you, now at last. You understand what I say?'

A gentle pressure on my hand.

'You had a child once, whom you loved and lost.'

A stronger pressure on my hand.

'She lived and found powerful friends. She is living now. She is a lady and very beautiful. And I love her!'

With a last faint effort, which would have been powerless but for my yielding to it and assisting it, he raised my hand to his lips. Then, he gently let it sink upon his breast again, with his own hands lying on it. The placid look at the white ceiling came back, and passed away, and his head dropped quietly on his breast.

Mindful, then, of what we had read together, I thought of the two men who went up into the Temple to pray, and I knew there were no better words that I could say beside his bed, than 'O Lord, be merciful to him, a sinner!'

The narrative prose in this extract is fairly muted, with none of those long multiple sentences punctuated by semicolons, which, as we have seen, often feature elsewhere in Dickens. Two of the most telling lines in the extract are not, strictly speaking, sentences at all since they contain no finite verb: 'A gentle pressure on my hand' and 'A stronger pressure on my hand.' The diction in both the narrative prose and dialogue is sparing and consists mainly of common words of one or two syllables. The prose is both compassionate and clinical, with precise observation of the way in which the light leaves and brightens Magwitch's face, a motif that is introduced in the second paragraph and runs through to the penultimate one.

The spoken dialogue is relatively sparse, but the speech styles of Magwitch and Pip are still carefully differentiated: Magwitch uses his characteristic colloquial style, established in the first chapter of the novel, which, in terms of Standard English, contains errors: 'I thought you was late' rather than 'I thought you were late'; 'I knowed you couldn't be that' rather than 'I knew you couldn't be that'; and – his last words – 'I don't complain of none' rather than 'I don't complain of any'. Pip, by contrast, uses Standard English, which is particularly evident in the line 'You had a child once, whom you loved and lost', with its carefully exact use of 'whom' rather than 'who' as the object pronoun. This dialogue-differentiation marks the persistence of class distinctions even in extremity – the approach of death does not dissolve them – but also emphasizes the extent to which Magwitch's project of making Pip into a gentleman has been successful.

In his last encounters with Magwitch, however, Pip shows himself to be a gentleman in more than an outward sense; he is a gentleman not only because he speaks correctly but also, and more profoundly, because he has become a gentle man in his relationship with Magwitch, tender and caring towards him in the way that Joe will later be tender and caring towards Pip himself. In a sense, Magwitch, who has claimed that he is Pip's 'second father' and that Pip is his 'son – more to me nor any son' (*GE* 315) – now occupies a position like that of Wemmick's Aged Parent, with Pip as the caring son – but one who was reluctant at first to play that role.

The language of hands that has been so significant earlier in *Expectations* recurs here, making an intratextual contrast to Magwitch's violent handling of Pip in their first encounter, to Mrs Joe's rough upbringing of Pip 'by hand', to Pip's refusal to respond to Magwitch when he first reappears, and to Pip's own intention of trying to lay restraining hands upon Magwitch at that fraught reunion. In their last exchanges Pip presses Magwitch's hand in silence when Magwitch affirms that Pip has never deserted him, and Pip cannot forget that he had once intended to do so. Pip, responsive to Magwitch's smile and touch, lays his hand on Magwitch's breast; Magwitch responds to Pip's words by a gentle, and then a stronger, pressure on his hand; and finally raises Pip's hand to his lips and lets it sink on his breast again, with his own hands lying on it. Hands speak at moments at which words – first Pip's, then Magwitch's – fail.

Religious discourse is employed in the first and final paragraphs. In the first paragraph, Pip thanks GOD – in capital letters – for the way in which criminals, 'malefactors', have shown themselves capable of kindness in nursing sick prisoners. There may be an oblique self-reference here to the way in which Pip himself, after the initial malefaction of rejecting Magwitch, has demonstrated that he is capable of kindness towards his benefactor, now a sick prisoner. In the last paragraph, he recalls his Bible reading with Magwitch and makes an intertextual reference to the parable, in Luke 18:9–14, warning against trusting in oneself as righteous and despising others. The parable tells of two men, a Pharisee and a publican (a collector of taxes for the

Romans), who went up into the temple to pray. The Pharisee thanked God that he was unlike others – 'extortioners, unjust, adulterers, or even as this publican' – and praised his own virtue: 'I fast twice in the week, I give tithes of all I possess.' In contrast, the publican 'would not lift up so much as *his* eyes unto heaven, but smote upon his breast, saying, God be merciful to me a sinner'. Jesus said that it was the publican rather than the Pharisee who left the temple justified: 'for every one that exalteth himself shall be abased; and he that humbleth himself shall be exalted'. Pip adapts the publican's words to apply to Magwitch – 'O Lord, be merciful to him, a sinner' – with the implication that Magwitch, who has recognized his guilt, is more 'justified' in the eyes of God than someone who boasts of his virtue. But in view of the original text, with its reference to 'me', Pip could also be speaking indirectly of himself, asking for mercy and suffering abasement after his earlier self-exaltation as a young man of 'great expectations'.

But neither Pip nor Magwitch has lost interest in social exaltation. Pip's last words to Magwitch tell him that his lost child lives and perform a primal act of restoration; if it were left at that, it might be the restoration of any lost child to any father; but, in this case, the mere fact of having survived is not enough; it is also important to tell Magwitch that his daughter, the child of a convict and a murderess, has risen socially. She has found 'powerful friends' and 'she is a lady and very beautiful'; in this latter sentence, her ladyhood comes first and her beauty, which might seem a quality that is at least partly independent of her social position, second; beauty is subordinate to her social status, an enhancement of her exchange value on the marriage market. Pip's final declaration is of his love for Estella, but it is clearly important, given that she is a lady, that he is a gentleman; if he were still a blacksmith, his love for Estella might raise the threat of a marriage that would be a social comedown for her, dragging her back towards the level from which she has risen, associating her with a 'forge' as she had once been associated with a 'forger', in the criminal sense, in the shape of her father.

Pip adumbrates a happy ending for himself and for the novel; that he will, eventually, marry Estella. But his position also raises a problem. Magwitch is Estella's biological father and Pip's surrogate father; a marriage between Estella and Pip could therefore seem incestuous, not in the technical sense but symbolically and psychologically. This perhaps helps to account for Dickens's difficulties, which we shall pursue in the next chapter of this book, in giving *Expectations* a conventionally happy ending.

Conclusions

Each of these extracts shows Dickens's skill in handling scenes which portray the approach of death, peacefully or tumultuously. Dickens orchestrates the scenes to produce emotions of pathos and sublimity and to provide perspectives on the lives both of the characters who are dying and those who remain. He shows that he is perfectly capable of concision and understatement as well as of more extended and elaborate effects. The scenes are not undisciplined squads of emotions but masterful marshallings of modes by which the human imagination can apprehend death. The first and fourth are deathbed scenes, but one is set at home, in domestic space, the other in prison, the site of penal subjection; the second unfolds in a courtroom and shows the passing of a collective death sentence, and the third takes place at sea, on the margins of the shore, with land tantalizingly close.

Dialogue plays an important role in the first and fourth extracts. In the first extract, it is the means by which Dora, showing a maturity and insight she has not previously articulated, passes a clear-eyed judgement on the likely failure of her marriage to David had she lived; this judgement elevates Dora and increases the poignancy of her death at a moment when she seems to have developed beyond the child-wife stage. In the prison scene, it is the means by which Pip assures Magwitch of the survival and social elevation of his daughter and of Pip's love for her. Direct-speech dialogue is, however, sparse in the courtroom and shipwreck extracts; in the former, only 'the prisoner', Magwitch, uses direct speech, and is swiftly hushed; in the latter, the only direct speech is Ham's, in his last words to David, and the minimal dialogue in which the fisherman tells David of the body that has come ashore. David recognizes whose it is (though his name is withheld until the start of the next chapter); but it is clear that dialogue has ceased between David and Steerforth.

The narrative prose in the account of Dora on her deathbed is strikingly restrained, deploying shortish sentences and monosyllables to imply emotions too large and deep for words. In the scene of the death of Ham and Steerforth, elaborate multiple sentences help to convey the tumult of the sea and the frantic activity of the rescue attempts, but these are varied with much shorter ones that denote key actions and states. In the third extract, present participles contribute to the sense of continuing stressful activity and occasional moments of stasis. Grammatical parallelism is employed in the first extract, to emphasize a movement from outer to inner. In both the first and third extracts, the present tense is used to enhance a sense of immediacy, of events unfolding in the present. The first extract also skilfully deploys other tenses – the perfect, the future, the perfect conditional – to increase the poignancy of the scene, and turns a grammatical fact into a painful existential reality when David registers that Dora is speaking of herself in the past tense.

In the Dora scene, the imagery is sparing, using common metaphors ('heart'), but the narrative prose provides a more extended metaphor when it calls David's belief that she will survive 'a pale lingering shadow', an image that seems also to apply to Dora herself at this point. The Steerforth scene contains much metaphor: the peaks and troughs of the turbulent waves become hills and valleys, as if a Wordsworthian landscape were loosed from stasis into motion, as if solid contours were transformed into liquid ones, as if geological upheavals lasting aeons were compressed into seconds. Wave and sail are personified; Steerforth's life hangs by the thread that Atropos will snip as he clings to the phallic mast; his red cap connotes social status, revolution and blood; the cracking planks ring, in anticipation, his death-knell. This riot of imagery, disciplined by Dickens's rhythmic prose, strengthens the impression of the riot of the waves.

The extracts contain several important intratextual links. In the Dora scene, there is an intratextual link to an earlier reference in *Copperfield* to the Gospel story of Lazarus. The Steerforth scene has seven intratextual links with earlier sections of the novel, thus contributing both to the comprehensibility and unity of the whole book, by reminding the reader of earlier passages and knitting different parts of the novel together. The gentle and supportive hand-holding and hand-pressure between Pip and Magwitch in the courtroom and prison scenes form an intratextual contrast with the violence or rejection of hands in earlier parts of *Expectations*, contributing to a kind of thesaurus of hand-language and its meanings and, as with the intratextual links in *Copperfield*, helping to knit the novel together.

Two important intertextual links to New Testament stories feature in the extracts: the Dora scene links with the story of Lazarus, and the Magwitch deathbed scene links with the story of the two men who went up into the temple to pray. The Lazarus allusion has ironic and alarming aspects, particularly if we follow the intratextual link mentioned in the previous paragraph, and recall the fear that the Lazarus story aroused in David as a small boy. The story of the two men who went up into the temple to pray, which Pip adapts to Magwitch, could also apply to Pip himself.

Death scenes in fiction involve reconfiguring the past and the future, looking back and looking forward. The first extract is striking for the way in which it starts to negotiate a transfer of the wifely role from Dora to Agnes, a negotiation in which, it seems, Dora herself will play an initiating role. The second extract shows Magwitch as subject to the inexorable processes of the law – necessarily so, in the sense that it helps to reintegrate his biological and surrogate children, Estella and Pip, fully into society, so that they no longer have a fugitive for a father – but it also suggests that the law is deficient in human understanding and spiritual vision, unable to accommodate Magwitch's emotional reasons for returning or achieve the absolute justice available in a divine perspective. The third extract brings together the two rivals for Em'ly's affections, Ham and Steerforth, her virtuous lover and her seducer, and shows them both perishing in their doomed encounter with the sublime power of the sea; this extract looks back to the past rather than the future, focusing inexorably on David's losses; despite the way forward that Dora has earlier prepared for him, the future is now a blank – but David, in contrast to Steerforth and Ham, has survived, so at least there is the possibility of a future. The fourth extract recounts the death of Magwitch, and Pip's final reassurance to him that his daughter lives, that she is a lady, and that Pip loves her, implies that in Magwitch's end there is a beginning, a future perspective in which Pip and Estella might marry. But all the extracts serve to bring the respective protagonists of *Copperfield* and *Expectations* closer to the point of crisis and it is their breakdowns and recoveries that our final chapter of analyses will explore.

Methods of Analysis

- We assessed the respective role of dialogue in each extract (e.g. the importance of the dialogue in which Dora assesses how her marriage to David might have developed; the dearth of direct-speech dialogue in the courtroom scene with its emphasis on indirect speech).
- We examined the length and structure of sentences in each extract (e.g. the shortish sentences in the Dora scene; the variation between extended and simple sentences in the Steerforth scene).
- We identified the use and effects of grammatical parallelism and repetition in the extracts (e.g. 'I hold her hand/heart in mine' in extract one, which progresses from outer to inner, from the physical to the emotional; the repetition of 'rising with the hills, falling with the valleys' in extract three that stresses the remorseless power of the waves over the human body).
- We highlighted the deployment of tenses (e.g. the present tense in the Dora and courtroom scenes, which increases the impression of immediacy; the past tense in which Dora speaks of herself in the first extract, thus stressing her imminent, inevitable death).
- We explored the imagery and its effects (e.g. the sparse imagery in the Dora scene, which enhances, by its restraint, the poignancy of her demise; the vivid and resourceful metaphors in the Steerforth scene, which reinforce the sense of the human and marine turbulence of the episode).
- We made significant intratextual links (e.g. in the Steerforth scene, between the corpse on the shore, lying with his head on his arm, and David's early sight of Steerforth at school, lying in the same posture; in the courtroom and prison scenes, between the benign use of hands and their violent uses earlier in *Expectations*).
- We traced important intertextual links (e.g. between the Dora scene and the story of Lazarus in St John's Gospel; between the prison scene and the story in St Luke's Gospel of the two men who went up to the temple to pray).

- We discussed the respective ways in which each extract reconfigures the past and future in the face of approaching death (e.g. Dora's intimation that she will hand over her wifely role to Agnes, thus opening a future for David; Pip's assurance to Magwitch about Estella, which raises the possibility that Pip may marry her).

Suggested Work

Analyse the two following passages. The first is the scene evoking Dora's final demise, which takes place 'offstage', after David has gone downstairs and Agnes has taken his place at Dora's bedside. The second describes Pip's confrontation with imminent death when Orlick kidnaps him and tells him he will kill him. Explore how the stylistic features of the passages work to evoke this 'offstage' death and this near-death experience and consider the complex attitudes to death they convey.

[a] *Copperfield*. From 'Agnes is downstairs' to 'blotted out of my remembrance' (*DC* 838–9)
[b] *Expectations*. From '"What are you going to do to me?"' to 'looking at me and enjoying the sight' (*GE* 436–8)

6

Breakdown and Recovery

Bildungsromane characteristically bring their protagonists to crises from which they emerge sadder but wiser and make some sort of settlement with themselves and with existing society. This pattern is vividly realized in *Copperfield* and *Expectations*. The severe losses which befall David and Pip culminate in breakdowns which make them feel close to death but ultimately help to reconfigure their identities and ways of life. David becomes a despairing wanderer in Europe and Pip collapses into fever and delirium, but both recover and, sooner or later, seek happiness in marriage. David finds this, but it is an open question whether Pip does so. We will look first at David's descent into the depths of despondency and the start of his awakening to hope.

Despondency to Dawn: *David Copperfield*, pp. 885–6

It was a long and gloomy night that gathered on me, haunted by the ghosts of many hopes, of many dear remembrances, many errors, many unavailing sorrows and regrets.

I went away from England; not knowing, even then, how great the shock was, that I had to bear. I left all who were dear to me, and went away; and believed that I had borne it, and it was past. As a man upon a field of battle will receive a mortal hurt, and scarcely know that he is struck, so I, when I was left alone with my undisciplined heart, had no conception of the wound with which it had to strive.

The knowledge came upon me, not quickly but little by little, and grain by grain. The desolate feeling with which I went abroad, deepened and widened hourly. At first it was a heavy sense of loss and sorrow, wherein I could distinguish little else. By imperceptible degrees, it became a hopeless consciousness of all that I had lost – love, friendship, interest; of all that had been shattered – my first trust, my first affection, the whole airy castle of my life; of all that remained – a ruined blank and waste, lying wide around me, unbroken, to the dark horizon.

If my grief were selfish, I did not know it to be so. I mourned for my child-wife, taken from her blooming world, so young. I mourned for him who might have won the love and admiration of thousands, as he had won mine long ago. I mourned for the broken heart that had found rest in the stormy sea; and for the wandering remnants of the simple home, where I had heard the night-wind blowing, when I was a child.

From the accumulated sadness into which I fell, I had at length no hope of ever issuing again. I roamed from place to place, carrying my burden with me everywhere. I felt its whole weight now; and I drooped beneath it, and I said in my heart that it could never be lightened.

When this despondency was at its worst, I believed that I should die. Sometimes, I thought that I would like to die at home; and actually turned back on my road, that I might get there soon. At other times, I passed on farther away, from city to city, seeking I know not what, and trying to leave I know not what behind.

It is not in my power to retrace, one by one, all the weary phases of distress of mind through which I passed. There are some dreams that can only be imperfectly and vaguely described; and when I oblige myself to look back on this time of my life, I seem to be recalling such a dream. I see myself passing on among the novelties of foreign towns, palaces, cathedrals, temples, pictures, castles, tombs, fantastic streets – the old abiding places of History and Fancy – as a dreamer might; bearing my painful load through all, and hardly conscious of the objects as they fade before me. Listlessness to everything, but brooding sorrow, was the night that fell on my undisciplined heart. Let me look up from it – as at last I did, thank Heaven! – and from its long, sad, wretched dream, to dawn.

This extract summarizes David's life over a period of time rather than presenting an individual scene. It explores the full emergence of his grief, constituting a kind of working-through of his sense of loss. It starts with a shortish one-sentence paragraph that introduces the metaphors of night and hauntedness to describe his prolonged period of mourning and gives a sense of the accumulation of painful past memories, stressed by the repeated phrase 'of many'. The second paragraph introduces an extended, almost epic simile, of an unusually martial kind for Dickens, in which David compares himself to a man mortally wounded in battle who scarcely registers how badly he is hurt.

David anatomizes the stages of his mourning as it intensifies. He becomes aware slowly – 'little by little' and 'grain by grain' – of how badly his emotions are wounded. He shows how these small awarenesses accumulate, deepening and widening hourly. He describes his initial feeling in general terms and then begins to identify its elements more exactly in the three interpolated clauses starting with 'of all that': there is 'love, friendship, interest' that he has 'lost'; then 'my first trust, my first affection'; and then a shift into metaphor, 'the whole airy castle of my life' that has been 'shattered'. A further metaphor describes what remains: the 'ruined blank and waste, lying wide around me, unbroken, to the dark horizon': the last image a desolate one indeed, that anticipates the bleak landscapes and mindscapes of Robert Browning's poem 'Childe Roland to the Dark Tower came' (1855) and T. S. Eliot's *The Waste Land* (1922).

David's full awareness of his grief is articulated in the three sentences starting with 'I mourn' – a further instance of Dickensian anaphora, of which we have seen several examples earlier. Here David is specific about his losses, though he eschews proper names: there is the child-wife (Dora); there is 'him who might have won the love and admiration of thousands' as he had won David's (Steerforth); there is 'the broken heart that had found rest in the stormy sea' (Ham's); and there is 'the wandering remnants of the simple home', the boat on the shore that had been the magical place of his childhood where Em'ly had once lived. All these losses create an 'accumulated sadness' from which he feels he will never emerge – a characteristic symptom of clinical depression. David becomes a wanderer on the face of the earth, always bearing a 'burden' of which he feels 'the whole weight'; the 'burden' is an intertextual reference to the burden borne by Christian, the protagonist of Bunyan's *Pilgrim's Progress*; but it is not easy to see, at this stage, how David will find salvation. Indeed, he drops to an emotional nadir in which he feels that he will die but cannot decide whether to go home to do so or to travel on; he becomes so confused that he loses his cognitive grasp on both past and future, a loss that the repeated 'I know not what' underlines.

David declares that he is incapable of describing the successive psychological phases through which he passed; following on from the earlier metaphors of night and hauntedness, he compares his experience at that time to a dream that eludes complete and precise description. He makes it clear that he is looking back, as narrator, from his present vantage point and visualizing his past experience – 'I see myself passing on among the novelties' – and he summarizes the places he visited and saw in generic plural nouns – 'foreign towns, palaces, cathedrals, temples, pictures, castles, tombs' – rather than itemizing them specifically; no place names are provided, no flashes of detail given. The places are also called, in an interpolation, 'the old abiding places of History and Fancy', as if they were locations that hovered between the real and the imaginary; the sense of the imaginary and dreamlike is enhanced by the link between 'Fancy', a term that is a contraction of 'fantasy', and the adjective 'fantastic' that occurs earlier in the same sentence, applied to streets, almost as if they were, anticipatorily, streets in a surrealist painting.

The phrase 'my painful load' echoes the image of the 'burden' used in the last paragraph but one. David sums up his experience in terms of 'listlessness', lack of enthusiasm and energy for anything except brooding sorrow, and uses the image of a 'night' that has fallen on 'my undisciplined heart'; this last phrase also occurred in the second paragraph of the extract and makes an intratextual link with its earlier uses in *Copperfield*, first by Annie Strong – when she expresses her thankfulness to her husband 'for having saved me from the first mistaken impulse of my undisciplined heart' (*DC* 730) – and then when it recurs in David's reflections (*DC* 733) and goes on to become 'almost always present to my mind': 'For I knew, now, that my own heart was undisciplined when it first loved Dora; and that if it had been disciplined, it could never have felt, when we were married, what it had felt in its secret experience' (*DC* 766). The phrase and the idea of 'the undisciplined heart' are key elements of *Copperfield*.

In the last sentence of the extract, David voices what could be both an imperative and a plea: 'Let me look up from it' may mean 'I must look up from it' and 'Allow me to look up from it'. Although he cannot quite comply with Jane Austen's imperative in chapter 48 of *Mansfield Park* (1814) – 'Let other pens dwell on guilt and misery' – he does want, in his capacity as autobiographical narrator, to move on from recollecting and recounting this dark night of the soul and to awaken from 'its long, sad, wretched dream, to dawn'. The image of the bad dream modulates into the image of morning and awakening and heralds the recovery that David will now describe. The 'Thank heaven!' interjected here is more than merely formal, but suggests David's sense that divine intervention did help his recovery.

In *Expectations*, Pip falls, as the next extract shows, into fever and delirium after Magwitch's death; he finds, however, that he is not alone, that a figure from the past has returned to help him through the crisis.

Turmoil to Tenderness: *Great Expectations*, pp. 471–2

That I had a fever and was avoided, that I suffered greatly, that I often lost my reason, that the time seemed interminable, that I confounded impossible existences with my own identity; that I was a brick in the house wall, and yet entreating to be released from the giddy place where the builders had set me; that I was a steel beam of a vast engine, clashing and whirling over a gulf, and yet that I implored in my own person to have the engine stopped, and my part in it hammered off; that I passed through these phases of disease, I know of my own remembrance, and did in some sort know at the time. That I sometimes struggled with real people, in the belief that they were murderers, and that I would all at once comprehend that they meant to do me good, and would then sink exhausted in their arms, and suffer them to lay me down, I also knew at the time. But, above all, I knew that there was a constant tendency in all these people – who, when I was ill, would present all kinds of extraordinary transformations of the human face, and would be much dilated in size – above all, I say, I knew that there was an extraordinary tendency in all of these people, sooner or later to settle down into the likeness of Joe.

After I had turned the worst point of my illness, I began to notice that while all its other features changed, this one consistent feature did not

change. Whoever came about me, still settled down into Joe. I opened
my eyes in the night, and I saw in the great chair at the bedside, Joe.
I opened my eyes in the day, and, sitting on the window-seat, smoking
his pipe in the shaded open window, still I saw Joe. I asked for cooling
drink, and the dear hand that gave it me was Joe's. I sank back on my
pillow after drinking, and the face that looked so hopefully and tenderly
upon me was the face of Joe.

At last, one day, I took courage, and said, '*Is* it Joe?'

And the dear old home-voice answered, 'Which it air, old chap.'

'O Joe, you break my heart! Look angry at me, Joe, Strike me, Joe.
Tell me of my ingratitude. Don't be so good to me!'

For, Joe had actually laid his head down on the pillow at my side and
put his arm round my neck, in his joy that I knew him.

'Which dear old Pip, old chap,' said Joe, 'you and me was ever friends.
And when you're well enough to go out for a ride – what larks!'

After which, Joe withdrew to the window, and stood with his back
towards me, wiping his eyes. And as my extreme weakness prevented me
from getting up and going to him, I lay there, penitently whispering,
'O God bless him! O God bless this gentle Christian man!'

This extract vividly conveys Pip's illness and the start of his recovery.
In a sentence that employs anaphora – the 'That I' which introduces
each of a series of relative clauses – it conveys his delirious and painful
delusions of entrapment and struggle, which clearly relate to his own
existential condition. He sees himself as a brick in a house wall asking
to be released and as a steel beam of a vast engine clashing and whirling
over a gulf; the latter image seems to combine the technology of the
industrial revolution with older visions of hell. Pip imagines himself
turned into what ought to be insentient parts of a whole, a brick and
a beam; but, paradoxically, he remains conscious and desperate to
escape from the totality that entraps him. This provides a powerful
metaphor of his enmeshment, not only in the complexities of his own
life, but also in a social system in which class, money and ultimately
prison and the law combine to try to keep each person in their place,
as if they were inert units subordinate to a structure like that of a
building or a machine. Ironically, to become a brick or steel beam – in
the sense of acquiring a fixed social identity, particularly in a 'giddy
place' – is exactly what Pip spent his boyhood and youth desiring

and which now figures in his fevered imagination as a nightmarish condition.

The narrator does draw back from total involvement to remind the reader that he is recalling rather than currently suffering these experiences and that, even at the time, he retained some idea of what was actually happening: 'that I passed through these phases of disease, I know of my own remembrance, and did in some sort know at the time'. If the main clause, 'I know of my own remembrance', were placed at the start of the sentence it would make the experience seem more distanced and controlled; by putting this near the end of the sentence, it plunges the reader more fully into the kind of febrile confusion evoked in the relative clauses, before eventually emerging to offer a more coherent perspective. The next sentence is similarly structured, with the relative clauses preceding the main clause. But in this sentence the emphasis changes from struggling with his own entrapment as a brick or beam – struggling against his conversion into an inert unit – to struggling with other people in the belief that they are murderers (an idea that shows how threatened he feels) before he realizes that their intentions are benign. But Pip has a clear cognitive grasp that, above the 'extraordinary transformations of the human face' that he experiences as he registers the presence of other people, there is 'an extraordinary tendency in all these people to settle down into one likeness'. The repetition of the adjective 'extraordinary' is important here, as marking how one form of extraordinariness, that involves metamorphosis and distortion, becomes another form of extraordinariness that reveals an underlying stability: the multitude who seem to attend on Pip fuse into the unfailing presence of a figure whose name is strategically withheld until the very last word of the paragraph: Joe.

The presence of Joe becomes the 'one consistent feature' of Pip's experience once his illness has passed its worst stage. His different attendants 'settle down' into Joe. In the next paragraph, four successive sentences, including the last, end with 'Joe', and one with 'Joe's', as if reinforcing Pip's increasing awareness of Joe's constant presence. Four of these sentences start in a grammatically parallel way, with first-person pronoun and finite verb – 'I opened' (twice), and then 'I asked' and 'I sank' – and all have Joe as their object. All this helps to strengthen the sense of Joe's constant presence. When Pip finally asks if it is indeed

Joe, the reply comes in the 'dear old home-voice', endowing Joe with homely associations, and his dialogue displays characteristic features of Joe's speech that we recall from earlier in the novel: the starting of statements with 'which' ('Which dear old Pip, old chap'); the use of singular rather than plural verb forms, and vice versa ('you and me was ever friends'); the distinctive vowel pronunciations ('Which it air [are], old chap'); and his most famous catchphrase, redolent of carefree, playful enjoyment: 'what larks!' Pip himself is overcome with guilt at Joe's affection and issues a series of imperatives: 'Look angry at me', 'Strike me', 'Tell me of my ingratitude', 'Don't be so good to me'. Joe ignores all these.

When Joe lays his head on the pillow and puts his arm around Pip's neck, in his joy that Pip has recognized him, he displays the maternal emotions and assumes the maternal functions conventionally ascribed to women which neither Pip's mother, because she is dead, nor his rampaging older sister, even when she was alive, could feel or perform. Joe is overcome with tears and has to go to the window and turn away. Pip is too weak to approach him physically and the maternal connotations modulate into religious ones, in the adverb 'penitently' and in Pip's call for a blessing which, significantly, includes the word 'gentleman', now fractured into two and with the adjective 'Christian' interpolated, indicating that Pip has arrived at a new understanding of the word 'gentleman' in which it is associated with charity, compassion and selflessness rather than social standing and money: 'O God bless this gentle Christian man!'

Nonetheless, the togetherness between Pip and Joe that Pip's illness and vulnerability make possible cannot last; Pip acknowledges that as he grows 'stronger and better', Joe 'becomes a little less easy with him' (*GE* 464) and thinks it is because Joe fears that, when Pip gets well, he will rebuff Joe as he had done in the past. One morning he finds that Joe has departed, leaving a short letter that says Pip 'will do better without' (i.e. without Joe). Pip resolves that he will try to restore his connection with the world of his native place by proposing to Biddy; but when he returns there three days later, he finds that Biddy has just married Joe. Pip's hopes of a matrimonial confirmation of his recovery have been baulked; but as the next extract shows, David will fare differently with Agnes.

Ever Undivided: *David Copperfield*, pp. 935–7

'Dearest Agnes! Whom I so respect and honour – whom I so devotedly love! When I came here today, I thought that nothing could have wrested this confession from me. I thought I could have kept it in my bosom all our lives, till we were old. But, Agnes, if I have indeed any new-born hope that I may ever call you something more than Sister, widely different from Sister! – '

Her tears fell fast; but they were not like those she had lately shed, and I saw my hope brighten in them.

'Agnes! Ever my guide, and best support! If you had been more mindful of yourself, and less of me, when we grew up here together, I think my heedless fancy never would have wandered from you. But you were so much better than I, so necessary to me in every boyish hope and disappointment, that to have you to confide in, and rely upon in everything, became a second nature, supplanting for the time the first and greater one of loving you as I do!'

Still weeping, but not sadly – joyfully! And clasped in my arms as she had never been, as I had thought she never was to be!'

'When I loved Dora – fondly, Agnes, as you know – '

'Yes!' she cried earnestly. 'I am glad to know it!'

'When I loved her – even then, my love would have been incomplete, without your sympathy. I had it, and it was perfected. And when I lost her, Agnes, what should I have been without you, still!'

Closer in my arms, nearer to my heart, her trembling hand upon my shoulder, her sweet eyes shining through tears, on mine!

'I went away, dear Agnes, loving you. I stayed away, loving you. I returned home, loving you!'

And now, I tried to tell her of the struggle I had had, and the conclusion I had come to. I tried to lay my mind before her, truly, and entirely. I tried to show her how I had hoped I had come into the better knowledge of myself and of her; how I had resigned myself to what that better knowledge brought; and how I had come there, even that day, in my fidelity to this. If she did so love me (I said) that she could take me for her husband, she could do so, on no deserving of mine, except upon the truth of my love for her, and the trouble in which it had ripened to be what it was; and hence it was that I revealed it. And O, Agnes, even out of thy true eyes, in that same time, the spirit of my child-wife looked upon me, saying it was well; and winning me, through thee, to tenderest recollections of the Blossom that had withered in its Bloom!

'I am so blest, Trotwood – my heart is so overcharged – but there is one thing I must say.'

'Dearest, what?'

She laid her gentle hands upon my shoulders, and looked calmly in my face.

'Do you know, yet, what it is?'

'I am afraid to speculate on what it is. Tell me, my dear.'

'I have loved you all my life!'

O, we were happy, we were happy! Our tears were not for the trials (hers so much the greater) through which we had come to be thus, but for the rapture of being thus, never to be divided more!

We walked, that winter evening, in the fields together; and the blessed calm within us seemed to be partaken by the frosty air. The early stars began to shine while we were lingering on, and looking up to them, we thanked our GOD for having guided us to this tranquillity.

We stood together in the same old-fashioned window at night, when the moon was shining; Agnes with her quiet eyes raised to it; I following her glance. Long miles of road then opened out before my mind; and, toiling on, I saw a ragged way-worn boy, forsaken and neglected, who should come to call even the heart now beating against mine, his own.

This extract is fascinating for the way in which, through narrative prose, direct-speech dialogue and indirect speech, it dramatizes the complex emotional, symbolic and spiritual negotiations David has to make to put himself into a position where marriage to Agnes might be possible, where indeed it might seem to provide a 'GOD'-given tranquillity. In David's declarations to Agnes, the diction offers a proliferation of terms in which David tries to define what Agnes means to him and to deal with his memory of his relationship with Dora. Agnes is his 'Dearest'; 'Sister'; 'guide'; 'best support'; 'second nature'. All these identifications, he claims, have distracted him from the truth that he loves her as a potential husband. He aims to acknowledge his love for Dora while she lived but to claim that Agnes was still necessary to complete and perfect it. He contends that Agnes now incorporates and transcends Dora – 'even out of thy true eyes, in that same time, the spirit of my child-wife looked upon me'; that Dora approves their match; and that Agnes serves as a memorial of Dora, imaged as 'the Blossom that had withered in its bloom!'

David's first declarations are in direct speech and his exchanges with Agnes are lubricated by her tears – but these are tears which brighten David's hope and express Agnes's joy rather than signalling sadness. He does most of the talking, though she interjects once, to approve of his expression of love for Dora – effectively telling him that this would be no obstacle between them. His first batch of direct-speech statements conclude with three grammatically parallel sentences that each have a first-person pronoun and finite verb at the start and the same phrase, consisting of a present participle and object pronoun at the end, an order of words that emphasizes the constancy of David's feelings: 'I went away, dear Agnes, loving you. I stayed away, loving you. I returned home, loving you.' The extract then moves into indirect speech in a more summary form, as David recounts what he told her. A short section follows in which Agnes asserts that she must speak; David is temporarily troubled, telling her he fears to speculate on what she may say, but her declaration removes his disquiet; in contrast to David's complex negotiations, Agnes simply affirms she has loved him all her life.

In the next section, David mainly employs the first-person plural pronoun, 'We', as if to emphasize the indissoluble unity they have now attained. Tears flow again but these mark their rapture rather than any distress. They are in a rural rather than urban environment, close to nature and the simplifying and clarifying effects of the frost, which, in an example of what the great nineteenth-century art critic and cultural commentator John Ruskin called 'the pathetic fallacy', in which natural phenomena that have no feelings seem to share those of human beings; the frosty air partakes of the 'blessed calm' within David and Agnes. The adjective 'blessed' introduces a religious note and this is strengthened by their thanking of GOD – Dickens again employs the convention of signifying spiritual importance by the use of capitals – for having guided them to this tranquillity.

The emphasis on tranquillity – rather than passion – is significant. Near the end of the extract, David speaks of Agnes's 'quiet eyes raised up' to the moon. In a sense, the adjective 'quiet' is curious since eyes do not make a noise; in this respect, it is an hypallage, a transferred epithet, from Agnes's demeanour as a person to her eyes; but it also indicates that her eyes – in contrast, say, to Rosa Dartle's – do not flash with passion and that she can gaze on the moon without the psychological disturbance that the moon is, superstitiously or mythically, said to produce (and also, implicitly, without the mood changes sometimes associated with menstruation). But Agnes's quietness and imperturbability, her lack of loudness and lunar disturbance, could also be a sign of low libido. In this respect, she exemplifies the way in which Dickens, especially in his portrayals of virtuous women, subdues an explicit sexual element, though it may show a limited erotic imagination to think that she is thereby rendered sexless. Indeed, the extract hints at a sexual element, for example in the earlier statement 'And clasped in my arms as she had never been, as I had thought she never was to be!', an embrace which might imply a stirring of desire, a glimpse of erotic fulfilment, on the part of David, freed from a 'child-wife' in a state of arrested development, and indeed on the part of Agnes, liberated from the obsessive devotion of her late father.

In narrative terms the mutual avowal of love between David and Agnes, which opens the way to marriage, makes a good conclusion to the story of David's crisis. This is emphasized, at the end of the extract, by a switch from the first-person plural to the first-person singular, as David, following Agnes's glances, raises his eyes to the moon, but sees '[l]ong miles of road' rather than moonscapes opening in his mind, taking him back to his past, making an intratextual link with his long and troubled boyhood trek from London to Dover (*DC* 233–47), and emphasizing that David, who was once 'a ragged, way-worn boy, forsaken and neglected', and who perhaps became partly so again during his continental travels after Dora's death, has now found an emotional and spiritual home.

As the end of *Expectations* approaches, Pip, who has been away in the East for eleven years, has no such home; Biddy, happily wed to Joe and with a son also called Pip, tells him he must marry, but he tells her it is not at all likely; then after dinner, in the early evening, he walks over to what was once Satis House:

Friends Apart? *Great Expectations*, pp. 491–3

A cold silvery mist had veiled the afternoon, and the moon was not yet up to scatter it. But, the stars were shining beyond the mist, and the moon was coming, and the evening was not dark. I could trace out where every part of the old house had been, and where the brewery had been, and where the gates, and where the casks. I had done so, and was looking along the desolate garden-walk, when I beheld a solitary figure in it.

The figure showed itself aware of me, as I advanced. It had been moving towards me, but it stood still. As I drew nearer, I saw it to be the figure of a woman. As I drew nearer yet, it was about to turn away, when it stopped, and let me come up with it. Then, it faltered as if much surprised, and uttered my name, and I cried out:

'Estella!'

'I am greatly changed. I wonder you know me.'

The freshness of her beauty was indeed gone, but its indescribable majesty and its indescribable charm remained. Those attractions in it, I had seen before; what I had never seen before, was the saddened softened light of the once proud eyes; what I have never felt before, was the friendly touch of the once insensible hand.

We sat down on a bench that was near, and I said, 'After so many years, it is strange that we should thus meet again, Estella, here where our first meeting was! Do you often come back?'

'I have never been here since.'

'Nor I.'

The moon began to rise, and I thought of the placid look at the white ceiling, which had passed away. The moon began to rise, and I thought of the pressure on my hand when I had spoken the last words he had heard on earth.

Estella was the next to break the silence that ensued between us.

'I have very often hoped and intended to come back, but have been prevented by many circumstances. Poor, poor old place!'

The silvery mist was touched with the first rays of the moonlight, and the same rays touched the tears that dropped from her eyes. Not knowing that I saw them, and setting herself to get the better of them, she said quietly:

'Were you wondering, as you walked along, how it came to be left in this condition?'

'Yes, Estella.'

'The ground belongs to me. It is the only possession I have not relinquished. Everything else has gone from me, little by little, but I have kept this. It was the subject of the only determined resistance I made in all the wretched years.'

'Is it to be built on?'

'At last it is. I came here to take leave of it before its change. And you,' she said, in a voice of touching interest to a wanderer, 'you live abroad still?'

'Still.'

'And do well, I am sure.'

'I work pretty hard for a sufficient living, and therefore – Yes, I do well.'

'I have often thought of you,' said Estella.

'Have you?'

'Of late, very often. There was a long hard time when I kept far from me, the remembrance of what I had thrown away when I was quite ignorant of its worth. But, since my duty has not been incompatible with the admission of that remembrance, I have given it a place in my heart.'

'You have always held your place in *my* heart,' I answered.

And we were silent again, until she spoke.

'I little thought,' said Estella, 'that I should take leave of you in taking leave of this spot. I am very glad to do so.'

'Glad to part again, Estella? To me, parting is a painful thing. To me, the remembrance of our last parting has been ever mournful and painful.'

'But you said to me,' returned Estella, very earnestly, '"God bless you, God forgive you!" And if you could say that to me then, you will not hesitate to say that to me now – now, when suffering has been stronger than all other teaching, and has taught me to understand what your heart used to be. I have been bent and broken, but – I hope – into a better shape. Be as considerate and good to me as you were, and tell me we are friends.'

'We are friends,' said I, rising and bending over her, as she rose from the bench.

'And will continue friends apart,' said Estella.

I took her hand in mine, and we went out of the ruined place; and, as the morning mists had risen long ago when I first left the forge, so, the evening mists were rising now, and in all the broad expanse of tranquil light they showed to me, I saw no shadow of another parting from her.

This evokes the final encounter between Pip and Estella, which concludes *Expectations*. The extract starts with an evocation of an atmosphere – the mist, stars, an imminent moon – of a twilight time, a liminal period between day and night and, for Pip, between past and present. The repetition of the relative adverb 'where' stresses the concern with physical location, the topography of Miss Havisham's paralysis, of Estella's entrapment, of Pip's humiliation; while the pluperfect 'had been', twice repeated, and understood in the last three 'where' phrases, indicates that the objects named, as if in an inventory, are now all in the past: house, brewery, gates, casks. Then a solitary figure appears: given the earlier mention of stars, there is an intratextual link with the figure who looked 'like a star', coming down a dark corridor, when Pip first saw Estella in Satis House, in the extract we discussed in chapter 2. But although the figure's gender is identified as a woman's, the pronoun 'it' rather than 'she' continues to be used until Pip utters Estella's name and the identification is confirmed – though Estella is surprised Pip should have been able to make it. She is older, lacking 'freshness' and her 'once proud eyes' have a 'saddened, softened light'; the alliterative sibilants of 'saddened' and 'softened' contribute to the sense given by the meaning of the words that unhappy experience has made her less hard.

Anaphora and grammatical parallelism are used to good effect on three occasions. There are the two sentences that start 'As I drew nearer', which build up to the moment of recognition when Estella utters Pip's name. There are the two clauses that start 'what I had never seen before' and describe, first, 'the saddened softened light of the once proud eyes' and, then, 'the friendly touch of the once insensible hand'. Here, the anaphora drives home the unprecedented nature of Pip's visual and tactile experience of Estella, and the repeated adverb 'once', here meaning 'formerly', underlines the contrast between her present and previous state. The two sentences that start 'The moon began to rise and I thought of' reinforce the intratextual link with the death of Magwitch – now known to be Estella's father. As we saw in our discussion of Magwitch's death scene in the previous chapter, the 'last words' that Magwitch 'had heard on earth' were 'And I love her', and there is a sense here that Pip may be about to try to fulfil the promise implicit in this declaration: that he will propose marriage to her.

Estella's first word is Pip's name, but this is not given in direct speech, as if to do so would be to create in the reader a sense of an intimacy too quickly achieved, after all their years apart and their painful early history. But Pip's exclamation of Estella's forename is given directly, and with an exclamation mark added, as if to stress the power and completeness, for Pip, of the moment of identification. Estella then does speak with remarkable frankness, if in general terms: 'I am greatly changed. I wonder you know me.' A language of hands operates between them, as Pip feels her 'friendly' touch.

A subdued dialogue between Pip and Estella takes place that nonetheless seems to be building up to a mutual declaration which would, as with David and Agnes in *Copperfield*, open the way to marriage. Estella's voice is 'of touching interest to a wanderer'; she has often thought of him and has kept a 'remembrance' of him and of what she had thrown away when she was quite ignorant of its worth, in her heart. There is an intratextual link here with her earlier denial to Pip that she had a heart in the emotional sense: 'I have a heart to be stabbed in or shot in ... and, of course, it if ceased to beat I should cease to be. But ... I have no softness there, no – sympathy – sentiment – nonsense' (*GE* 259). Now she acknowledges that she does have a heart in the sense of a capacity for sympathetic and sensitive feeling. Pip, carrying on the metaphor, declares that Estella has always held a place in his 'heart' and this seems a cue for a mutual declaration of love that would open the way to matrimony. But they fall silent again, and when Estella breaks the silence, it is to talk of parting from Pip; when Pip objects that parting is painful, and recalls his last parting with Estella, she asks that he show the same consideration and goodness now and tell her they are friends; Pip accepts that they are friends, and Estella draws the line there when she says: 'And will continue friends apart' – an ambiguous phrase which could mean 'we will continue to be friends who stay apart' or 'we can only continue to be friends if we stay apart'. Here, as earlier in the novel, Estella is an anti-Agnes who inverts conventional expectations of womanly behaviour.

The language of hands is used again when Pip takes Estella's hand in his, and they leave 'the ruined place'. There is an intertextual link here with the famous lines describing Adam and Eve departing from the Garden of Eden at the end of Milton's *Paradise Lost* (1667): 'The world was all before them, where to choose / Their place of rest, and Providence their guide: / They hand in hand, with wandering steps and slow, / Through Eden took their solitary way'. But the Garden

Pip and Estella are leaving has been an infernal, fallen one, a place in which nature has been warped and frozen, and it now seems that the only force that will reanimate it is the commercial system of buying and selling – as Estella tells Pip, it is now to be built on.

Two balanced clauses contrast the morning mists when Pip left the forge for London with the evening mists rising now. There is an intratextual link back to the end of chapter 20: 'And the mists had all solemnly risen now, and the world lay spread before me' (we may notice the intertextual link to *Paradise Lost* here as well, with the last clause echoing Milton's line 'The world was all before them'). In the departure of Pip and Estella, there is an emphasis on expansion – 'broad' – and on tranquillity. But the world spread before them at the end of *Expectations* is not the mythical founding moment of human society in which there was no social division, the moment said to have been evoked by John Ball (d. 1381), a key figure in the 1381 Peasants' Revolt: 'Whanne Adam dalfe and Eve span, / Who was þanne a gentil man?' ('When Adam delved [dug] and Eve span, / Who was then a gentleman?'). It is a world in which the stratified social system that helped to produce the plights of Pip and Estella, as it turned them into a gentleman and a lady, is firmly in place and will continue to constrict them.

Pip's final statement remains ambiguous: 'I saw no shadow of another parting from her' could mean they will stay together and marry, but it might show that Pip, in believing that this will be the case, falls once more into the illusory optimism that originally sustained his great expectations. The statement could also mean that he and Estella will remain friends apart, or that this will be the last time they see each other – there will be no other parting because they will not meet again. The alternative phrasing of the final clause, 'I saw the shadow of no parting from her', is again ambiguous, since it could mean the idea of not parting from her, even of marrying her, casts a shadow, perhaps because of their dark mutual history – that the idea of 'no parting from her' is a gloomy rather than joyous prospect.

There is also the original ending, in which Pip and Estella meet in Piccadilly in London when Pip is with little Pip, Joe and Biddy's son. Pip knows of Bentley Drummle's death and Estella tells him she is now married to a Shropshire doctor. She seems to think little Pip is Pip's own child. This ending concludes with Pip's reflection that Estella's face and voice and touch have given him 'the assurance, that suffering had been stronger than Miss Havisham's teaching, and had given her a heart to understand what my heart used to be'. There is no hint here that Estella and Pip might ever marry, and the closing paragraph suggests that Pip may be emotionally atrophied, as Estella once was, and that he has accepted this. It is a less ambiguous and much more downbeat, modern ending. The coexistence of the alternative endings demonstrates the extent to which *Expectations* is not a fixed, definitive work but a mobile and ambiguous one – and this awareness can feed into interpretations of other Dickens novels, such as *Copperfield*, sections of which also exist in the alternative versions that Dickens prepared for his public readings.

Conclusions

We will aim here to summarize the results of our analyses in each chapter of the book, including this one, and to provide a succinct final assessment of Dickens's achievement in *Copperfield* and *Expectations*.

Sons and Patriarchs

Both novels show the impact of threatening male figures on young boys who have lost their fathers. David's father died six months before he was born, and he is happy with his mother and nurse; Murdstone disrupts this idyllic state, insinuating himself into Mrs Copperfield's affections and marrying her while David is away at Yarmouth – so that he returns to Peggotty's announcement 'You have got a Pa!' (*DC* 92). Both Pip's mother and father, and his five small siblings, are dead and Magwitch rises up, like his father's ghost, in the churchyard where they lie. Dickens powerfully evokes the different kinds of threat that Murdstone and Magwitch pose: the first is masked in the middle-class politeness of an apparent gentleman; the second is the raw menace of a hungry, desperate outlaw. But once Murdstone is married and, aided and abetted by his sister, has established his patriarchal authority, the mask comes off to reveal a sadistic control freak, and a violent conflict ensues that leaves David feeling frightened and guilty, as though he were not merely a bad boy, but a criminal. Magwitch also induces terror and guilt in Pip, turning him into a thief. Murdstone will send David away to school, estranging him from his mother and nurse, literally labelling him as vicious ('*He bites*' (*DC* 130)), and pitching the vulnerable boy into a life of isolation. Magwitch will be recaptured and, for a long time, disappear from the story, but he later reveals himself as Pip's secret benefactor and claims he is Pip's 'second father' – a role that involves both paternal benevolence and patriarchal manipulation. Both boys' lives are profoundly changed by the intervention of these patriarchal figures who bring violence and a strong awareness of the wider system of crime and punishment into their lives.

Ladies and Gentlemen

Em'ly, in *Copperfield*, wants to rise in society by becoming a lady; Pip, in *Expectations*, wants to rise in society by becoming a gentleman. Em'ly's desire to be a lady has elements of generosity, whimsicality, naivety, materiality and practicality; she wants to provide her uncle, rather than herself, with luxurious and colourful appurtenances, help the rest of her family and dispense charity to those who will remain fishermen and who, as she recognizes, have a hard and dangerous life. Pip's desire to be a gentleman is driven by his admiration for Estella and the humiliations to which she has subjected him, making him aware of his status as a 'common labouring boy', his coarse hands and boots and his inappropriate vocabulary. Neither Em'ly nor Pip question social division since their aspirations depend on its continued existence. In both cases, their desire leads them into moral danger and unhappiness. Em'ly becomes vulnerable to Steerforth, who affirms that she should have been a lady and that her virtuous suitor, Ham, is unworthy of her. Pip becomes distant from Joe and treats him in a patronizing way that makes him partly a common butt but cannot take away his fundamental dignity. Through Em'ly and Pip, Dickens explores the complex and sometimes contradictory meanings of the ideas and ideals of gentility and ladyhood, showing their basis in social inequality, the potential confusions between outward show and inner virtue, and the moral and social dangers that may arise from the desire to be a lady or gentleman.

Obsessives and Eccentrics

In *Copperfield* and *Expectations*, Dickens creates memorable obsessive and eccentric figures who fascinate, alarm, amuse or endear themselves to the reader. They are vivid examples of modes of psychological deviance that take to extremes feelings and forms of behaviour that are part of most people's lives, and they relate to wider social phenomena, for example the position of women, the treatment of those judged insane, and the split between private and working life. The boundaries between obsessive and eccentric characters are often blurred, since obsession and eccentricity feed each other. Rosa Dartle and Miss Havisham are both malign wounded women, obsessed by the idea of how men have damaged them; Steerforth by his rejection of Rosa, Compeyson by his jilting of Miss Havisham. In Rosa, the outward and visible sign of the wound is a scar, or seam, on her face, which alters the shape of her mouth; this distortion of the orifice through which words come can be linked to the oblique manner of speaking that she adopts with Mrs Steerforth until her outburst against her. In Miss Havisham, the outward and visible sign of the wound is her repeated ritual re-enactment of the moment of jilting, with the dressing of the bride still incomplete and the clock stopped at twenty to nine. Both, in their respective ways, exemplify the relative powerlessness of many women in Victorian England, for whom marriage offered the only acceptable social identity. Mr Dick is a harmless, benign eccentric but he does have an obsession with King Charles's head and he cannot bear to use his family name because his brother wanted to confine him to an asylum; in this last respect, Mr Dick highlights the way in which psychological deviance might be policed by incarceration. John Wemmick's eccentricities – and his more human side – are likewise benign and harmless and have only a tincture of the obsessive. But his house and garden constitute a kind of microcosm of key aspects of Victorian England and his division of his life between work and home makes him representative of a much wider social tendency to split the two spheres, reserving one's humanity for the home and repressing it at work. Dickens's obsessives and eccentrics provide powerful portraits of psychological deviance and illuminate large areas of nineteenth-century English life.

Moments of Truth

Dickens's novels characteristically lead up to revelations of truth. These often take melodramatic, theatrical forms but they are also psychologically penetrating. The denunciation of Heep provokes him to drop his mask of servility and display his full rancour; but David's intensive abuse of Heep in his narrative prose suggests that Heep may be David's dark double, an incarnation of aspects of himself David wants to disown, while Micawber's indictment of Heep displays Micawber's capacity for self-dramatization and reflects to some extent on his own manipulative behaviour. When Rosa denounces Mrs Steerforth, she vividly reveals long-suppressed aspects of herself; the fact that David makes no serious attempt to silence Rosa is also revealing, suggesting that he may share her strength of feeling for Steerforth and her belief that the mother bears the blame for the son's waywardness and is, in a sense, glad to let Rosa articulate these. Magwitch's dramatic return reveals the true identity of Pip's benefactor and shows both the manipulative patriarchal aspects of the source of his expectations – his desire to claim Pip as a surrogate son and to see how he has moulded a vulnerable boy into a gentleman – and the limitations of Pip's own self-concept and sympathies as he learns he is being bankrolled by an ex-convict rather than an eccentric but high-class old lady and has to start to reconfigure his life radically. Miss Havisham's conversion to penitent sinner releases long-frozen emotions but threatens to lock her into repetition again, this time of remorse; it also reflects on Pip's own behaviour towards Magwitch. In each case, melodrama combines with psychological revelation, not only about the chief subject of the revelation but also about others, particularly the narrators.

Dying in Style

Key characters in Dickens die in style – that is, their demise is skilfully orchestrated by Dickens to arouse appropriate emotions in the reader and to contribute to the overall meanings of the works in which they feature. Dickens is sometimes thought of as a writer who summons up the rhetorical equivalent of a full orchestra to his deathbeds to play bittersweet strains that flood the eyes with tears; but his portrayals of death are more varied and often, even in their more plangent phases, engage the intellect as well as the emotions. Dying in Dickens's fiction, as in life, is a time for reconfiguration, reorientation and reflection on the part of all those closely involved. The scene at Dora's deathbed – though she does not actually die at this stage – is muted, and much of the dialogue is devoted to Dora's assessment of her marriage to David and the unlikelihood of their future matrimonial happiness had she survived; she is clear-minded, offering herself and David a means of consolation and preparing the way for the possibility of David's marriage to Agnes. The courtroom scene in which Magwitch and 31 others are condemned to death dramatizes both the inexorability and the inadequacy of the law by setting it in a larger spiritual perspective; the scene also comes to serve as a universal image, not confined to the courtroom: every one of us is condemned to die sooner or later. The deaths of Ham and Steerforth are intensely dramatic, calling forth Dickens's rhetorical powers and conjuring up the sublime forces of nature; but the end of the scene, leading up to David's sight of Steerforth's body, is muted and economical. The scene of Magwitch's death is also muted; unlike the scene with Dora, it does show the actual moment of Magwitch's passing, but it resembles that earlier scene in its economy and simplicity and in the way in which it negotiates a settlement that offers hope for the future: as David may marry Agnes, so Pip may marry Estella. But those hopes are not enough to sustain the narrators immediately; each has to descend further into the depths before they can return to life.

Breakdown and Recovery

These extracts trace the different trajectories of David and Pip as the cumulative force of all their experiences drives them to breakdown. In David's case, the loss of Dora, and then of Steerforth and Ham, leaves him physically intact but in a state of despondency that turns him into a purposeless European wanderer who likens himself to a mortally wounded soldier gradually becoming aware of the extent of the damage and who comes to feel that he is likely to die. But a glimmer of hope wakens in him that is a harbinger of a better future. Pip, dunned by creditors, falls into a delirious fever in which he experiences frightening hallucinations of being an inert unit in a building or machine and of people trying to kill him; but these eventually pass and he becomes aware of a constant, comforting, caring presence whom he finally identifies as Joe and who shows himself to be a true gentle man, in the idealistic, ethical sense. David returns to England and at last proposes to Agnes; for him, this is a complex process in which he must reconcile his memory of Dora, and his sense of Agnes as a guide and a sister rather than a lover, with the prospect that Agnes will become his wife; Agnes herself willingly accepts David's proposal and David can feel that Dora has been incorporated into Agnes and that Dora sanctions the marriage – that, indeed, she already, on her deathbed, handed over David to Agnes. Pip's idea of marrying Biddy is quickly crushed when he finds she has married Joe, and Pip then goes to work abroad, returning 11 years later and making his way to the site of Satis House, where he meets Estella. The possibility that he might at last marry Estella, however, is intimated but left suspended; the ending – and alternative endings – of *Expectations* remain ambiguous.

Copperfield and *Expectations* are two of the great novels of English and world literature. As our analyses have shown, Dickens draws on a rich rhetorical repertoire to dramatize and explore his themes: he varies sentence structure, length and rhythm to achieve different effects; uses grammatical parallelism and anaphora to reinforce his meanings; skilfully balances the proportions of narrative prose, dialogue and indirect speech; suits dialogue to his different speakers, using dialect or Standard English as appropriate; employs elaborate or simple diction as required; uses imagery to enliven his scenes and their significance and to contribute to broader symbolic structures; constructs intratextual links within each novel that enrich specific scenes and give the whole work greater weight and import; and makes intertextual links to other works, such as the Bible, and to other genres, such as fairy tales and melodrama, to provide wider dimensions and perspectives. Dickens also shows a proto-cinematic awareness that was to be developed with the invention of film. *Copperfield* and *Expectations* magnificently exemplify and extend the possibilities of the *Bildungsroman*, the formation-novel that shows the development of its protagonists, their education-by-life; but they also interweave and enrich the other genres on which they draw.

Through his command of generic and rhetorical resources, Dickens is able to explore crucial themes in *Copperfield* and *Expectations*: how children and adults relate to each other, especially sons to surrogate fathers; how aspirations to upward mobility may be compromised by materialism and social division; how human beings, driven by psychological and social pressures, may take strange shapes, obsessive or eccentric, that affect those who encounter them; how truth can emerge in dramatic, life-changing moments; how dying reconfigures those who suffer it and those who survive; how the cumulative weight of painful life-experience may produce both physical and mental breakdown; and how people may recover and reorient themselves in an improved or impoverished future. In these novels, as throughout his fiction, Dickens's overall concern is how to live: what is the proper way to conduct one's life that will balance the demands of self and society and the desires for happiness and goodness? *Copperfield* and *Expectations* provide no simple, one-size-fits-all answers to those questions but, through their use of language and structure to evoke character, scene and event, the novels allow the reader to experience imaginatively the pilgrim's progress of their two protagonists to some kind of hard-won solution. Wherever lives are to be lived, and readers to be found, *Copperfield* and *Expectations* will have vital contributions to make to our knowledge and understanding of the conditions and possibilities of human existence.

PART II

THE CONTEXT AND THE CRITICS

7

Charles Dickens: Life and Works

The life of Charles Dickens was a spectacular success story. From humble beginnings, with little in the way of money, formal education or family connections, he made his mark at the age of 24 with *The Pickwick Papers* (1837) and went on to complete 13 more novels and to become nationally and globally famous. A man of great creativity, enormous energy, strong self-discipline and intense conviviality, he packed a vast amount into his 58 years. But his success was not unshadowed. Some of his experiences in boyhood and early adolescence, especially his spell of employment in a blacking factory at the age of 12, haunted him throughout his life; his marriage to Catherine Hogarth produced ten children but ended in a separation that he procured with ruthless cruelty; his embroilment from his mid-forties with Ellen Ternan, a woman 27 years his junior, left him deeply unhappy; his punishing programmes of public readings in his later years had a manic, near-suicidal quality. The world-class writer, the indefatigable worker, the genial host, the passionate performer, was also a melancholy, driven man; but these painful elements of his life helped to enrich his books.

Charles John Huffam Dickens was born at Mile End Terrace, Landport, Portsmouth on 7 February 1812, the second child of John and Elizabeth Dickens, who had married in 1809. Their first child, Frances Elizabeth ('Fanny'), had been born in 1810. They were to have eight children in all, five sons and three daughters (though one of each gender would die in infancy). Charles's paternal grandparents were servants –William Dickens the butler, Elizabeth the housekeeper – in the Crewe household, a family of wealthy landowners. His maternal grandfather, Charles Barrow, was a senior official in the Navy Pay Office who had to flee England in 1810 after he was discovered to have embezzled public funds. Dickens's own father had worked in the Navy Pay Office since 1805 but retained his post and enjoyed promotion despite the Barrow scandal; his income should have been adequate but for his financial imprudence.

In June 1812, the Dickens family moved to 116 Hawke Street, Portsmouth, the first of a series of moves during Dickens's childhood prompted sometimes by John Dickens's different postings and sometimes by his money problems. In December 1813, the Dickenses went to live at 39 Wish Street, Southsea, and in 1815 they made a much larger move, to London, because John Dickens had been recalled to the Admiralty Offices, then in Somerset House in the Strand. They lodged in Norfolk Street (now Cleveland Street) in Marylebone. But they left the capital early in 1817 for Sheerness, where John Dickens was briefly stationed, and then, in April 1817, progressed to a six-roomed house at 2 Ordnance Terrace, Chatham. In April 1821, they took a slightly smaller house, 18 St Mary's Place, Chatham, perhaps because of John Dickens's financial difficulties. While living there, Charles and his eldest sister Fanny were sent to a nearby school, which seems to have been a good one, run by William Giles, a Baptist minister.

John Dickens was recalled to Somerset House again in June 1822, and the family returned to London, living first of all in a small house at 16 Bayham Street, Camden Town. On 9 April 1823, Fanny, then aged 12, became a pupil at the recently opened Royal Academy of Music; but no money seemed available to allow Charles to pursue his education. In December 1823, the family moved to Gower Street North (now Gower Place), Camden, where Mrs Dickens tried to alleviate their shortage of funds by starting a school; but she acquired no pupils.

Early in 1824, possibly on 9 February, Charles was sent to work at Warren's, a shoe-blacking business run by a Dickens relative, James Lamert. It was located at 30 Hungerford Stairs, off the Strand (where

Charing Cross Station now stands). Charles's main task was to cover and label pots of shoe polish for ten hours a day. The experience was deeply humiliating. In an autobiographical fragment, he famously recalled:

> It is wonderful to me how I could have been so easily cast away at such an age. It is wonderful to me that, even after my descent into the poor little drudge I had been since we came to London, no one had compassion enough on me – a child of singular abilities, quick, eager, delicate, and soon hurt, bodily or mentally – to suggest that something might have been spared, as certainly it might have been, to place me at any common school.

But these feelings were only made public after his death, in John Forster's biography (1872–74). During his lifetime Dickens kept silent about his blacking-factory experience apart from a few oblique references, like Joe's statement, in the *Expectations* extract we discussed in chapter 2, that he and Wopsle 'went off straight to look at the Blacking Ware'us' on their visit to London (*GE* 244).

John Dickens was arrested for debt in February 1824 and confined in the Marshalsea Prison. Soon afterwards, his wife and three younger children went to live with him. Charles himself lodged in Little College Street, Camden Town, and then in Lant Street, nearer the prison. On 28 May 1824, John Dickens was released from the Marshalsea, after going through the insolvency court and inheriting money from his late mother; but there was no immediate release from the blacking factory for his eldest son; Dickens seems to have stayed there for nine or ten more months. John Dickens then quarrelled with the owner and withdrew Charles from the job; but his mother tried to get him re-employed there, which left an indelible wound: 'I never afterwards forgot, I never shall forget, I never can forget, that my mother was warm for my being sent back.'

John Dickens moved with his family to 29 Johnson Street, Somers Town in December 1824. The following year, on 9 March 1825, he retired early from the Navy Pay Office on medical grounds, with a pension after 20 years of service. He then, in April 1825, sent Charles back to formal education, this time at Wellington House Classical and

Commercial Academy in Hampstead Road. Two years later, in March 1827, his father was again in financial difficulties, the Dickens family was evicted for non-payment of rates, and Charles's schooling was cut short once more. The Dickenses moved to 17 The Polygon, a ring of houses close to their previous address, and Dickens, now aged 15, started work as a solicitor's clerk at Ellis and Blackmore of Raymond Buildings, Gray's Inn, Holborn.

In 1828, in a move that would have implications for his son's career, Dickens's father went to work for his brother-in-law, John Barrow, who was starting a newspaper, *The True Sun*, which aimed to compete with *Hansard* in providing reports of parliamentary debates. Dickens left Ellis and Blackmore in November of that year and worked for another solicitor, Charles Molloy of Symond's Inn. After mastering shorthand, he left in 1829 to work at Doctors' Commons, as David does in *Copperfield*. When he turned 18 in 1830, he obtained a ticket for the British Museum Reading Room, where he pursued his self-education. In May the same year, he began a painful and protracted stage of his sentimental education when he met Maria Beadnell, fell in love with her and pursued her in vain for three years. Meanwhile, in 1831, he began working as a reporter for the *Mirror of Parliament* and then also for *The True Sun*. In 1832, he witnessed and recorded the debates on the great Reform Bill of that year. He was a very quick, efficient and accurate reporter but his experience of debates contributed to the scorn for parliamentary politics evident in his fiction, for example *Bleak House*.

Dickens first achieved publication with the story 'A Dinner at Poplar Walk', which appeared in the *Monthly Magazine* in December 1833, and further stories quickly followed. In August 1834, he secured a permanent post as a reporter on the *Morning Chronicle* and in September started to write a series of 'Street Sketches' of London life for the newspaper; he would produce 20 'Sketches of London' for the *Evening Chronicle* and 12 'Scenes and Characters' for *Bell's Life in London*. But in November of that year, John Dickens was once more arrested for debt and taken to Sloman's sponging house, a place of detention for debtors. His eldest son had to pay to get him released. In summer 1835, Charles became engaged to Catherine Hogarth and in December he left his parents' home and took rooms at 13 Furnivall's Inn, Holborn.

Events moved quickly the following year. His debut book, *Sketches by Boz, First Series*, compiled from his newspaper sketches and with illustrations by George Cruickshank, came out on 8 February 1836, the day after he turned 24. It was a collection of essays, stories and sketches, many of them previously published in periodicals, which ranged widely and vividly over aspects of contemporary life, from amateur dramatics to Newgate Prison, and anticipated concerns he would pursue in his fiction. *Boz* enjoyed a good reception and greater success soon followed, coupled with changes in Dickens's personal life. On 17 February 1836, Dickens moved to 17 Furnivall's Inn; the first monthly instalment of *The Pickwick Papers* appeared on 31 March; and two days later, on 2 April, Charles and Catherine were married.

The first four instalments of *Pickwick* sold reasonably well, but sales really took off when the character of Sam Weller appeared in the fifth instalment in August. *Pickwick Papers* would run until November 1837. This loosely shaped episodic novel, which had begun as a series of sketches, follows the hilarious misadventures of Samuel Pickwick and his three fellow Pickwick Club members, Tracy Tupman, Augustus Snodgrass and Nathaniel Winkle, incorporating, among many other incidents, a satirical portrait of a corrupt election campaign at Eatanswill and a breach-of-promise-of-marriage case brought by Mr Pickwick's landlady, Mrs Bardell, that results in his temporary imprisonment and deepens the shadow over the comic proceedings already cast by the interpolated tales in the novel such as 'The Convict's Return'.

The year 1836 ended with the publication, in December, of Dickens's *Sketches by Boz: Second Series*. The first issue of *Bentley's Miscellany*, edited by Dickens, appeared around the start of 1837, and on 6 January his first child, Charles ('Charley') Culliford Boz, was born. In February 1837, the second issue of *Bentley's Miscellany* carried the first of 24 instalments of what would become the novel that would follow Oliver Twist's journey from the workhouse in which he was born, to Fagin's den of boy-thieves in London, to his eventual adoption, after many vicissitudes, by the benevolent Mr Brownlow. *Twist* is memorable for its workhouse scenes (particularly the one where Oliver asks for more gruel); these constitute an attack on both the old Poor Law workhouses and, more topically, the new ones produced by the 1834 Poor Law Amendment Act. *Twist* also aimed to counter the romanticization of crime in contemporary 'Newgate fiction' such as Bulwer Lytton's *Eugene Aram* (1832). The novel was a further success for Dickens.

Dickens, Catherine and her sister Mary Hogarth, and the infant Charley, moved in March 1837 to a 12-roomed house at 48 Doughty Street in London. It seemed that life was steadily improving: then came a harsh blow. On 6 May 1837, Mary, aged 17, fell ill and died the next day. Her death devastated Dickens and he would idealize her memory. It was in the months after Mary's death that Dickens's friendship with John Forster, whom he already knew slightly, developed; they would become lifelong friends (though less close after Forster's unexpected marriage late in life), and Forster would be Dickens's first biographer.

Between 30 January and 6 February 1838, Dickens made a trip to Yorkshire with his illustrator and friend Hablot K. Browne (known as 'Phiz'), where he visited a school on which he drew for the portrait of Dotheboys Hall in *Nicholas Nickleby*. Catherine Dickens gave birth to their second child and first daughter, Mary ('Mamie'), on 6 March 1838. The first of 20 monthly instalments of *Nicholas Nickleby* came out on 31 March 1838. This lively and loosely-structured work follows the fortunes of Nicholas and his sister Kate after their impoverished father dies and they are sent out to work. It is notable for its portrayal of Dotheboys Hall and its brutal owner, Wackford Squeers, its account of Nicholas's life as a strolling player with Vincent Crummles's troupe, its evocations of London life, and its presentation of the vulnerable and ultimately doomed orphan Smike. *Nickleby* proved a huge success, selling nearly 50,000 copies.

Dickens resigned as editor of *Bentley's Miscellany* on 31 January 1839; but he would launch the first of his own magazines the following year. His third child and second daughter, Catherine ('Katey') Elizabeth Macready, was born on 29 October 1839 and in December Dickens moved with his family to 1 Devonshire Terrace, which would be his home until 1851 and where he would write *The Old Curiosity Shop*, *Barnaby Rudge*, *A Christmas Carol*, *Martin Chuzzlewit* and *Copperfield*. The first issue of Dickens's new weekly magazine *Master Humphrey's Clock* appeared on 4 April 1840 and sold nearly 70,000 copies; but sales of subsequent issues fell quickly when readers realized it was not a new Dickens novel. Dickens decided to produce a full-length novel in instalments, *The Old Curiosity Shop*, which ran in the magazine from 25 April 1840 until February 1841. It tells the story of Nell Trent – better known as Little Nell – and her grandfather, the old curiosity shop's proprietor, who flees to the country, taking Nell with him, when he is unable to repay the money he borrowed from the malevolent Daniel Quilp; Nell and her grandfather become beggars and Nell dies before her great-uncle, who is trying to trace her, can find her. The novel attracted a strong following, with readers writing to Dickens to beg him not to let Little Nell die.

On 8 February 1841, Catherine gave birth to Dickens's fourth child and second son, Walter Landor, and on 13 February, the first instalment of Dickens's fifth novel, *Barnaby Rudge*, appeared in *Master Humphrey's Clock*. Its final episode would appear on 27 November of that year, in the last issue of the magazine. *Rudge* was a historical novel set at the times of the anti-Catholic riots in 1780 incited by Lord George Gordon. Its plot turns on the unsolved murder of Reuben Haredale, committed 20 years previously. After the riots, Mr Rudge, Haredale's ex-steward, is unmasked as the murderer and hanged; his half-crazed son, Barnaby, almost shares his fate. The novel, which has never enjoyed great popularity or critical acclaim, is particularly notable for its riot scenes which, while set in the past, touched on contemporary anxieties about the violent potential of Chartism.

At the start of the following year, on 4 January 1842, Dickens took ship with Catherine for America. He arrived in Boston later that month to an enthusiastic reception and then moved on to Worcester, Hartford, New York, Philadelphia, Washington DC, Richmond, Baltimore, Pittsburgh, Cincinnati, Louisville, St Louis, Columbus, Buffalo and Niagara Falls, returning to New York after a visit to Canada that took in Toronto, Montreal and Quebec. Dickens was often fêted on his travels through the States but caused offence and provoked press attacks by raising the topic of international copyright in some of his speeches; the works of English writers enjoyed no copyright protection in the USA and the writers lost out financially, Dickens to a considerable extent, given the popularity of his fiction in America. Dickens enjoyed many aspects of the USA but detested slavery and disliked some American manners, such as the habit of chewing and spitting out tobacco. It was with some relief that he boarded ship at New York on 7 June 1842 for his return voyage to England. He arrived back in Liverpool on 29 June, and set to work on his account of his travels, *American Notes*, which appeared on 19 October. Its sales were good in England and huge in the USA, but it came under fire from some sectors of the American press.

In 1842, Georgina Hogarth, Catherine's 15-year-old sister, moved in permanently with the Dickens family at 1 Devonshire Terrace; she would become Dickens's preferred companion at social events and would stay with him until his death, even after he separated from Catherine. In January 1843, the first instalment of *Martin Chuzzlewit* appeared. *Chuzzlewit* was originally conceived as a study in selfishness and shows its title character escaping the selfishness that is a family inheritance. But it was not popular at first; its first instalment sold only 20,000 copies, much less than Dickens had hoped. In an attempt to raise sales, Dickens packed his young hero off to America; this also gave him the opportunity to unleash some of the stronger criticisms of the USA he had excluded from *American Notes*. But the sales of the novel's instalments never climbed above 23,000. *Chuzzlewit* is notable, however, for the energy and invention that drive its sometimes apparently disorganized narrative and for the characters of Mrs Gamp, the drunken midwife, and Pecksniff, the pompous architect to whom Martin is originally apprenticed.

A story that also tackled the theme of selfishness, *A Christmas Carol*, appeared on 19 December 1843 and was a much greater commercial success, selling 6,000 copies in the short pre-Christmas period and continuing to enjoy good sales into the spring of 1844, by which time it had run through seven editions. It was the first of Dickens's five 'Christmas Books', which would first be published together in 1852. Meanwhile, Dickens's friend, the immensely wealthy heiress and philanthropist Angela Burdett-Coutts, had asked him for his opinion of 'Ragged Schools' for poor children and he sent her an account of his visit to such a school in Saffron Hill. This was the start of a collaboration between Dickens and Coutts on philanthropic projects that would last until the break-up of Dickens's marriage.

Dickens's fifth child and third son, Francis Jeffrey, was born on 15 January 1844. The last episode of *Chuzzlewit* came out on 30 June and on 2 July, Dickens and his family left to live in Genoa in Italy, where they would stay for almost a year. On 16 December 1844, Dickens's second Christmas Book, *The Chimes at Midnight*, was published, and immediately sold 20,000 copies, making Dickens a profit of £1500. His Christmas Books, like the Morecambe and Wise Christmas shows on twentieth-century British television, were becoming an event to which many people looked forward keenly. Dickens returned to England on 9 June 1845 and on 25 October Catherine gave birth to his sixth child and fourth son, Alfred D'Orsay Tennyson. Dickens's third Christmas book, *The Cricket on the Hearth*, was published on 20 December 1845; its first edition of 16,500 copies sold out before the end of the year and went on selling through numerous reprints.

Early in 1846, a newspaper, *The Daily News*, briefly appeared under Dickens's editorship but he resigned as editor within a month. The literary fruits of his Italian sojourn, *Pictures from Italy*, came out on 18 May 1846, to a lukewarm reception but reasonable sales. Later that month he wrote to Angela Burdett-Coutts about his idea of establishing a refuge for fallen women, a major charitable project that they would pursue together with the establishment of Urania House in Shepherd's Bush in London. At the end of May, Dickens left with his family for a stay in Switzerland and lived in Lausanne between June and November, where he started to write *Dombey and Son*. He and his family then moved on to Paris. The first episode of *Dombey* appeared in October 1846 and the Christmas Book for that year, *The Battle of Life*, was published on 19 December; its first printing of 24,000 copies sold out before Christmas Day and earned Dickens £1300 by the end of 1846.

Dombey ran in 20 monthly parts until April 1848. It was Dickens's most carefully planned and unified novel to date, a powerful study of emotional repression and the freezing effects of an obsession with money and property. It traced the cold and severe Mr Dombey's successive losses: of his first wife; of his young son, Paul; of his second wife, who deserts him; of his health; and finally of his business. It is only when all seems lost that he acknowledges the love of his daughter, Florence, who has always loved him but whom he has previously rejected. One of the most notable passages in the novel is the account in chapter 20 of Mr Dombey and Major Bagstock's train journey from London to Birmingham, the most sustained encounter with the transformative, ambivalent power of the railway in Dickens's fiction.

Dickens and his family lived in Paris from November 1846 to 28 February 1847. Soon after their return to England, Dickens's seventh child and fifth son, Sydney Smith Haldimand, was born on 18 April 1847. Dickens's own eldest sister, Fanny, died of consumption on 2 September 1848. *The Haunted Man and the Ghost's Bargain*, the last Christmas Book (there had not been one in 1847), came out on 19 December 1848. It immediately sold 18,000 copies but sales dropped off later. Dickens would continue to write short stories for Christmas but not 'Christmas Books'. Early the following year, on 15 January 1849, Catherine gave birth to their eighth child and sixth son, Henry Fielding; he would live until 1933 and prove the most successful of Dickens's sons, becoming a High Court judge and earning a knighthood; one of his granddaughters, Monica Dickens, became a bestselling author in her own right in the twentieth century. Dickens had called his son Henry Fielding after the great eighteenth-century English novelist; according to Forster, this was 'a kind of homage to the style of the novel he was about to write': *David Copperfield*.

Copperfield came out in 20 monthly parts from April 1849 to October 1850. While he was working on it, the first number of his weekly magazine *Household Words* appeared, dated 30 March 1850. It took its title from a line in the king's speech before the Battle of Agincourt in Shakespeare's *Henry V*, 'familiar in our mouths as household words' (4.3.54), but its focus was on the domestic rather than martial associations of the image. *Household Words* quickly became an established periodical, combining fiction and social commentary and not missing an issue until its final closure on 28 May 1859. Dickens's many contributions, sometimes co-written with others such as his chief assistant on the magazine, W. H. Wills, covered a wide range of contemporary topics. for example, the unhealthy conditions at Smithfield Cattle Market; popular theatres for working-class people; panoramas and dioramas; the solitary confinement of prisoners; the writers of begging letters; Pre-Raphaelite painting (Dickens savaged Millais's *Christ in the House of his Parents* (1849–50)); the establishment of the Detective Branch of the Police; banknote forgeries; the large fees that the York Minster ecclesiastical registry charged for administering wills; the cost of establishing a patent; the papal bull restoring the Roman Catholic hierarchy in England; railway strikes; midwifery; bill-sticking; capital punishment; Bradshaw's *Railway Guide;* the Kent seaside resort of Broadstairs; the National Temperance Society; the new London to Paris rail link; the 'Bloomer' movement for reforming women's dress; the treatment of the insane; pawnbrokers; betting shops; the Duke of Wellington's state funeral; the river police; an asylum for prostitutes; the Preston cotton-mill workers' strike of 1853–54; the language of barristers; the effect of railway construction on Camden Town; the mismanagement in the Crimean War; and the Northcote–Trevelyan Report on civil service reform. It was also in *Household Words* that Dickens published, irregularly between 25 January 1851 and December 1853, *A Child's History of England.*

Dickens's ninth child and third and last daughter, Dora Annie, was born on 16 August 1850. If her forename was a tribute to the dead Dora of *Copperfield*, this proved sadly appropriate. On 14 April 1851, soon after the death of Dickens's own father on 31 March, which affected him deeply, Dora Annie suddenly went into convulsions and died. In October 1851, Dickens and his family moved to Tavistock House in Bloomsbury, and the first instalment of *Bleak House* appeared in March 1852. On 13 March, Catherine gave birth to their tenth and last child, and seventh son, Edward Bulwer Lytton ('Plorn'). *Bleak House* ran for 20 instalments, the last appearing in September 1853. This massive, sombre, superbly constructed novel remorselessly explores the interactions between the law, money and human irresponsibility, tracing the stories of three people, Esther Summerson, Ada Clare and Richard Carstone, whose lives are overshadowed by the seemingly interminable case of Jarndyce v. Jarndyce in the Court of Chancery. The novel is also notable because it features, for much of the time, a female first-person narrator in the shape of Esther Summerson, who combines moral perception with proper submissiveness and whom we might see partly as Dickens's version of Fanny Price, in Jane Austen's *Mansfield Park*, and partly as his riposte to a recent novel with a perceptive but rebellious first-person female narrator-protagonist, Charlotte Brontë's *Jane Eyre* (1847) – a book which Dickens certainly knew about, though he might not have read it. *Bleak House* also offers, in the character of Inspector Bucket of the Detective Police and in the mystery of who shot the solicitor Tulkinghorn, an anticipation of key elements of the detective story genre.

From October to December 1853, after the completion of *Bleak House*, Dickens went on a tour of Switzerland and Italy with his friend and fellow-writer Wilkie Collins and the painter Augustus Egg. Near the end of 1853, he gave two public readings at Birmingham Town Hall: *A Christmas Carol* on 27 December and *The Cricket on the Hearth* on 29 December. This was a harbinger of the public readings to come. Between 1 April and 12 August 1854, Dickens's tenth novel, *Hard Times*, his only one set in the industrial north of England, appeared in parts in *Household Words*. A compressed, powerful novel, it contrasts the unfeeling world of fact, embodied by Thomas Gradgrind and enacted in the schools and mills of Coketown, with the world of fancy, embodied in the abandoned child Sissy Jupe who grows up in Gradgrind's household and in Sleary's circus. It also follows the progress of an industrial dispute and the fate of the honest workman Stephen Blackpool, expelled from the community and under suspicion of a crime actually committed by Gradgrind's son, Tom.

Little Dorrit, Dickens's eleventh novel, was serialized in 20 instalments in *Household Words* from December 1855 to May 1857 and offers a potent study of corruption and incorruptibility. Amy Dorrit, known as 'Little Dorrit', the youngest daughter of William Dorrit, is born in the Marshalsea Prison, where her father is confined for debt, as Dickens's own father had been. Arthur Clennam befriends them, and his mother gives Little Dorrit a job as a seamstress. Then, in a sudden change of fortune, the Dorrit family become wealthy due to an inheritance, leave prison, and travel in style to Italy, where William dies. Back in England, Clennam ends up in the Marshalsea himself after falling victim to a huge fraud masterminded by Merdle the financier. Little Dorrit discovers Arthur there and he acknowledges her love; when the Dorrit fortune is lost again, the couple are reunited.

While *Little Dorrit* was appearing in serial form, Dickens completed the purchase of Gad's Hill Place in Rochester on 14 March 1856. But the following year his marriage plunged into crisis. He fell for an 18-year-old woman, Ellen ('Nelly') Lawless Ternan, whom he met when she played the minor part of Lucy Crayford in a Manchester production of Wilkie Collins's play *The Frozen Deep* on 21, 22 and 24

August 1857. Ellen's mother Mrs Ternan was cast as Nurse Esther and Ellen's sister, Maria, as the heroine, Clara Burnham. Dickens himself took the lead role of Richard Wardour, Clara's rejected suitor, who rescues his successful rival Frank Aldersley in the Arctic at the cost of his own life. As Dickens's interest in Ellen deepened he found his wife increasingly intolerable. In early September he confided to Forster his feeling that 'Poor Catherine and I are not made for each other and there is no help for it', and the following year, on 9 May 1858, he wrote to Angela Burdett-Coutts, saying 'no two people were ever created, with such an impossibility of interest, sympathy, confidence, sentiment, tender union of any kind between them, as there is between my wife and me'. By then, he and his wife had arranged to separate, with Catherine initially accepting Dickens's settlement terms that gave her a house of her own, £400 a year and a brougham (a four-wheeled carriage). But when Dickens heard that Mrs Hogarth and her daughter Helen had started to circulate rumours that he had an unnamed mistress (by implication, either Georgina Hogarth or Ellen Ternan), he became angry and refused to make any settlement unless they retracted the rumours in writing. After almost two weeks, they capitulated.

Dickens then published a strong denial of the rumours about his association with an unnamed woman in a statement that first appeared in The *Times* on 7 June 1858, and then, headed 'PERSONAL', on the front page of *Household Words* on 12 June: 'I most solemnly declare, then – and this I do both in my own name and my wife's name – that all the lately whispered rumours touching the trouble at which I have glanced are abominably false.' Dickens also gave his manager Arthur Smith a copy of the Hogarths' statement of retraction and a letter that he had himself written in which he claimed that 'some peculiarity of [his wife's] character has thrown all the children on someone else' – that is, that she had been unable to look after her children and that Georgina Hogarth had taken care of them: 'I do not know – I cannot by any stretch of fancy imagine – what would have become of them but for this aunt.' He went on to assert that his wife's 'always increasing estrangement made a mental disorder under which she sometimes labours'. As Dickens had told Smith that he could show the letter to anyone 'who wishes to do me right' or 'may have been misled into doing me wrong', Smith let a journalist see it and it later appeared in the New York *Tribune* and then in English newspapers, bringing more condemnation on Dickens's head for his aspersions on Catherine's maternal capacities and mental stability.

Between 29 April and 22 July 1858, Dickens conducted his first season of public readings in London for money, and from 2 August to 13 November, he undertook his first provincial reading tour. It was a strenuous schedule, with 87 appearances in England, Scotland and Ireland. The tour made him a lot of money – over 1000 guineas a month after expenses – and the affection, indeed adulation, of his audiences gratified him and offset the wounding rumours that had surrounded his separation from his wife. Meanwhile, Ellen Ternan was living with her sister Maria in their family lodgings at 31 Berners Street, off Oxford Street in London. Dickens had now taken the whole Ternan family under his wing. In March 1859, Mrs Ternan and Maria bought the lease of 2 Houghton Place, Ampthill Square, possibly bankrolled by Dickens, though there is no documentary evidence of this. A year later they sold the lease to Ellen when she turned 21 and could own property herself.

Dickens broke with the publishers Bradbury and Evans in 1859 and the last issue of *Household Words* appeared on 28 May that year. In the meantime, he had launched a new weekly magazine, *All the Year Round*, which would prove a great success, its sales surpassing those of its predecessor. Its debut number, which came out on 30 April, contained the opening instalment of his twelfth novel, *A Tale of Two Cities*, which appeared weekly up to 26 November. Like *Barnaby Rudge, Two Cities* was an historical novel, but set this time during the French Revolution. It interweaves the stories of Dr Manette, released after 18 years' wrongful imprisonment in the Bastille; his daughter Lucie, brought up in England; her husband Charles Darnay; and the high-minded ne'er-do-well Sydney Carton, who loves her and who looks very much like Darnay physically. When Charles returns to France and is condemned to death, Sydney Carton, relying on their resemblance, takes his place and goes to the guillotine in chapter 15 with the famous words: 'It is a far, far better thing that I do, than I have ever done.' *Two Cities* proved popular and it can be related both to the potential of unrest in the London of Dickens's time and to the 'Indian Mutiny'.

Dickens undertook a second reading tour through the Midlands from 10 to 27 October 1859, appearing at a new venue nearly every night, and in London, between 24 December 1859 and 2 January 1860, he conducted a series of Christmas readings. On 28 January 1860, his 'Uncommercial Traveller' series, consisting of essays with autobiographical elements, started in *All the Year Round* and would appear at irregular intervals until 5 June 1869. He settled into Gad's Hill Place, supported emotionally and practically by his sister-in-law Georgina, who had followed him there after his separation from Catherine, and by his eldest daughter, Mamie. But he was upset when, on 17 July 1860, his second eldest daughter, Katey, married, against his advice, the painter Charles Allston Collins, younger brother of Wilkie Collins and one of the original members of the Pre-Raphaelite Brotherhood. Her husband would die of cancer in 1873 and Katey then married another painter, Charles Edward Perugini; their one child, Leonard Ralph Dickens, would die in infancy in July 1876, but Katey would become quite a successful artist in her own right, exhibiting at the Royal Academy.

Dickens severed a further link with his past on 21 August 1860, by selling the lease of Tavistock House. *All the Year Round* continued to enjoy good sales until the serialization of Charles Lever's *A Day's Ride* seemed to cause a decline. In October Dickens called 'a council of war' at the magazine's offices. 'It was perfectly clear that the one thing to be done was, for me to strike in.' He struck in with *Expectations*: the first episode appeared in the magazine on 1 December and instalments would continue until 3 August 1861. Conscious that the hero began the novel as 'a boy-child' like the protagonist of *Copperfield*, he reread the earlier novel '[t]o be quite sure I had fallen into no unconscious repetitions'. *Expectations* would become one of Dickens's most successful and critically esteemed works.

Between 14 March and 18 April 1861, Dickens gave six public readings in London, in St James's Hall, Piccadilly, and from 28 October 1861 to 30 January 1862 (with a hiatus due to Prince Albert's death on 14 December), he made a second highly successful reading tour of the provinces. He gave further public readings in London between 13 March and 27 June 1862. He went to stay in Paris, with Georgina and Mamie, in October 1862, and while there, he gave readings for charity at the British Embassy, between 17 and 30 January 1863. On his return to England, he gave 15 readings in London from March to June. On 7 August 1863, he began work on *Our Mutual Friend*. His mother, who had been senile for a long time, died on 12 September and on the last day of the year his son Walter died in Calcutta at the age of 22. Throughout all this time, he continued his relationship with Ellen Ternan, though it is unknown whether it was physically unconsummated, whether it was consummated without issue, or whether, as has been suggested, Ellen had a child by Dickens that miscarried, was aborted, died in infancy or lived on. No conclusive documentary evidence is extant.

Our Mutual Friend, a complex, multiplotted work, appeared in 20 monthly instalments between May 1864 and November 1865. Its main story is that of John Harmon, who is thought to have drowned and conceals his real identity so he can find out about Bella Wilfer, whom he must, by a condition of his father's will, marry to acquire his inheritance. The novel also interweaves the story of Lizzie Hexam and the rivalry for her affections between the lazy barrister Eugene Wrayburn, whom she loves, and the intense schoolmaster Bradley Headstone, who loves her and who eventually tries to kill Wrayburn before meeting his own end in a mutually fatal struggle with his blackmailer, Rogue Riderhood. These stories and the symbolic aspects of the novel, such as its great dust heaps of metropolitan refuse that are also sources of wealth, combine to form an intense, oppressive montage of a fragmented modern society corrupted by materialism.

During the serialization of *Our Mutual Friend*, Dickens, returning from France with Ellen and Mrs Ternan on 9 June 1865, was involved in a serious railway accident in Staplehurst, Kent which killed ten people and badly injured many more. He showed great presence of mind, rescuing the mother and daughter, and the manuscript of part of *Our Mutual Friend*, from a teetering carriage and ministering to the injured and dying with brandy and water from his top hat. After finishing *Our Mutual Friend*, Dickens wrote, with Wilkie Collins, the sketch *Dr Marigold's Prescriptions*, which appeared in the Christmas number of *All the Year Round* and proved a great success, selling more than a quarter of a million copies.

Dickens undertook a further series of public readings between 10 April and 12 June 1866. Organized by Chappell and Company, these began and ended at St James's Hall in London, in the meantime taking in cities such as Liverpool, Manchester, Edinburgh, Glasgow and Aberdeen. The readings went well but took their toll on his already failing health. He was able to recuperate for six months and to produce a Christmas story, 'Mugby Junction', for *All the Year Round*. From 15 January to 13 May 1867, he undertook a second series of readings for Chappell, performing for 42 nights for £2500, moving on an almost weekly basis between London and the provinces and back again. In June he started to rent Windsor Lodge, in Linden Grove, Peckham, for Ellen Ternan and it was there, on 26 June, that he completed the story 'George Silverman's Explanation', which would first be published in the American magazine *The Atlantic Monthly* and the story-series 'A Holiday Romance' which would appear in the American children's monthly, *Our Young Folks*.

Dickens took ship for Boston on 9 November 1867 for his second American visit, which would begin on 2 December and last until 20 April 1868. He undertook 76 readings, a very demanding programme for a man in his fifties in failing health. But he was always able to summon the necessary energy to perform well and the readings proved highly popular and profitable. On 22 April he set off from New York to sail back to England, arriving at Queenstown Harbour on 30 April. Between 6 October 1868 and 20 April 1869, he undertook his 'Farewell Reading Tour'. On 14 November 1868, when his readings were suspended in that month due to a general election, he tried out, for the first time, his reading of the scene of Bill Sikes's murder of Nancy, adapted from *Twist*, before a specially selected audience of 50 critics, artists and writers at St James's Hall. It proved compelling and Dickens gave his first fully public performance of the scene on 5 January 1869. He went on to give 27 more performances. But on 22 April his health collapsed at Preston and his doctor, Frank Beard, forbade further readings, so that he had to return to Gad's Hill Place with 25 readings still outstanding. He started work on *Edwin Drood* in September 1869. On 11 January 1870, he began a series of 12 public readings in London for Chappell, and concluded his last reading on 15 March with the valediction: 'from these garish lights I vanish now for evermore, with a heartfelt, grateful, respectful and affectionate farewell'. His words foreshadowed his more final vanishing act on 9 June 1870 when, after a day's work at Gad's Hill Place on *Edwin Drood*, he died of a cerebral haemorrhage. His death caused a widespread sense of loss in Britain and abroad.

Six of the planned twelve instalments of *Drood* appeared between April and September 1870, the last three posthumously. Dickens tantalizingly left an unfinished novel that many others have tried to complete, along with a huge body of finished work. His oeuvre is remarkable for its rhetorical resourcefulness and its intense curiosity about human life in many of its manifestations at a time of wide-ranging and fast-moving change. It is to this time of change, the historical, cultural and literary context of his life and writing, which we now turn.

8

The Historical, Cultural and Literary Context

The Historical Context

Charles Dickens was born in the year of Napoleon's retreat from Moscow and three years later, in 1815, Wellington's victory over the French emperor at Waterloo marked the end of the Napoleonic Wars and the start of almost a century in which Britain would be free of military involvement in major European conflicts. In June 1837, when Dickens was 25 and publishing the first instalments of *Pickwick Papers*, the young Queen Victoria came to the throne and remained there until her death in 1901. By then, Dickens had been dead for 31 years but he had helped to define the Victorian age. Victoria reigned over, and Dickens wrote in, a country of contradictions: national prosperity and widespread poverty; increasing industrialization and burgeoning anti-industrial attitudes; sharp social divisions and spectacular instances of upward mobility (Dickens himself being a notable example); government regulation (for example, in factory working conditions) and free trade; eschewal of war in Europe and engagement in conflicts further afield; imperial consolidation and armed resistance (most notably in India). Key features of the era were the ongoing industrial revolution; the spread of the factory system; the expansion of the railway; the growth of towns and cities; a rise in population and in emigration to the USA and to British colonies; legislation affecting provision for the poor and working conditions in factories; the triumph of the ideology of free trade; Parliamentary reform that gradually and patchily gave more adult males the right to vote; working-class agitation that focused in Chartism and then the growth of trade unions; the Great Exhibition of 1851; and the Crimean War of 1853–56. We shall look at each of these in turn.

The largest change of the period, which had begun in the later eighteenth century, was what the historian Arnold Toynbee, in 1881, called the industrial revolution. The accuracy of the term 'revolution' is debatable but the phrase has caught on, and, if used circumspectly, it remains a convenient shorthand way to indicate those multiple, partial, diversely paced changes in productive processes and ways of life that took place in Britain before and during Dickens's time and which no society had ever experienced before. A crucial component of industrialization was the factory system, in which production was concentrated in factories where workers – women, children and men – worked in conjunction with and usually in subordination to, machines; as James Kay Shuttleworth put it, 'the animal machine … is chained fast to the iron machine, which knows no suffering and no weariness'. In the 1830s and 1840s it was mostly the textile industries that used the factory system, which displaced the older domestic system, in which textile production had been the task of individual handloom-weavers working in their homes. *Hard Times* was Dickens's most direct portrayal of the factory system.

The railway was both an industry in itself and a key element in the transport and distribution infrastructure of other industries. In the 1830s and 1840s, the growth of the railway absorbed some surplus capital and labour and contributed to a more diversified economy. By 1840 almost 2,400 miles of track joined London to Birmingham, Manchester and Brighton and the later years of the decade of the 1840s were marked by the spread of 'railway mania', partly promoted by George Hudson, known as the 'Railway King', who illicitly used capital raised to build new branch lines to pay dividends on existing routes and had to flee the country when this malpractice and others were exposed in 1848. But by this time railway track mileage had increased to more than 8,000 and the railway network had spread from Aberdeen to Plymouth. The railways did not reap huge profits: by 1849 £224.6 million had been invested, while receipts did not rise above £11.4 million, and although they climbed to £24.4 million by 1859, they gave at best only a relatively small return on investment and could be a way of losing money. Nonetheless they seemed a visible sign of British dynamism and Dickens would register their impact, for good and ill, in his fiction, most vividly in *Dombey and Son*.

Despite industrialization, agriculture remained Britain's largest national industry, employing, according to the 1851 census, about 1,790,000 people. There were also more than a million people who worked in domestic service. But over 1,650,000 people were employed in textiles and more than 65,000 in railways. By 1871 over three-quarters of a million worked in the metal, engineering and shipbuilding trades, with 106,000 engaged in machine-making, and 50,000 in mines and factories. The 1851 Census showed that, for the first time, more people – slightly over half of the population of England and Wales – lived in towns and cities rather than in the countryside.

In 1801, the UK population was 15.74 million; by 1831, it had risen to 24.15 million and by 1851, the year after *Copperfield* was published in volume form, it reached 27.39 million. It increased further by about 5 million between 1851 and 1871, with the birth rate rising from 33.9 per 1000 to 35.3 per 1000 and the death rate falling from 22.7 per 1000 to 22.4 per 1000. In 1830, emigration from Britain to the colonies and USA increased suddenly to 60,000, from a previous maximum of 30,000 annually. It was more than 100,000 in 1832, rose to 130,000 in 1842 and rose considerably above 250,000 in 1847–49. The emigrants went mainly to the USA and to the Canadian provinces, and to the Antipodes, Australia and New Zealand. By 1840 Australia had about 130,000 white inhabitants and persuaded the British government to stop using the colony as a destination for transported convicts (like Magwitch in *Expectations*). In *Copperfield*, Mr and Mrs Micawber, their children, Mr Peggotty, Em'ly, Mrs Gummidge and Martha Endell (Em'ly's childhood friend and later a London prostitute) all go to Australia and improve their lives.

Emigration, in fact as well as fiction, seemed to offer escape from poverty in Britain. The Poor Law Amendment Act of 1834 had addressed the issue of poverty, but with unintended consequences that were to produce some of Dickens's most memorable earlier writing. The Amendment was supposed to remedy the problems caused by the system of outdoor relief for the able-bodied that had emerged during the Revolutionary and Napoleonic Wars. On 6 May 1795, the justices at Speenhamland (now north Newbury) in Berkshire, faced with the rise of the price of bread to an all-time high, set up a system that would provide outdoor relief for families on a sliding scale according to the price of a loaf. Many other places took up this system but it was condemned as very costly and counter-productive, encouraging farmers to pay low wages knowing the poor rate would provide a supplement, and further pauperizing people who were already poor by removing the incentive to work more and inviting them to have more children in order to gain more relief. The Poor Law Amendment Act of 1834 stipulated the provision of indoor relief, in the form of workhouses, for the able-bodied, rather than outdoor relief, and required that the workhouses should be almost as bad as prisons to deter people from entering them. In *Oliver Twist*, the story of a boy born in a workhouse, Dickens highlighted abuses that had already existed under the pre-1834 Poor Law as well as abuses that had emerged due to the Amendment; but the overall effect of *Twist* was to fuel the growing perception that the post-Amendment workhouse was a place of deprivation and brutality whose inmates were famished and fearful.

As well as being concerned with the effect of the new Poor Law, Dickens also took an interest in legislation to improve the conditions of factory workers. The politician and philanthropist Lord Shaftesbury had seen the first effective Factory Act through Parliament in 1833, which forbade the employment of children under 9 in textile factories and tried to limit the working hours and improve the conditions for children aged between 11 and 13. Unlike two earlier ineffective Factory Acts, which lacked any means of enforcement, the 1833 Factory Act was enforced by a team of four inspectors. The 1844 Act limited female labour in textile industries to 12 hours a day and children to 6½ hours but let them be employed from 8 years old. It also introduced measures about fencing machinery and paying compensation for accidents, though this was confined to those under 18. But Shaftesbury was unable to secure anything more than the nominal extension of such legislation to other trades, especially mining. The 1847 Factory Act stipulated that women and young persons should work only a 10-hour day, but employers evaded this requirement.

In 1842, Dickens had written to the *Morning Chronicle* applauding Shaftesbury's attempts to ban women and children from working in mines and attacking the Marquess of Londonderry, a colliery owner who had criticized Ashley's proposals. Between March 1854 and January 1856 eight articles, seven by Henry Morley and one by Morley and Dickens, appeared in *Household Words*, attacking mill owners, and those who supported them with legal arguments, for evading their duty to ensure workers' safety as the 1844 Factory Act demanded. Counter-attacks came from employers' groups and the writer Harriet Martineau; this marked the end of her friendship with Dickens and of her contributions to *Household Words*.

In economic policy, the key debate from the end of the Napoleonic Wars and the 1840s was between protectionism and free trade, and it focused on the Corn Law of 1815 and the campaign to repeal it. The 1815 Corn Law was a protectionist measure, passed after a collapse in prices following the end of the Napoleonic Wars, which forbade the import of corn until the home market price attained 80 shillings per quarter. Its aim was to make landlords, farmers and land labourers more prosperous and secure, but by raising the price of bread it left poor people with less money to buy other farm produce such as eggs, milk and meat and thus reduced the overall profits of agriculture. It also resulted in large price variations because corn prices rose on a bad harvest, then quickly fell as dealers imported corn. An attempt to remedy these problems by introducing a sliding scale in 1828, which imposed high duties, rather than a complete ban, on corn imports when home prices were low, and which gradually lowered the duties as home prices rose, failed because corn-trade dealers and speculators stored imported corn in bonded warehouses (that is, customs-controlled warehouses for holding imported goods until the duty owed on them is paid) and then released it into the market when home prices were peaking, thus again creating a pattern of slump-and-glut.

The Corn Law controversy was a clash between the landed interest, that wanted prices maintained at a high level, and the industrial and commercial interests, that wanted to keep prices low to allow wages to buy more, keep down wage bills and the consequent cost of manufactured goods, and make the corn-exporting countries more prosperous so that they would provide larger markets for British-manufactured cotton goods. Growing agitation led to the foundation in Manchester in 1839 of the Anti-Corn Law League, led by Richard Cobden and John Bright, which campaigned for Corn Law repeal and more generally for free trade. The pressure for repeal was increased by the bad harvests and deep trade depression between 1839 and 1843 that led to these years being dubbed 'the hungry forties'. The economic distress of this period could be attributed to the Corn Laws which, it was argued, raised the price of food and the cost of living by curtailing purchasing power and deterring the export of manufactured goods in exchange for imported corn. Sir Robert Peel, Tory prime minister from 1841 to 1846, lowered the duty on corn in 1842 and, after the failure of the potato crop in Ireland in 1846 raised the spectre of famine, pushed through the repeal of the Corn Law in 1846, although this resulted in his own fall from power and a split in the Tory party (though there were no organized political parties in a twenty-first-century sense at this time). The Whig Lord John Russell replaced him as prime minister and the Tories would hold power for only five of the next thirty years. It was a victory, not only for the Anti-Corn-Law League, but also for the Whigs, who would modulate into the Liberal Party; for the manufacturers in their battle with the landed interest; and for the whole ideology of free trade and *laissez-faire* – the idea that the economy worked best when governments did not try to interfere in it.

In the field of parliamentary reform, the 1832 Reform Act produced only a modest extension of the franchise. It added 217,000 voters to an existing electorate of 435,000, an increase of just under 50 per cent, by giving the vote to such categories as the £10 householder in the towns and, in the counties, the £10 copyholders (holders of land based on manorial records). The Act was more significant for its redistribution of seats: 56 'rotten' boroughs, which had been entitled to return MPs with very few voters, lost separate representation, and 30 others lost one of their two members in the Commons. Representation was given to 40 other boroughs which had lacked it, mostly big new industrial and commercial northern towns such as Manchester, Birmingham, Sheffield and Leeds. 65 more seats went to the counties. The Act also stipulated that potential electors had to register to gain the right to vote. But there was no secret ballot, so it was possible to bring illicit pressure to bear on voters in all kinds of ways. Dickens's portrayal of the Eatanswill election in *Pickwick Papers*, a classic point of reference for accounts of nineteenth-century electoral processes, was set after, not before, the 1832 Reform Act. As the previous chapter observed, Dickens, in his capacity as Parliamentary reporter, had witnessed and recorded the debates on the 1832 Act, but he had little respect for Parliament, reformed or unreformed. The 1832 Act was important in the longer term, however, because it set the precedent that the voting system was not immutable but could be changed by Act of Parliament and because it did provide a modicum of parliamentary representation and increased power to upwardly mobile men from the middle classes – men like Dickens himself. A second Reform Act would not, however, get on to the statute books until 1867. This, in effect, enlarged the middle-class vote in the counties and extended it to the artisans and better-off workers in the towns. It did not stipulate a secret ballot but this measure would finally become law in 1872, two years after Dickens died. The 1867 Act also made it likely that further parliamentary reform would occur before too long, as it did 14 years after Dickens's death, in 1884.

In the 1830s and 1840s, however, the slow pace of parliamentary reform, coupled with increasing industrialization, economic difficulties and the hardships produced by the Poor Law Amendment Act, contributed to the development of the movement of the working classes called Chartism. Its 'People's Charter', drawn up by William Lovett and Francis Place in 1838, consisted of six points: manhood suffrage (that is, all adult males, though no women, should have the vote); a secret ballot; equal electoral districts; abolition of property qualifications for MPs; payment for MPs; and annual parliaments. It presented three large petitions to Parliament, in 1839, 1842 and 1848, and all were rejected. Despite mass demonstrations, some local agitation and violence, and the advocacy of physical force by some of its leaders, it largely collapsed in the later 1840s as a result of growing economic prosperity. In a longer historical perspective, however, all but one of its points (annual parliaments) had been adopted, in effect, by 1918 and have become key features of modern British parliamentary democracy.

With the repeal of the Corn Laws, the collapse of Chartism, and a prospering economy, Britain, though still marked by gross inequalities, entered the 1850s as a richer and more stable society that seemed to unite the interests of commerce, industry and land. It was possible to imagine that the harmony finally achieved at the end of *Copperfield* had also prevailed on a national scale. The start of the decade was marked by a celebration of British achievement in the 1851 Great Exhibition, with Joseph Paxton's Crystal Palace in Hyde Park displaying British scientific, technological, commercial and imperial artefacts. Over 6 million tickets were sold and on one day over 100,000 people visited the exhibition. The profits were later used to build the great South Kensington museums that still thrive in the twenty-first century. But Dickens himself was not overenthusiastic about the Great Exhibition and it is interesting that its name shares an adjective, and the first syllable of a noun ('Great Ex – '), with the title of the novel that Dickens would complete ten years later: *Great Expectations*; a novel which, in its broader social implications, questions the mid-Victorian optimism that the Great Exhibition exalted.

This optimism was qualified in the 1850s by industrial conflict, as the Preston strike on which Dickens drew for *Hard Times* demonstrated; but working-class people were organizing into trade unions rather than into anything resembling the radical mass movement, agitating for national political reform, that Chartism had been; these unions were more limited in their aims but more effective. So, on the whole, the domestic scene in England did seem to be settling down after the privation and unrest of 'the hungry forties'. But there was trouble in foreign parts. Dickens, like many others, was particularly disturbed by the maladministration revealed in the conduct of the Crimean War of 1854–56. The war had come about because of the desire of Britain and France to counter the threat of Russia to the ailing Ottoman Empire, 'the sick man of Europe', and to secure the British sea route to India. After a campaign that was mostly made up of a succession of sieges, whose stasis anticipated the deadlocks of the First World War, the British and French finally succeeded in checking Russian expansive ambitions. But the long supply lines between England and the Crimea produced unprecedented problems in provisioning British troops, and the medical care was appalling – it was at this point that

Florence Nightingale emerged as a national heroine with her efforts to ensure adequate hospital care for wounded or sick British soldiers. The Crimean War was the first in which newspaper reports of the sufferings of British soldiers reached the home country by means of the new technology of the telegraph. Such reports helped to stir up public anger, not only against the Russians, but also against what was seen as the bureaucratic ineptitude of the British government. It led Dickens to create his most memorable image of obstructive bureaucracy: the Circumlocution Office that features in *Little Dorrit*.

The Circumlocution Office is one of the many ways Dickens's novels engage with the historical context in which they emerge. His novels also issue from, and feed into, a rich and complex cultural and literary context, and we now explore this.

The Cultural and Literary Context

Romanticism was the greatest cultural change of the later eighteenth and early nineteenth century, sweeping across literature, painting, music and thought. Its most notable British literary representatives were poets – Blake, Coleridge, Wordsworth, Shelley and Byron – and the many differences between their work exemplify the more general truth that Romanticism was a rich, complex, multifaceted, uneven and sometimes contradictory set of developments which it is important not to oversimplify. But its broad features can be suggested. Romanticism stressed emotion rather than reason; intuition rather than intellect; vision rather than analysis; organic wholes rather than mechanical parts; the concrete rather than the abstract; the particular rather than the general. Whereas the emphases earlier in the eighteenth century had been on reason and a sober acceptance of limitations, and then on enlightenment and the capacity of the rational human mind to illuminate and improve the human condition, Romanticism stressed those irrational, sometimes dark aspects of human experience that could lead to a deeper vision than mere reason could provide, but also to violence and self-destruction.

Historical events may have given rise to these concerns and certainly seemed to confirm their importance: the French Revolution, ostensibly based on enlightenment principles, had at first looked like an exhilarating liberation – 'bliss was it in that dawn to be alive', as Wordsworth's *Prelude* famously put it – but had turned into a bloody mechanism of destruction, devouring even its own supporters. Napoleon's conquests seemed to re-create mythic heroism in the modern world – as Stendhal wrote in the opening of his novel *La Chartreuse de Parme* [*The Charterhouse of Parma*] (1839), Napoleon's entry into Milan on 15 May 1796 'taught the world that after so many centuries Caesar and Alexander had a successor' – and to announce the triumph of the individual will, Faustian and Promethean, rather than the march of an impersonal reason. Even the industrial revolution, whose dark satanic mills and regimented Coketowns might seem anti-Romantic, could be regarded, from another perspective, as an astonishing combination of human imagination and natural energies that drove furnaces and factories and would lead, in the Victorian era, to the visionary but viable projects of Isambard Kingdom Brunel.

In nineteenth-century England, however, Romanticism had a powerful philosophical and practical rival: Utilitarianism. The leading exponent of this philosophy was Jeremy Bentham, who saw human beings as primarily motivated by their desire to pursue pleasure and avoid pain and who proposed the happiness principle – the greatest happiness of the greatest number – as the criterion for moral and social evaluation and action. Bentham's ideas were the basis of the approach of the 'philosophic Radicals' and proved highly influential in the social reforms of Victorian England. Utilitarianism was closely associated with two other major movements of thought: Malthusianism, and political economy (what we now call 'economics'). Malthusianism was derived from Thomas Malthus's *An Essay On the Principle of Population As It Affects the Future of Society* (1798) which argued that, as unchecked population 'increases in a geometrical ratio' while subsistence 'increases only in an arithmetical ratio', population must always exceed the means of subsistence unless controlled by 'preventive' checks (not marrying), 'positive' checks – 'the distresses which they [the lower classes] suffer from the want of proper and sufficient food, from hard labour and unwholesome habitations' – and 'vicious customs with respect to women, great cities, luxury, pestilence, and war'. This could seem to imply that hunger, arduous toil and poor housing were necessary to control the population and prevent more widespread hunger.

The 'classical' version of political economy that became dominant in nineteenth-century Britain had been formulated by Adam Smith, in *The Wealth of Nations* (1776; 1784), and developed by David Ricardo in *On the Principles of Political Economy and Taxation* (1817; 1821) and James Mill in *Elements of Political Economy* (1821). Political economy argued that free trade, the unrestricted operation of markets without government interference, would result in greater prosperity and harmonize a multitude of differing individual interests and activities by the working of what Smith memorably called 'an invisible hand'.

Utilitarianism, Malthusianism and classical political economy were enormously influential in shaping ideas, ideology and economic and social policy in nineteenth-century Britain, but they came under attack for being too abstract and mechanical, for denying the human emotions, needs and complexities that Romanticism had highlighted. The philosopher John Stuart Mill, brought up by his father, James Mill, as a disciple of Utilitarianism, came to feel that it was too arid a philosophy which should be supplemented by the kinds of insights that the Romantics, particularly Coleridge and Wordsworth, could provide. Utilitarian elements feature in Dickens's disciplined, hard-driving conduct of his personal life, his finances and his writing and editing career, and in his philanthropic projects, such as Urania House, the home he and Angela Burdett-Coutts established for fallen women and for which he drew up a distinctly Utilitarian regime. But Dickens was more allied by temperament to Romanticism rather than Utilitarianism, and *Hard Times* is a concentrated attack on Utilitarian excesses applied to education and the organization of social life.

Hard Times is dedicated to Thomas Carlyle, who was a major influence on Victorian thought, both through his social analysis, which mixed reactionary and radical perceptions, and his bravura style, with its vivid dramatization of issues, and its quirky coinages that could capture the quintessence of a topic. He had risen to fame with *The French Revolution* (1837), a history of the upheaval that cast its sanguinary, sublime shadow over the nineteenth century, and, in the later 1830s and early 1840s, he produced several key works of social and cultural criticism. *Chartism* (1839) affirmed that 'for the idle man there is no place in this England of ours', but attacked the 1834 Poor Law Amendment Act, which had been intended to drive every able-bodied man to work or to the workhouse, as an attempt to obscure rather than obviate poverty: 'To believe practically that the poor and luckless are here only as a nuisance to be abraded and abated, and in some permissible manner made away with and swept out of sight, is not an amiable faith' (12). He attacked *laissez-faire* and what he called 'self-cancelling Donothingism' and argued that 'Cash Payment' had become 'the universal sole nexus of man to man' – 'and there are so many things which cash will not pay!' *On Heroes, Hero-Worship and the Heroic in History* (1841) contended that 'Universal History, the history of what man has accomplished in this world, is at bottom the History of the Great Men who have worked here' and that the hero as Man-of-Letters, that new and 'very singular phenomenon', 'must be regarded as our most important modern person', thus constructing a dominant and heroic role for writers like himself or Dickens. *Past and Present* (1843) addressed the apparent paradox, in the 1840s, of unprecedented prosperity and unparalleled privation: 'We have more riches than any Nation ever had before; we have less good of them than any Nation ever had before.' *Past and Present* contrasted the medieval and modern worlds and stressed the importance of the hero.

The man of letters was not, however, the only Victorian contender for the role of modern hero. Carlyle himself had spoken of 'captains of industry' and Samuel Smiles cast inventors and entrepreneurs as the heroic figures of the industrial age in such biographies as *George Stephenson* (1857), *Lives of the Engineers* (1861–62) and *Lives of Boulton and Watt* (1865). Smiles's best-known book, *Self-Help: With Illustrations of Character and Conduct* (1859) assembled a range of success stories to show what self-reliance and individual effort could supposedly achieve – an emphasis that fitted in well with classical political economy. *Self-Help* sold very well and many of its ideas concurred with those of Dickens; its final chapter 'Character – The True Gentleman' delineates an ideal – 'Gentleness is indeed the best test of gentlemanliness' – close to that upheld in *Expectations*. Dickens also satirized, however, the possible distortions of the 'self-help' mentality, for example in Josiah Bounderby in *Hard Times*.

If ideas of self-help chimed conveniently with classical political economy, they were also rooted in the religious cultures of nineteenth-century England, particularly its nonconformist varieties. In the previous century, Methodism had mounted a vigorous challenge to a rather inert Anglican church and the first response within Anglicanism had been the development of Evangelicalism. Particularly important in this respect was the 'Clapham Sect', a loose association of wealthy Evangelicals which was so named because most of its members lived near and worshipped in Clapham in London; their most famous member was William Wilberforce, leader of the campaign to abolish slavery. Evangelicalism emphasized personal conversion and living one's life in the spirit of biblical precepts. Evangelicals were prominent in missionary work, the establishment of the British and Foreign Bible Society in 1804, the growth of Sunday Schools, and working for social reform. In 1846, the interdenominational Evangelical Alliance was formed, to promote 'an enlightened Protestantism against the encroachments of Popery and Puseyism'.

'Popery' was Roman Catholicism and 'Puseyism' was one of the names for the High Church Tractarian movement that had begun as the Oxford Movement in the 1830s when Edward Pusey, John Henry Newman, John Keble and Richard Froude, all Fellows of Oriel College, and Isaac Williams, Fellow and Dean of Trinity, had preached and written against liberal theology. They contributed to a series of *Tracts for the Times* which appeared between 1833 and 1841 and mutated from pamphlets to theological treatises. Newman, who had written the first tract, also wrote the last, *Tract XC* [90], which argued, explosively for the time, that the Anglican 39 articles and Roman Catholic doctrine were compatible. The controversy this provoked brought the series to an end and four years later, in 1845, Newman became a Roman Catholic, leaving Pusey as the leader of the High Church movement within the Church of England; Pusey remained an Anglican but sought a rapprochement with Rome. The High Church movement pushed the Evangelicals closer to the Nonconformists. Dickens himself had little taste for doctrinal debate, but he had read and approved the controversial collection *Essays and Reviews* (1860), which advocated a liberal Christianity that accommodated modern biblical scholarship and recent scientific findings, and a broad current of religious feeling, based upon the New rather than the Old Testament and emphasizing compassion, repentance and forgiveness, runs through his novels, as our analyses of *Copperfield* and *Expectations* have shown.

The arguments between Anglicanism and Roman Catholicism and, within Anglicanism, between High, Low, Broad and Evangelical churches were arguments within a general assumption that Christianity, and the existence of God, were valid beliefs. There were two main challenges to this assumption. One came from the 'Higher Criticism', developed by eighteenth- and nineteenth-century German scholars, which read the Bible as literature by diverse hands rather than the divinely inspired word of God. David Friedrich Strauss's *Das Leben Jesu* [*The Life of Jesus*] (1835–36), which redefined the supernatural elements of the Gospels as mythic rather than miraculous, made an especially significant impact on English culture. George Eliot's English translation of this book appeared in 1846 and its arguments contributed to her later loss of faith.

The other challenge to religion came from science, particularly in the form of two books accessible to a general reader. One was Sir Charles Lyell's *Principles of Geology* (1830–33), which argued, from geological evidence, that the earth was much older than the biblical account suggested – in *Annales Veteris et Novi Testamenti* (1650) Archbishop Ussher had worked out from the Bible that it was created on 23 October 4004 BC. Then in 1859 Charles Darwin's *On the Origin of Species* proposed that human beings and other species had evolved by natural selection rather than being created by God. Darwin's 'bulldog', T. H. Huxley, vigorously defended the theory of evolution and coined the word 'agnosticism' to indicate the position that nothing is or can be known of the existence of God. Dickens owned copies of *Principles of Geology* and *Origin of Species* and was interested in geological discoveries; the first paragraph of *Bleak House* evokes a muddy November in London in which 'it would not be wonderful to meet a Megalosaurus, forty feet long or so, waddling like an elephantine lizard up Holborn Hill'. Science and the Higher Criticism seem to have left Dickens's own faith undisturbed; these developments did, however, contribute to a cultural climate in which the religious element in his novels might seem insufficient to counteract their darker aspects.

All the cultural elements we have discussed are closely involved with printing which, in the absence of radio, television or the internet, was still the major means of disseminating fiction, poetry, history and ideas. Blake, Coleridge, Wordsworth, Shelley, Byron, Ricardo, Mill senior and junior, Carlyle, Smiles, Pusey, Newman, Keble, Froude, Williams, Strauss, Lyell, Darwin, Huxley: all spread their work through the printed word in the form of books, pamphlets, and articles in influential periodicals such as the *Fortnightly Review* and the *Cornhill Magazine*. In this fertile and multifaceted cultural scene, the novel became increasingly important. The 1840s marked the start of an especially rich period for fiction: as well as Dickens's work, there was Thackeray's *Barry Lyndon* (1844) and *Pendennis,* and the appearance of several debut novels: Anthony Trollope's *The McDermots of Ballycloran* (1847), Charlotte Brontë's *Jane Eyre*, Emily Brontë's *Wuthering Heights* and Mrs Gaskell's *Mary Barton* (1848).

Mary Barton was an example of a kind of fiction that became significant in the 1840s, stimulated and influenced by Chartist agitation and by the writings of Thomas Carlyle in *Chartism* and *Past and Present*. This was the 'Condition of England' novel that dealt with contemporary social problems, particularly those of the industrial poor, and tried to suggest remedies for them – usually ones that stopped short of legislative change and whose main ingredient was a change of heart. Examples included Mrs Gaskell's later *North and South* (1855), Disraeli's *Coningsby* (1844) and *Sybil* (1845), Charlotte Brontë's *Shirley* (1849), Charles Kingsley's *Alton Locke* (1850) and *Yeast: A Problem* (1851) and Dickens's own *Hard Times*.

Dickens thus worked, in the years in which he was writing *Copperfield* and *Expectations*, among a particularly rich and various crop of novelists, who differed with, learnt from and competed against one another, who extended the technical and thematic range of fiction, who showed the capacity of the novel both to entertain and to engage with a wide range of personal and social issues, and who enjoyed wide and involved readerships, particularly through the medium of serial publication, which made readers want to know what happened next and even try to intervene to change it (as with the pleas Dickens received, while writing *The Old Curiosity Shop*, to reprieve Little Nell). It was a cultural and literary context in which novelists could thrive and Dickens took full advantage of it.

Even in his own lifetime, however, a change was coming about in attitudes to the novel that would cast a colder, more critical light on his work. The fertility, variety and popularity of the novel led to a sense, especially among more intellectual writers such as George Eliot and her partner G. H. Lewes, that it should be brought under control, turned into a respectable art form rather than an apparently rough-and-ready means of dealing with experience, and that this reshaping should be achieved by applying to the novel ideas derived from Romantic aesthetics: the novel should be an organic unity and produce a seamless illusion of reality. This sense becomes apparent in George Eliot's work and is later adopted and elaborated by Henry James, who memorably calls certain kinds of nineteenth-century novels 'large loose baggy monsters, with their queer elements of the accidental and the arbitrary'; his examples are Thackeray's *The Newcomes* (1853–55), Alexander Dumas's *The Three Musketeers* (1844) and Tolstoy's *War and Peace* (1869), but it is easy to see how Dickens's novels might fit the description. We will pursue the question of Dickens's critical standing in the next chapter, where we sample key readings of *Copperfield* and *Expectations*.

9

A Sample of Critical Views

Both *Copperfield* and *Expectations* won great praise in early reviews, but with some reservations. For example, the *Athenaeum* (23 November 1850) voiced its strong opinion that *Copperfield* was 'in many respects [Dickens's] most beautiful and highly finished work', but it did detect 'one or two strained incidents and forced scenes', such as Rosa Dartle's tirade against the fallen Em'ly. Eleven years later, the *Atlantic Monthly* (September 1861) called *Expectations* 'an artistic creation' that 'demonstrates that Dickens is now in the prime ... of his great powers' but found less 'quotable epithets and phrases' than in *Dombey* or *Copperfield*. These reservations foreshadowed the shape of things to come: in the years after Dickens's death, an increasingly critical view of his work developed, fostered by figures such as G. H. Lewes. This persisted into the mid-twentieth-century, culminating in the exclusion of Dickens from the top rank of English novelists by the most influential British literary critic of the time, F. R. Leavis. In *The Great Tradition* (1948), Leavis dismissed Dickens's 'genius' as that of a 'great entertainer' who (with the exception of *Hard Times*) failed to offer the 'adult mind' a 'challenge to an unusual and sustained seriousness' (Leavis 9). This edict inhibited the development of Dickens criticism in Britain and meant that original critical work on the country's most famous novelist progressed more quickly in the USA. It is to a notable example of such criticism that we turn first.

J. Hillis Miller

J. Hillis Miller's *Charles Dickens: The World of His Novels* (1958) chooses 'the theme of the search for a true and viable identity' as a 'salient approach' to Dickens's 'imaginative universe' (Miller x). *Copperfield* is the first Dickens novel 'to organize itself around the complexities of romantic love' and see 'marriage, in a more than conventional way' as 'a solution to the problem of solitude and dispossession' (Miller 150). It is above all 'a novel of memory, a *Bildungsroman* recollecting from the point of view of a later time the slow formation of an identity through many experiences and sufferings' (Miller 152), and it possesses 'a duration and a coherence denied to all the third-person narratives among Dickens' novels'; the 'spiritual presence of the hero organizes all these recollected events, through the powerful operation of association, into a single unified pattern which forms his destiny'. But the novel also contains 'repeated references to a very different kind of unifying presence' (Miller 155): 'the power of divine Providence'. This creates a dilemma: does David make himself through his organization of his memories, or is he a product of Providence? To consider how the novel resolves this dilemma is 'to reach the very heart of its central dramatic action: the developing relationship between David and Agnes' (Miller 156).

In contrast to earlier critics such as G. K. Chesterton and George Orwell, who see David's marriage to Agnes as an artistic flaw, Miller finds it crucial to the resolution of the novel. 'David has that relation to Agnes which a devout Christian has to God, the creator of his selfhood, without whom he would be nothing.' It is only 'in the perspective of his total recollection of his life' that David can see that it is less 'his own mind' than 'the central presence of Agnes which organizes his memories and makes them a whole' (Miller 158). David has thus 'both made himself and escaped the guilt which always hovers, for Dickens, over the man who takes matters into his own hands' (Miller 159).

Miller finds *Expectations* 'a radical revaluation' of the 'solution of Dickens' central problem' offered by *Copperfield* (Miller 159). It is 'the most unified and concentrated expression of Dickens' abiding sense of the world', and we could call Pip 'the archetypal Dickens hero' (Miller 249). Dickens needed 100 pages at the start of *Copperfield* to express what the brief, concentrated opening of *Expectations* conveys much more potently. Like other Dickens heroes and heroines, Pip is isolated, without ties to nature, family or community, and feels guilty because of his very existence, and because he must generate his own values, fashion his own aim, grasp his place in a society which seems to offer only one kind of human relationship: 'that of oppressor to oppressed', or vice versa (Miller 254). For example, Wemmick, dominated by Jaggers, dominates in his turn the prisoners whose 'portable property' he acquires. But becoming an oppressor, even on a small scale, brings guilt. One way to try to avoid this is to attempt to avenge one's oppression through another person, as Magwitch does by making Pip into a gentleman, whose social role will justify his disdain for other people, or as Miss Havisham does through making Estella the instrument of her revenge upon men. In this way, neither Magwitch nor Miss Havisham will feel guilty because it is someone else, not themselves, who is carrying out the oppression; Pip will not feel guilty because he will see the status of gentleman as his right rather than something he has grasped of his own volition; and Estella will not feel guilty because she has no heart. But the 'attempt to transcend isolation without guilt, by paradoxically both being and not being another person whom one has created, in both cases fails' (Miller 259). Miss Havisham wants to eliminate Estella's compassionate and loving feelings for men while securing Estella's love solely for Miss Havisham herself, thus creating an ideal relationship of the kind she failed to have with Compeyson; but Estella turns against her. Magwitch returns to see the gentleman he has made, but once Magwitch tells Pip that he made him, Pip stops believing that he is a gentleman, because his maker is a convicted criminal, and recoils from Magwitch with horror. Both Estella and Pip turn against the person who has made them because of the way in which they have been made.

A third way of trying to establish a place in society, while staying free of the guilt involved in trying to grab a place for oneself, is to fantasize that one's place has already been prepared. This is what happens when Jaggers tells Pip he has 'great expectations', and Pip believes Miss Havisham is probably his benefactress and Estella his destined bride. But when he becomes a gentleman, before he knows who his benefactor is, he still feels unsettled and guilty, frittering away his time and money, and experiencing a lack of direction and identity, and a continued sense of isolation from any community. Once he discovers that his benefactor is Magwitch, his claim to the title of gentleman collapses and he is returned to the original moment of the story and his initial sense of social isolation on the marshes, compounded by an awareness that his own actions and self-deceptions have led him (back) to this state.

Pip finds his escape from this depth of despair through love, first of all for Magwitch.

> His acceptance of Magwitch is not only the relinquishment of his great expectations; it is also the replacement of these by a positive assertion that he, Pip alone, will be the source of the meaning of his own life. Pip finally accepts as the foundation of his life the guilt which has always haunted him: his secret and gratuitous act of charity to the escaped convict …he cannot erase this act from existence. He can only betray it, or reaffirm it.   (Miller 274, 275)

Pip chooses to reaffirm it. This enables him to join with Estella in a relationship in which he can fuse with her but also acknowledge and uphold 'the irreducible otherness, the permanent area of mystery in the loved one' (Miller 277). Only when each of them has been, in their respective ways, humbled – Pip by his discovery of his benefactor, Estella by her marriage to Bentley Drummle – can they escape from oppressive relationships and meet in mutual recognition. In contrast to critics like George Gissing and Edmund Wilson, Miller prefers the revised ending, asking whether Dickens would really have accepted Lytton's suggestions without good reasons of his own and asserting that 'the second ending, in joining Pip and Estella, is much truer to the real direction of the story' and that they 'go forth from the ruined garden into a fallen world' in which 'their lives will be given meaning only by their own acts and by their dependence on one another' (Miller 278).

Miller provides interpretations of *Copperfield* and *Expectations* which are both philosophically sophisticated and rooted in the detail of the text. We can move from this to the more empirical, down-to-earth reading, also rooted in textual detail, by the English critic Barbara Hardy.

Barbara Hardy

In *The Moral Art of Dickens* (1985), Barbara Hardy contends that Dickens's fiction is 'primarily concerned with the nature of society' and portrays socially conditioned characters, but includes 'a continuing fantasy about the ideal, the unconditional virtue', and it is this virtue that often survives. Dickens's novels 'show a division between the society he rejects and the humanity he believes in, and that humanity, in different ways, is somehow preserved, frozen, shut off, and saved from the social pressure'. One of the main characteristics of his fiction is 'the double emphasis, on the power and glory of human love, and the power and horror of contemporary society' (Hardy 4–5).

Copperfield contains less overt social criticism than Dickens's other work. It lacks the detachment of *Expectations*, in which the psychological themes express social ones and which is simultaneously a portrayal of an individual and of key elements of the broader society. In *Copperfield*, David 'often reveals – or rather *betrays* – Victorian limitations' invisible to the author but all too glaring to 'the modern reader' (Hardy 123, 124; original emphasis). Such a reader is unlikely to share David's assumption, in regard to Dora, that 'every man deserves a good housekeeper', though they can still sympathize with David's attempt to accept Dora for what she is. They may also find it difficult to credit what Hardy calls 'one of the strangest portraits of an artist ever written', in which David's principal quality as a writer is a capacity for hard work, though they may assent to the characteristics of 'humane curiosity and shrewd observation' that David displays from his earliest days as signs of the novelist-to-be (Hardy 124, 125).

Hardy also feels that Dickens's reliance on 'a context of religious reverence' to achieve some of his effects – for example likening Agnes to a figure in a stained-glass window (*DC* 280)– will probably 'send a fair number of his modern readers racing off in the opposite direction' (Hardy 127). While acknowledging the historical relativity of such responses, she nonetheless finds that 'the religious/feminine ideal presented in Agnes is repulsive, and the childlike/feminine/sickly appeal of the dying Dora only slightly less so' (Hardy 127–8).

Hardy praises the portrayal of childhood in *Copperfield* while stressing that we should see it 'as part of the psychology of the whole character [of David], a study in isolation and the novelist's imagination' (Hardy 128). But the unevenness of the novel means that we can see David as 'a complex thinking and feeling character' only to a certain extent. Hardy accepts the view of critics such as Gwendolyn B. Needham (see 'Further Reading') that *Copperfield* is unified around the theme of the 'undisciplined heart' (*DC* 730, 733, 885, 886), but denies that this is the key to *Copperfield*'s power. The novel's force comes, rather, from 'the intense and local shafts which strike deep as human insights, honest revelations, and dramatic communications' (Hardy 129). In Hardy's view, *Copperfield*'s 'very neat graph of progress' shows Dickens falling into the 'moral and psychological fallacy' of 'identifying diagnosis with remedy' (Hardy 130): once David recognizes his undisciplined heart, he can fairly easily bring it under control. But we are only *told* that David comes to terms with his marriage to Dora, rather than shown it in dramatized scene and psychological detail. Summary and evasion replace in-depth portrayal of 'the disenchanted life' and Dora's death, fusing the Victorian literary convention of 'the Providential death' with 'wish-fulfilling fantasy', releases David for a new start (Hardy 131, 132).

Turning to *Expectations*, Hardy focuses on the significance of meals in the novel. She does not see the meals as symbols; they 'convey no more ... than the elementary implications of natural domestic and social order, given particularity by the context of the novel' and involve 'nothing of the movement from a first term to a second associated with symbolism' (Hardy 140–1). But they do accumulate significance. The first meal is '*demanded*', with menaces, by Magwitch, in chapter 1 of the novel (Hardy 141; original emphasis). But Pip turns Magwitch's rough meal into a ceremonious repast, treating him politely and feeling compassion for him, and arousing Magwitch's gratitude. 'I said I was glad you enjoyed it'. / 'Thankee, my boy. I do' (*GE* 50). Hardy argues that this meal provides 'a model of ceremony' which 'controls our response to the many related descriptions of meals' later in the novel (Hardy 143–4). Gratitude and compassionate love recur in chapter 5, when Magwitch, to shield Pip, claims that he stole the food himself and Joe responds by saying 'God knows you're welcome to it – so far as it was ever mine ... We don't know what you have done, but we wouldn't have you starved to death for it, poor miserable fellow-creatur. – Would us, Pip?' (*GE* 71).

There is a contrast between the first rough but ceremonious meal in *Expectations* and Pip's first meal at Satis House, where Estella gives him 'some bread and meat and a little mug of beer'. Like Magwitch's meal in the cemetery, this takes place in the open air; but there is no politeness or sign of compassion: Estella 'put the mug down on the stones of the yard, and gave me the bread and meat without looking at me, as insolently as if I were a dog in disgrace' (*GE* 92). But Pip still eats, and the meal is adequate and energizing: the 'bread and meat were acceptable, and the beer was warming and tingling, and I was soon in spirits to look about me' (*GE* 93). Back at the forge, however, he lies elaborately and inventively about the meal, creating an antithesis of the reality that nonetheless preserves its hierarchical and 'bizarre' features (Hardy 145): 'cake and wine on gold plates', eaten in 'a black velvet coach' (*GE* 97). Pip does so out of fear of being misunderstood and because he feels 'that there would be something coarse and treacherous in my dragging [Miss Havisham] as she really was (to say nothing of Miss Estella) before the contemplation of Mrs Joe' (*GE* 95). So his lies are due to a desire to protect not only himself but others, Miss Havisham and Estella, as Magwitch lied to the soldiers to protect Pip; and also to a desire to endow his first meal at Satis House with due ceremony.

The first meal in the novel is echoed again on Magwitch's return. In telling Pip his story, he recalls working in Australia as 'a shepherd in a solitary hut' and sometimes, in his isolation, seeing Pip's face: 'I drops my knife many a time in that hut when I was a eating my dinner or my supper, and I says, "Here's the boy again, a looking at me whiles I eats and drinks!".' Magwitch links this with his determination, if he gets money and freedom, to 'make that boy a gentleman' (*GE* 337). But, as Hardy points out, the gentleman Magwitch has made now looks at Magwitch eating with none of the compassion that the boy once did but finds him repellent – 'uncouth, noisy, and greedy' (*GE* 346). As Hardy puts it, 'the food is not sauced with ceremony' (Hardy 146).

For Hardy, Miss Havisham is one of the most salient failures in love in *Expectations* and food provides graphic evidence of this. 'Her love-feast is preserved in its decay to make the most conspicuous contribution to the themes of love and nature.' A 'gruesome parody of ceremony' is all that remains of 'the expectations of Satis House'

(Hardy 153). As Jaggers points out to Pip, we never see Miss Havisham eat and drink.

> Miss Havisham's rejection of ordinary public meals is like her attempt to shut out the daylight. Food in *Great Expectations*, as in *Macbeth*, is part of the public order, and the meals testify to human need and dependence, and distinguish false ceremony from the ceremony of love. They are not literary symbols but natural demonstrations.   (Hardy 154–5).

Hardy's emphasis on 'natural demonstrations' rather than literary symbols provides an interesting alternative to Miller's attention to the philosophical implications of the novels. A third perspective is offered by Harry Stone, who acknowledges the natural elements of *Copperfield* and *Expectations*, but sees them as strengthened and enhanced by supernatural, fairy-tale features.

Harry Stone

In *Dickens and the Invisible World: Fairy Tales, Fantasy, and Novel-Making* (1979), Harry Stone explores how fairy tales, in an extended sense that includes 'folklore, myths, legends, enchantments, dreams, signs, recurrences, correspondences … entered Dickens' imagination and shaped his art' (Stone xi). Stone sees *Copperfield* as 'the first consummate rendering' of his 'mature … fairy-tale method', while *Expectations* offers 'a late example' of that 'method' and shows 'how Dickens translated ordinary encounters and everyday circumstances into rich fairy-tale fabling' (Stone xi, xiii).

The 'presiding atmosphere' of *Copperfield* combines 'realism and storybook enchantment' (Stone 194). Thus, for example, 'Betsey Trotwood is David's fairy godmother' but also seems 'a flesh-and-blood reality' (Stone 197, 200). David's journey to Dover after he flees Murdstone and Grinby is 'a pilgrimage from storybook nightmare to storybook felicity' in which the scene at the old man's shop where he sells his jacket (*DC* 239–42) 'combines meticulous realism with wild expressionism' (Stone 211, 215). Uriah Heep is, on the plane of sociological realism, a clerk consumed by envy and resentment, but he is also 'a devil' and 'David's double' (Stone 220).

Steerforth displays 'a host of fairy-tale attributes', most obviously '[m]agical charm, protean changefulness, and spell-like enchantment', and is both a 'larger than life' and 'realistic' character (Stone 227). A 'magical predictiveness, which goes beyond ordinary dramatic irony or foreshadowing, and approaches the occult regions of magic glasses and second sight … plays all over Steerforth's comings and goings' (Stone 228). Steerforth, 'a fallen Lucifer, still astonishingly bright and attractive, still powerful and dominating but evil', is 'David's bad angel' who contrasts with his good angel, Agnes (Stone 230).

Stone proposes that, by 'touching Agnes with supernal and Steerforth with infernal powers, Dickens universalizes the conflict within David and makes it cosmic' (Stone 232). Dickens also intimates from time to time 'that Steerforth is David's double', that they have 'a subtle alter-ego relationship'. Steerforth is 'a completion of the evil in David' and thus 'the mirror image of Agnes who represents …a completion of the good in David' (Stone 233, 237). But Agnes is not a wholly convincing good angel; David's ultimate fusion with her is 'storybook wish fulfillment pure and simple', 'in [Dickens's] old fairy-tale manner'. Agnes does, however, contribute to 'the newer, less arbitrary fairy-tale designs that govern so much of *Copperfield*', when, near the end of the novel, she is 'at the center of a deep movement of recapitulation, recurrence, and closure' (Stone 271, 273).

Rosa Dartle is both 'a storybook character of great power and potency' and, in realistic terms, 'an acute and penetrating psychological portrait' (Stone 238, 239). Although she exhibits 'an unmistakable strain of the ranting, evil, melodrama queen' and her 'scenes of towering passion sometimes topple into stagy clichés and histrionic poses', these elements are 'partly redeemed by the fairy-tale air which surrounds' her. For example, Dickens counterpoints Rosa, 'the cruel princess', to Em'ly, 'the baseborn fairy-tale rival' (Stone 241). Dickens also 'surrounds benign characters with enchantment', as in his account of David's early rapture with Dora (Stone 246).

Stone finds that the 'old fairy-tale method of arbitrarily transforming some character or event', used in the pre-*Dombey* novels, sometimes features in *Copperfield*, but that most of 'its fairy-tale elements … are rooted in verisimilitude'; 'storybook motifs and portents are usually fused to the central realism of the novel and work throughout' to assist its realistic aspects and to expand and deepen Dickens's meanings. This, for Stone, is Dickens's 'new or mature fairy-tale method' which forms 'the mainstay of the fairy story in *Copperfield*' (Stone 275).

In *Expectations*, the 'many other realistic characters who reflect or extend or illuminate Pip's personality' contribute to an 'intricate counterpoint' that 'gives [the novel] structure and meaning' (Stone 303). Orlick's 'sinister relationships and heightened fairy-tale attributes', for example, 'accentuate rather than diminish his realism and his significance'. He is 'an objectification of Pip's darkest desires and aggressions' and 'also an independent manifestation of primal evil' (Stone 303–4). This ambiguity makes him an especially effective character and contributes to Pip's own complex psychology. In *Expectations*, Orlick plays 'his triple role as swarthy journeyman, malignant devil, and [Pip's] dark alter ego' (Stone 305). His role as Pip's double is evident, for instance, in the scene where he holds Pip prisoner and tells him that he, Pip, was his sister's real attacker: 'it warn't Old Orlick as did it; it was you. You was favoured, and he was bullied and beat ... You done it; now you pays for it' (*GE* 437).

Magwitch, a more central character, contributes to 'the great structuring nodes of the novel', 'the fairy-tale pattern, the psychological elaboration, the mythic fall and redemption'. Moreover, like other crucial characters in *Expectations*, he 'integrates additional themes': 'society's guilt in producing criminals; the tainted nature of Victorian wealth and gentility; and, by means of his social, business, or blood relationships, the intricate unity of society, the universality of guilt and responsibility' (Stone 309). Like Orlick, Magwitch is Pip's double, but even more so. Miss Havisham also has a 'storybook role' as 'a veritable witch' (Stone 310), while being realistically located in time and place. Her dwelling, Satis House, is both 'a real English manor house and a wild fairy-tale nightmare' (Stone 320).

In his conclusion, Stone affirms that *Expectations* is

> a narrative that partakes of fairy-tale transformation, ... that fuses autobiographical, sociological, psychological, and mythological elements into a deeply resonant unity ... that is at once esoteric and realistic. .. In ... *Expectations*, Dickens' early experiences and fantasies, his fairy-tale finales and godmother figures, his later disappointments

and insights, have been transmuted into a subtle, endlessly ramifying fable that concentrates reality and deepens our apprehension of life. (Stone 337)

Stone argues persuasively for the importance of the fairy tale, in its widest sense, in enhancing the reader's grasp of reality in both *Copperfield* and *Expectations*. Emily Rena-Dozier, to whom we now turn, focuses on feminist and formal issues of gender and genre to provide an original perspective on *Copperfield*.

Emily Rena-Dozier

Emily Rena-Dozier's essay 'Re-gendering the Domestic Novel in *David Copperfield*' (2010) considers the question of whether *Copperfield* is 'a domestic novel'. The term 'domestic novel' is, Rena-Dozier acknowledges, a slippery one, but she identifies three main interweaving elements: in terms of setting, it is located in the domestic sphere, understood as that part of one's life-experience concerned with home and family; in terms of plot, it is focused on personal relationships within the family and with romantic extra-familial relationships; in terms of narrative form, it means a kind of narration which bases its authority on the domestic sphere. In mid-nineteenth-century England, where a strong ideology of separate spheres reserves the economic sphere for men and the domestic sphere for women, the domestic novel comes to mean the feminine novel, either written by women or showing feminine characteristics. We can see *Copperfield* as Dickens's attempt to show that writing domestic fiction is a suitable activity for men.

Copperfield portrays a man writing domestic fiction – or at least, since we do not know what kind of books he writes, producing them from within a domestic setting. Rena-Dozier quotes David's statement that 'I was at home and at work – for I wrote a good deal now, and was beginning in a small way to be known as a writer' (*DC* 712). But to be at home and at work was a questionable position in terms of the ideology of separate spheres in which work at home primarily meant housekeeping by women, and any other home-based activity, such as novel-writing, would thereby seem feminine. In *Copperfield*, Dickens tries to rescue the domestic novel for masculinity in two ways:

> First, Dickens proposes an androgynous domestic space, in which masculine virtues such as Copperfield's work ethic and powers of concentration infuse the domestic sphere with rigor and purpose, and feminine virtues such as Agnes's gentleness soften and humanize the realm of commerce. Second, Dickens attempts to evade domestic fiction's persistent association with femininity by recasting his domestic novel as a revision of the great masculine novel of the eighteenth century, Henry Fielding's *Tom Jones*.   (Rena-Dozier 814)

In *Copperfield*, Dickens aims both to prove that a man can write a domestic novel and to improve on the manly novels of the eighteenth century by retaining their masculinity but eliminating their immorality and thus signalling the ethical advance the nineteenth century has achieved. Women, by producing domestic fiction, had eliminated the immoral elements of the eighteenth-century novel; now both men and women could produce fiction that eschewed such immorality. By taking *Tom Jones* as his major model for revision, Dickens could effectively replace Fielding as the father of the novel by producing a work that combined 'masculine literary greatness and feminine domestic propriety' (Rena-Dozier 815). As we saw in the 'Life and Work' chapter, and as Rena-Dozier points out, Dickens, as he was preparing to begin *Copperfield*, even named his son Henry Fielding Dickens 'as a kind of homage to the style of the novel he was about to write'.

In *Copperfield*, a small selection of mostly eighteenth-century fiction is David's main legacy from his father: as well as *Tom Jones*, there are Smollett's *Roderick Random*, *Peregrine Pickle* and *Humphry Clinker*, Goldsmith's *Vicar of Wakefield* and Defoe's *Robinson Crusoe*. As Rena-Dozier says: 'In a novel overstocked with missing fathers, bad fathers, and incompetent fathers, the eighteenth-century novel is the only inheritance upon which one can rely.' But Rena-Dozier observes that the works David cites were not seen as children's books, and indeed some were rather ribald, which is why David has to insist that they 'did me no harm; for whatever harm was in some of them was not there for me; *I* knew nothing of it' (*DC* 105). In effect, David, as a boy, instinctively edits the books he reads to make them suitable not only for himself but also for Victorian readers; he 'domesticate[s] the eighteenth-century novel' (Rena-Dozier 817).

As Rena-Dozier points out, David, as a schoolboy, become Steerforth's storyteller, who recounts, from memory, the eighteenth-century fiction he has read and makes, in Steerforth's words, 'some regular Arabian Nights of it' (*DC* 144). Steerforth's reference feminizes David as Scheherazade, the female narrator of the Arabian Nights, and this feminization, Rena-Dozier suggests, ensures that the originally ribald eighteenth-century tales he tells will be purified. This purification is necessary to avoid any implication that David's tales might have corrupted Steerforth, might have provided bad examples that he followed in his seduction of Em'ly. David's schoolboy storytelling prepares him for his later role as a novelist who retells but also revises eighteenth-century fiction to make it suitable for Victorian readers.

Copperfield has to undertake this revision while avoiding the emasculation that domestic fiction may seem to entail. One way it does this is by undermining female authority in the home. Apart from the apotheosis of Agnes as both good housekeeper and spiritual guide, *Copperfield* contains many 'representations of hostile, misguided, or simply incompetent feminine authority, ranging from the cruel (Miss Murdstone, Rosa Dartle, and Mrs. Steerforth) to the hapless (Mrs. Micawber, Clara Copperfield, and Dora Copperfield)' (Rena-Dozier 820). In particular, there is a contrast between David and Dora; David's work in the home, his writing, is a success, but Dora's, her housekeeping, is a shambles, as chapter 44 attests in detail (*DC* 701-16). By this contrast, Dickens implies both the existence of masculine domesticity and its superiority to feminine domesticity. He thus both challenges the ideology of separate spheres and asserts male dominance *within* the domestic sphere which that ideology reserves for women.

Dickens does not only do this through David. Traddles, his wife Sophy, and Sophy's sisters all live in Traddles's law-chambers, so Traddles's place of work is also his home and the domestic, women's sphere and money-earning man's sphere fuse. *Copperfield* implies that this fosters rather than impedes Traddles's career, and by the end of the novel he is set fair to become a judge, even though he keeps 'his papers in his dressing-room and his boots with his papers' (*DC* 949). 'The ideal family, then, integrates the domestic and the professional', but '[m]en, not women, supervise Dickens's integrated domestic realms' (Rena-Dozier 821).

Dickens's attempt to reclaim the domestic novel for masculinity was not wholly successful in or beyond his lifetime. For example, the *Saturday Review* (August 1858) remarked that 'Mr. Dickens's literary progeny seem to us to be for the most part of the feminine gender', while Walter Bagehot in the *National Review* (October 1858) observed Dickens's 'deficiency in those masculine faculties' of 'the reasoning understanding and firm far-seeing sagacity'. (quoted in Rena-Dozier 823). Subsequent critics have tended to see *Copperfield* as falling on either side of a gender divide – either David, as a male artist, distances himself from his feminine characteristics (Margaret Myers (1995)) or succumbs to them (U. C. Knoepflmacher (1968)). As Rena-Dozier puts it: 'critics prefer to either assert that Dickens is not a proper domestic novelist (because he is male) or that he is not a proper male (because he is a domestic novelist)' (Rena-Dozier 825). In Rena-Dozier's view, *Copperfield* shows the need to develop a more complex understanding of domestic fiction and the domestic sphere that avoids fusing the domestic with the feminine.

Our final sample of criticism draws on psychoanalysis and feminism to consider the incarnation of victim-aggressor roles in three female characters in *Expectations*.

Adina Ciugureanu

In 'The Victim-Aggressor Duality in *Great Expectations*' (2011), Adina Ciugureanu offers a 'psychological and feminist' analysis of Miss Havisham, Mrs Joe and Molly which aims to explain 'aspects of their behaviour usually perceived as strange' (Ciugureanu 347). In psychoanalytical terms, all three can be diagnosed as suffering from 'narcissistic personality disorder' but we can also relate them to Victorian ethics and 'debates on sexuality, crime, marriage, and divorce' (Ciugureanu 347).

The key question about Mrs Joe is: why, after Orlick has attacked her, does she want to keep on seeing him every day? She may not know that Orlick was her attacker: as Orlick himself says when he admits his crime to Pip, 'I come upon her from behind' (*GE* 437), and she may not have seen him. What is this strange connection between them? To pursue that question, Ciugureanu returns to Mrs Joe's behaviour before the attack and her aggressive treatment of Pip and Joe. Her aggression, Ciugureanu suggests, is linked 'with her psychotic belief that she is actually the victim of both' (Ciugureanu 348). When she turns on them, she employs 'the apron and the duster, the symbolical objects of a housewife, as weapons of enslaved womanhood' (Ciugureanu 349). Pip, even from an adult perspective, has no insight into his sister's frustrations at being forced to marry beneath her and do her own housework without a servant. Indeed, Ciugureanu suggests, Pip fails to understand any of the women he encounters, including the 'good' woman, Biddy. Ciugureanu relates this to Dickens's own attitudes to women, progressive in certain areas (higher pay, educational opportunity, marriage and divorce arrangements) but conservative in that he felt women should remain in the private, domestic sphere and should be submissive, within that sphere, to men. His portrait of Mrs Joe might have been, in part, a satire on the growing feminism of his time, a stereotypical picture of a woman who has appropriated undue power to herself. Frances Power Cobbe, a campaigner for feminism in the 1850s and 1860s, compared the husband–wife relationship, in many instances, to that of master and slave: Mrs Joe calls herself 'a slave with her apron never off' (*GE* 53) but controls her husband's earnings and beats both him and her brother. On one level, she could be seen as comic; on another level, there is a tragic element that is linked with narcissism.

Ciugureanu summarizes the definition of a psychotic narcissist in Elsa F. Ronningstam's *Identifying and Understanding the Narcissistic Personality* (2005). Such a person 'shows contempt and depreciation of others, lacks empathy and understanding, is egotistical, craves to be the center of attention, becomes enraged for unreasonable causes and, whenever cross, becomes authoritarian and aggressive'. Mrs Joe certainly fits this description. She depreciates and speaks contemptuously of both brother and husband, calling Pip a 'monkey' (*GE* 41) and Joe a 'staring great stuck pig' (*GE* 43). She shows no empathy with or understanding of Pip's illnesses, insomnia, accidents and injuries (*GE* 59). She tries to make people notice her by registering how clean her house is and by how she dresses and what she carries when she goes out: 'a very large beaver bonnet ... a basket like the Great Seal of England in plaited straw, a pair of pattens, a spare shawl, and an umbrella', although it is 'a fine bright day' (*GE* 127). She gets angry, often without reasonable cause, and asserts her authority aggressively, sometimes going 'on the Ram-page' (*GE* 40). When the party that has gone out with the soldiers returns, Mrs Joe, for no apparent reason, grabs Pip 'as a slumberous offence to the company's eyesight' and pulls him up to bed 'with such a strong hand that I seemed to have fifty boots on, and to be dangling them all against the edges of the stairs' (*GE* 73). In the scene prior to Orlick's assault on her, she inflames a situation Joe has tried to defuse and deliberately works herself into a rage, becoming 'blindly furious by regular stages' (*GE* 142).

These narcissistic aspects indicate 'psychological depth in Dickens's portrayal of secondary characters' (Ciugureanu 351). Such depth is also evident in Dickens's representation of Mrs Joe's docility and dependency after the attack. Pip expects her to denounce Orlick when he first visits her, but she shows 'every possible desire to conciliate him' and her 'bearing' towards him is that of 'a child towards a hard master' (*GE* 151). As the word 'child' suggests, Mrs Joe regresses to an infantile stage and order only returns to the house when Biddy arrives. Mrs Joe's passivity could be read as repentance; but it could also be a continuation of narcissism by other means; she is now, as victim rather than aggressor, the centre of attention she has always wanted to be.

Miss Havisham, like Mrs Joe, takes on the patriarchal Victorian world and exemplifies the restricted opportunities it offers women: 'marriage, celibacy, or prostitution' (Ciugureanu 354). Unlike Mrs Joe, who chooses marriage (though to a social inferior), Miss Havisham, rejected as a potential wife, makes no further attempt to marry and flaunts her celibacy. She both loves and hates her self-dramatizing situation, which seems to further her project of revenge (through Estella), but stops her from loving others. 'The desire for love pitted against the desire for revenge creates the victim–aggressor duality, which overlaps with the narcissistic pattern' (Ciugureanu 356).

Molly – housekeeper to Jaggers, sometime wife to Magwitch and biological mother of Estella – is an ex-tramp and murderess with a violent temper. At first a victim of society's exclusions, she becomes an aggressor. At the time she committed the murder, she was 'a perfect fury in point of jealousy' (*GE* 405). Jaggers's instructions to her defence counsel get her off but give him power over her so that she can serve as a mirror to reflect and enlarge his own narcissism. He treats Molly like a wild animal he has tamed. She has apparently made the transition from aggressor to victim, but she still seems dangerous to Pip, reminding him of the witches in *Macbeth* (*GE* 235). There is still a sense that Molly might start to change back from victim to aggressor, to turn against her tamer, to speak her own story, and thereby diminish Jaggers's narcissism.

Ciugureanu sums up her argument thus:

> The aggressor–victim duality in *Great Expectations* reveals itself to be triangular: each of the three female characters suffers some kind of victimization before she unveils her aggressive nature … the three female characters are made to suffer the consequences of their own behavior and become victims of their own aggression … (Ciugureanu 360)

Reading about these women, Ciugureanu concludes, offers three different – and dubious – sorts of pleasure: 'misogynic' – 'seeing a woman put in her place'; 'voyeuristic' – 'peeping into a woman's boudoir'; and 'sadistic' – 'holding a woman prisoner of her own faults and misfortunes' (Ciugureanu 360). But these pleasures are limited by the awareness that these three characters cannot escape from narcissism and the victim–aggressor duality – except, as Miss Havisham does, through death.

By highlighting not only the much-discussed Miss Havisham, but also the relatively neglected figures of Mrs Joe and Mollie, Ciugureanu demonstrates the continued power of *Expectations* to yield meanings and the fruitfulness of an approach that combines psychoanalytic and feminist perspectives with considerations of the discourses of Dickens's time.

We have sampled five interpretations of *Copperfield* and *Expectations* from the voluminous criticism of the novels that has appeared in the past 55 years. Each of these readings approaches the novels from different angles but argues its case convincingly and supports its arguments by specific examples from the text of the novels and, where appropriate, from other relevant texts. We should treat these interpretations, like any others, as provisional and test them against our own knowledge and understanding of the novels, weighing the arguments and the textual evidence for and against them. They are part of the rich critical conversation that *Copperfield* and *Expectations* have generated over the years; we should listen to them, sift what they say, and consider how we might, in presentations, seminars and essays, contribute to the conversation ourselves.

Further Reading

Other works by Dickens

Among Dickens's 12 other completed novels, *Nicholas Nickleby* (1838–39), with its portrayal of its protagonist's mother and of his experiences as a teacher at Dotheboys Hall, and its loose structure encompassing elements of comedy, sentiment and melodrama, is interesting to read in relation to the themes and form of *Copperfield*. *Oliver Twist* (1837–39), with its account of Oliver's harsh childhood and its comparatively tight focus, can profitably be read alongside *Expectations*. *Martin Chuzzlewit* (1843–44) is, like *Expectations*, a portrait of a selfish young man, but with notable differences in style, structure and attitude. *Dombey and Son* (1846–48), the novel which preceded *Expectations*, and two of the novels which followed it in the 1850s, *Bleak House* (1852–53) and *Little Dorrit* (1855–57), give a sense of Dickens's increasing seriousness, social engagement and structural control in the later phase of his fiction. *Bleak House* is also interesting in relation to *Copperfield* and *Expectations* for its use of a first-person female narrator to sustain a crucial strand of the story. As well as Dickens's fiction, it is worth sampling Dickens's journalism, which he continued to write while he was working on fiction and which has a close, though not always direct, relationship to his novels. His magazines, *Household Words* and *All the Year Round*, are both available at the free, open-access 'Dickens Journals Online' site at http://www.djo.org.uk/household-words.html and http://www.djo.org.uk/all-the-year-round.html.

Key novels by other writers

There are three contemporary *Bildungsromane* which illuminatingly relate to *Copperfield* and *Expectations*. One is Thackeray's *The History of Pendennis* (1848–50), which appeared around the same time as *Copperfield* and with which it has often been compared, though it is a third-person rather than first-person narrative. The other two are written by women and have female protagonists: Charlotte Brontë's *Jane Eyre*, told in the first person by its titular heroine, and George Eliot's *The Mill on the Floss* (1860), the story of Maggie Tulliver, told in the third person and ending with a Dickensian death scene in which the heroine and her brother drown. *Expectations* can also be compared in some respects to *The Scarlet Letter* (1850) by the American writer Nathaniel Hawthorne.

It is interesting, especially in relation to *Copperfield*, to sample some of the eighteenth-century novels which are mentioned in *Copperfield* as part of the 'small collection of books' left by his father which David reads as a lonely boy, and which Dickens sometimes echoes and amends: Henry Fielding's *The History of Tom Jones, A Foundling* (1749), Tobias Smollett's *The Adventures of Roderick Random* (1748) and Oliver Goldsmith's *The Vicar of Wakefield* (1766).

A further intriguing field to explore is that of fiction with intertextual references to *Copperfield* and *Expectations*; for example, in the USA, F. Scott Fitzgerald's *The Great Gatsby* (1925), whose title character is a man of gargantuan 'great expectations' on an American scale, and J. D. Salinger's *The Catcher in the Rye* (1951), whose narrator, Holden Caulfield, starts by repudiating 'all that David Copperfield kind of crap' but shares *Copperfield*'s fascination with pre-pubertal innocence. In England, John Fowles's *The Magus* (1966; revd edn 1977) and Hanif Kureishi's *The Buddha of Suburbia* (1990) both, in their different ways, echo and reinscribe aspects of *Expectations* as they recount the adventures of their respective protagonists, Nicholas Urfe and Karim Amir.

Biography

John Forster's *Life* (1872–74) is indispensable because of its author's close personal knowledge of Dickens. An abridged and revised version of Forster's biography by George Gissing, in which he has sometimes substituted 'remarks of his own for Forster's critical comments on each of the novels', is interesting because Gissing was both a notable Dickens critic and a practising novelist. Peter Ackroyd's *Dickens* (1990; author-abridged edn, 2002) is in a class of its own as a biography, exhaustively researched, absorbing to read, and fascinating as the record of a sustained encounter between Dickens and a biographer who is himself a significant modern novelist. Una Pope-Hennessy's wartime biography (1945), though limited in the documentary sources consulted, remains readable and reasonably reliable; Edgar Johnson (1952; revd and abridged edn, 1977) is the most fully researched biography up to the early 1950s; and more recent biographies by Fred Kaplan (1988), Michael Slater (2009) and Claire Tomalin (2011) are all lucid, enjoyable and informative. Tomalin's *The Invisible Woman: The Story of Nelly Ternan and Charles Dickens* (1970) is also worth consulting. Grahame Smith's *Charles Dickens: A Literary Life* (1996) concentrates on Dickens's networking with his public and publishers. Robert Douglas-Fairhurst's *Becoming Dickens: The Invention of a Novelist* (2011) is a lively study of Dickens at a time when his future was uncertain.

Criticism

General critical books on Dickens

George Gissing's *Charles Dickens: A Critical Study* (1898) is a pioneering analysis organized by topics such as 'Characterization', 'Women and Children' and 'Style'. G. K. Chesterton's *Charles Dickens* (1906) and his introductions to the Everyman editions of Dickens's novels, collected as *Appreciations and Criticisms of the Works of Charles Dickens* (1911), are vigorous and perceptive. George Orwell's 'Charles Dickens', first collected in *Inside the Whale* (1940), and Edmund Wilson's 'Dickens: The Two Scrooges', collected in *The Wound and the Bow* (1941), are major revaluations, one English, one American, from a mid-twentieth-century perspective, both written with great clarity and insight. Humphry House's *The Dickens World* (2nd edn, 1942) is a classic work of historical contextualization. K. J. Fielding's *Charles Dickens* (1958; revd edn, 1965) is a lucid and perceptive survey of all Dickens's books from *Boz* to *Drood*. J. Hillis Miller's *Charles Dickens: The World of His Novels* (1958), which we sampled in chapter 9, is a compelling analysis of Dickens that establishes the philosophical complexity of Dickens's work. Barbara Hardy's *The Moral Art of Dickens* (1970; 1985), also sampled in chapter 9, is worth reading for its general chapters on 'Society and the Individual' in Dickens as well as for its interpretations of specific novels. Robert Garis's *The Dickens Theatre: A Reassessment of His Novels* (1965) offers an original approach to

Dickens as the practitioner of 'a theatrical art' that constantly makes the reader aware of Dickens as performer. Harry Stone's *Dickens and the Invisible World: Fairy Tales, Fantasy, and Novel-Making* (1979), the third of our critical samples in chapter 9, is a mine of information and insights and develops a persuasive overall argument. Steven Connor's *Charles Dickens* (1985) is a stimulating reinterpretation of Dickens in light of modern critical theory. Two twenty-first-century books on Dickens which offer fresh perspectives are Jay Clayton's *Charles Dickens in Cyberspace: The Afterlife of the Nineteenth Century in Postmodern Culture* (2003) and Holly Furneaux's *Queer Dickens; Erotics, Families, Masculinities* (2010).

George H. Ford's *Dickens and His Readers* (1955) is a valuable account of the critical reception of Dickens's work from the late 1830s to the mid-twentieth century. Key critical anthologies are Martin Price (ed.), *Dickens: A Collection of Critical Essays* (1967); A. E. Dyson (ed.), *Dickens: Modern Judgements* (1968); Stephen Wall (ed.), *Charles Dickens: A Critical Anthology* (1970); and Wendell Stacy Johnson (ed.), *Charles Dickens: New Perspectives* (1982). *The Cambridge Companion to Charles Dickens* (2001), ed. John O'Jordan, contains 14 original essays on a range of textual and contextual topics.

Critical books, essays and anthologies about *Copperfield*

Copperfield has attracted less in the way of monographs and critical anthologies than *Expectations,* but Philip Collins's *Charles Dickens: David Copperfield* (1977) is a concise and perceptive study by a leading Dickens scholar and John Peck (ed.), *Charles Dickens: David Copperfield and Hard Times* (1995), is a key anthology of *Copperfield* criticism informed by modern literary theory.

The classic *Copperfield* essay cited by Barbara Hardy (see chapter 9) is Gwendolyn B. Needham, 'The Undisciplined Heart of David Copperfield' (*Nineteenth-Century Fiction,* 9:2 (September 1954), 81–107). The essays cited by Emily Rena-Dozier in chapter 9 are Margaret Myers, 'The Lost Self: Gender in *David Copperfield*', in Peck (1995, details above), 108–24, and U. C. Knoepflmacher, 'From Outrage to Rage: Dickens's Bruised Femininity', in Joanne Shattock (ed.), *Dickens and Other Victorians: Essays in Honor of Philip Collins* (1968), 75–96. Significant and as yet uncollected post-2000 essays on *Copperfield* (possibly accessible from school and university databases) include David Thiele, 'The "transcendent and immortal … HEEP!": Class Consciousness, Narrative Authority and the Gothic in *David Copperfield*' (*Texas Studies in Literature and Language,* 42:3 (September 2000), 201–21); Julia F. Saville, 'Eccentricity as Englishness in *David Copperfield*' (*Studies in*

English Literature, 1500–1900, 42:4 (Autumn 2002), 781–97); Sharon E. Sytsma, 'Agapic Friendship [David and Steerforth]' (*Philosophy and Literature*, 27:2 (October 2003), 428–35); Annette R. Federico, '*David Copperfield* and the Pursuit of Happiness' (*Victorian Studies*, 46:1 (Autumn 2008), 69–95); Maria McAleavey, 'Soul-Mates: *David Copperfield*'s Angelic Bigamy' (*Victorian Studies*, 52:2 (Winter 2010), 191–218); and the essay sampled in chapter 9, Emily Rena-Dozier, 'Re-gendering the Domestic Novel in *David Copperfield*' (*SEL Studies in English Literature 1500–1900*, 50:4 (Autumn 2010), 811–29).

Critical books, essays and anthologies about *Expectations*

George R. Thomas's *Charles Dickens: Great Expectations* (1964), Anny Sadrin's *Great Expectations* (1994), Nicola Bradbury's *Charles Dickens: Great Expectations* (1990) and Douglas Brooks-Davies's *Charles Dickens: Great Expectations* (1989) all contain interesting and useful material.

Key critical anthologies include Michael Cotsell (ed.), *Critical Essays on Charles Dickens's Great Expectations* (1990); Norman Page (ed.), *Charles Dickens: Hard Times, Great Expectations and Our Mutual Friend* (1979); and Roger D. Sell, *Great Expectations: Charles Dickens* (1994). Nicolas Tredell (ed.), *Charles Dickens: Great Expectations: A Reader's Guide to Essential Criticism* (1998) tracks the critical reception of *Expectations* from its first reviews to the 1990s, with substantial extracts from the writings of key critics. Significant and as yet uncollected essays on *Expectations* (possibly accessible from school and university databases) include Jerome Meckier, '*Great Expectations* and *Self-Help*: Dickens Frowns on Smiles' (*Journal of English and Germanic Philology*, 100:4 (October 2001), 537–54); Ankhi Mukherjee, 'Missed Encounters: Repetition, Rewriting, and Contemporary Returns to Charles Dickens's *Great Expectations* [i.e. in three novels, Kathy Acker's *Great Expectations* (1982), Sue Roe's *Estella, Her Expectations* (1982) and Peter Carey's *Jack Maggs* (1997) and in Alfonso Cuarón's film *Great Expectations* (1998)]' (*Contemporary Literature*, 46:1 (Spring 2005), 108–33); and the essay sampled in chapter 9, Adina Ciugureanu, 'The Victim-Aggressor Duality in *Great Expectations* (*Partial Answers: Journal of Literature and the History of Ideas*, 9:2 (June 2011), 347–61).

Index

Printed in China